BRING CLEM HUME

The Fall of a Texas Judge

A NOVEL BASED ON A TRUE STORY

KIRK MCCLELLAND

Copyright © 2018 Kirk McClelland
All rights reserved
First Edition

PAGE PUBLISHING, INC.
New York, NY

First originally published by Page Publishing, Inc. 2018

ISBN 978-1-64214-013-2 (Paperback)
ISBN 978-1-64214-015-6 (Hardcover)
ISBN 978-1-64214-014-9 (Digital)

Printed in the United States of America

Dedicated
to my Carol, who always said I should write this
and
to my Cheryl, who helped me write it better…

TEXAS

Key Locations

1 Houston
2 Huntsville
3 Belton
4 Austin
5 Marlin
6 Laredo/Nuevo Laredo

FOREWORD

Bring Clem Home exposes one of this country's first Media-driven prosecutions. In 1950 Clement McClelland was elected Probate Judge in Houston, Texas, and then in November of 1962, he was found Guilty of *Conversion of Estate Funds* and sentenced to ten years in prison. The case against him was one of nine indictments handed down by a Houston Grand Jury, the large number guaranteeing that the ruthless District Attorney in charge would eventually obtain a conviction. The city of Houston watched this case closely since the news media there had brainwashed and prejudiced everyone against Clem, except for me and my family.

My name is Kirk McClelland, and I was born fourteen years before Clem's conviction. Clem and my mother, Doris, had tried twice before to have a son, so my birth was presumably a positive omen of great things to come. Indeed, the memories of my early years were happy ones, and my world was filled with goodness and light. As Clem's nightmare unfolded, I saw that light fade, but since I was young and naive, I believed it would still stay lit. When Clem's nightmare transformed into a monster and the good light failed, my happy Houston family was suddenly and brutally challenged. This is our story over the first eighteen years of my life.

Kirk, Micki, Doris, Clem, and Anne

**Clem McClelland 1937
Sigma Chi, University of Arkansas**

**Doris and Clem played host to
weekly parties at our Mid Lane home**

CHAPTER ONE

IT COULD HAPPEN HERE, 1937–1954

My father's full name was Clement Bramlette McClelland. He received his undergraduate Bachelor of Law degree at the University of Arkansas on June 7, 1937, and when his name was automatically engraved on the sidewalk that led to the emblematic "Old Main" building, he was proud to have the longest name ever inscribed on that walkway.

Clem then decided he'd attend the University of Texas to achieve a Master Law degree. When he graduated from Texas, he moved to Houston, where he started a law practice and met and married Doris Cook. As they raised their family of two daughters and me, they contributed to the well-being of all Houstonians through Clem's association with the Shriners of Arabia Temple and Doris's reign as the chairwoman of the March of Dimes. To better understand how my family lived back then, I studied every family scrapbook and watched all the old 8 millimeter home movies that Clem had shot with his Kodak camera. I analyzed the good times, the smiling faces, and together these images helped me better understand how far we all fell.

As a child, some of my earliest and happiest memories were parties held in our small house at 2704 Mid Lane to help raise funds and attract volunteers for the different causes Clem and Doris had adopted. I remember looking up at the tall legs of adult party members. When I was discovered, I heard, "*Oh, look! There he is! Isn't he just the sweetest?*" as I was picked up and held high for display. I remember hearing happy and loud voices as I ran through the living room where most guests sat with their drinks. I remember a strong arm catching me and, again, raising me up. Clem looked at me as he hoisted me and he said, "*Make a wish, boy.*"

I looked into his commanding and kind eyes and replied, "*I wish I'd never come in here.*"

As the guests laughed and applauded, Clem set me down so I could make my escape.

Clem stood 6 feet 4 inches tall, looked like Burt Lancaster, and spoke with the poise and confidence of Gregory Peck playing Atticus Finch. He loved to smoke his classy cigars, and whether he was wearing his black judge's robe or one of his expensive dress suits, he looked like and *was* a solid, trustworthy man. Whenever I watched him talk to Doris or one of his brothers or sister, I saw a complete man in a giving attitude and comfortable with whatever he was saying. I loved to watch him. I was called *The Phantom* by my parents and their friends because I used to hide under a table or crouch behind a standing indoor houseplant where I'd look at and analyze Clem. I was a serious *Phantom*, and I learned a lot by watching Clem's example.

I remember Clem being tall

There were many happy times from that period that Doris recited years later when things grew dark and any memory of past good times might help. One of our favorite stories: I was four years old, and Doris was training me to add small sums using my fingers hidden behind my back. I was taught by my parents to perform. One day, to impress a Doris friend, she asked me, "*Kirk, how much is 3 plus 4?*"

With hands and fingers behind my back I counted on my fingers and proudly declared, "*Seven!*"

Then she asked, "*Kirk, how much is 5 plus 4?*"

To which I answered, "*Nine!*"

Finally she asked, "*Kirk, how much is 6 plus 6?*"

I pondered, then frowned and complained, "*What you think I got? 3 hands?*"

Another happy memory in the early fifties occurred late on Christmas Eve. I'd been tucked into bed by Doris and as she closed the door to my room I thought I heard the faraway sound of sleigh bells high in the sky outside my window. There was no doubt in my mind that this was Santa, and the bells that were ringing were on his sleigh. Years later Doris told the truth about the "*Christmas bells*" and described

Clem standing outside my window with a bottle of Jack Daniels whiskey in one hand and jangling sleigh bells in the other.

In those early years, I was a sound sleeper, and on that night, while I slept soundly, Clem stayed up until morning putting together a huge electric train set in our Mid Lane garage that included ten passenger cars, four baggage cars complete with three towns, hills, snow, and train stations. There were also over a hundred scale-modeled citizen figures walking to work or walking their dogs. When I awoke on Christmas morning, I heard the train whistle blowing, and I ran to the garage to behold this enormous present laid out by Santa, with Clem at the train controls grinning and wearing a new train conductor's hat as he smoked his signature cigar.

My second favorite present that Christmas was a Peter Pan Coloring Book with all the Disney characters from the 1953 animated movie. Two days after Christmas, due to a mistake in court scheduling, Judge Clem was forced to preside in his probate courtroom at the Harris County Courthouse. He decided to let his five-year-old son go with him to watch him work. To impress everyone, Doris dressed me up in a suit complete with a red-striped bow tie, *"Your father's going to be so proud of you, but remember don't fidget or distract him."*

Helen Smith, Clem's fifty-year-old devoted secretary, took my hand, said, *"I've got him, Doris,"* and led me into Clem's courtroom through the judge's side entrance. I saw and heard a large, noisy room (with very high ceilings) filled with people.

Helen Smith was devoted to Clem

I dressed up for Clem's court

I studied Helen's constant smile, and her flowered suit as she led me to the witness box located to the right of where Clem sat in his long black judge's robe. As I walked with her I saw the faces of people smiling and nodding to each other as if they knew me. I saw Clem's nameplate but I was too young to know that it read JUDGE CLEM MCCLELLAND.

I continued to look around and saw two large men in uniforms who Helen whispered to me were called *Bailiffs*. I remember thinking, *"Why'd I come here when I could be home playing with my new train set?"* and then I thought about my coloring book. I sat down, looked at Clem, and then I attacked Captain Hook's coat with a fiery red crayon as Clem banged his gavel, "*Ladies and gentlemen, let me introduce you to my son, Kirk McClelland. He'll be joining us today to observe the workings of my probate court, so I suggest you behave accordingly.*"

I saw everyone laugh since it would've been bad form to offend the judge. And then I saw a woman in her midthirties with red hair, similar in color to the hue I'd just crayoned Captain Hook's coat. I found out later she sat at the plaintiff's table and that her name was Mildred Henderson. I was beginning to become interested in how adults conducted business, and it looked like she was desperate to say something to the judge, with no concern about upsetting him.

Her attorney was a man named Guy Price, whom I'd seen before at our house for fund-raising, and he was trying with no success to calm Mildred down. At the other table was the defendant, Arthur Henderson. He was Mildred's brother, and he was laughing at something that his attorney, another friend of Clem's named Bryson Martin, had just said to him.

I put down my crayon and engaged my eyes/ears since I enjoyed watching adults about to participate in what Clem and Doris called *"disappointing disagreements."*

Clem called the court to order and said, "*Next up is case number 5477782, Henderson versus Henderson. I've reached a decision and I find for Arthur Henderson. This decision was simple for me since the evidence offered by Mildred Henderson did not change the fact that Arthur and Mildred's father, Wilfred, wanted Arthur to receive the bulk of the Henderson estate. I think that . . .*"

At that moment Mildred jumped out of her chair and yelled as she pointed at her brother, "*Who cares what Your Honor THINKS if you're gonna agree with this moron!*"

The Bailiffs moved to restrain her but Clem waved them back to hear more of her outburst, "*And don't have a cow, Your Honor. I know all about you and how you do business.*

I also know a royal shaft when I see one!"

Then she launched herself over her table, ran across the aisle and hit her brother Arthur, hard, with her purse. I remember I said, "*Wow!*" but Clem didn't notice me since he was busy waving at his Bailiffs to grab this crazy lady, and directing Guy Price, "*Mr. Price, please control your client and help her gather up her things . . .*" since her purse had emptied on the floor. Then the judge said to the winning attorney, "*Mr. Martin, I'll see you and your client in my Chambers after lunch.*"

Two notes about that day in Clem's court: No. 1 it's a small world since in the near future I'd have Mildred Henderson as my fourth grade teacher at Will Roger's Elementary School, and No. 2 when she smacked her brother Arthur, everyone in the courtroom had gasped out loud except for one man. His name was Assistant District Attorney Frank Briscoe, and he was in the courtroom to observe and take notes relating to Judge McClelland. Frank Briscoe was tall and thin with a mean and hungry look as he scribbled his notes on a legal pad. Oblivious to Briscoe at that time, Clem banged his gavel and called out, *"Next case"* while I used my green crayon to color Peter Pan's costume . . .

It was during this time that Clem and Doris bought an empty lot on a bare street just behind our Mid Lane house. The new street was called Ivanhoe and, when it was built, our new home's address would be 4514 Ivanhoe. I remember my parents looking at pictures and blueprints and renderings that covered our breakfast table as they designed their two-story dream house so it would fit our family.

Construction began quickly and every day when Clem returned home from working as a probate judge, he and I would go behind our Mid Lane house, go through the backyard barbed-wire fence, and walk half a block to monitor the progress of the new building. I remember having to trot double-time to keep up with his 6'4" stride.

Clem met with his plump construction supervisor, Fred Ball, who wore a yellow construction helmet to assure the judge that he was on the job.

Fred said to me, *"Hi there, Kirk, you can call me Freddy"* which made me feel right at home.

While Clem and Freddy talked, I explored this two-story residential palace that would someday be the center of my life.

Then, after meeting with Freddy, Clem carefully laid down his rule to me, *"Listen close, boy. You don't ever come to this place unless your mother or I bring you. Do you understand?"*

I nodded to him because he was 6 feet 4 inches to my 3 feet 6 inches, and, with his trademark gray Stetson hat, he was 6 feet 6 inches. Would I dare disobey? Was I five years old?

I had two new friends named Chris Hale and Steve Taylor. I met them both at the Houston Boy's Club which is where Clem decided he'd introduce me to the world of athletic competition. I learned how to swim, to run, and to box for MEDALS! I was fast and I liked getting out in front in a race and turning to run backward so I could wave at all the slower boys behind me. Clem was forced to deal with the predictable complaints from losing parents, but I enjoyed winning since every time I won, he'd put his arm around me and say, *"That's my boy!"*

One day after a session at our preschool, Chris and Steve came over to play in my Mid Lane back yard. While Doris entertained their mothers inside the house, the three of us slipped through the barbed-wire fence and ran to Freddy's construction site so I could show my new friends our new fortress. Since on that day Freddy and his workers were absent, we happily stood on this perfect playground site and considered its possibilities.

A quick note: The previous week Chris and I had competed in a boxing match at the Boy's Club. Neither of us had set foot inside a boxing ring before and it didn't matter that the gloves were too heavy for Chris and that all his small arms could manage was a roundhouse swing instead of a glove-to-nose punch. What mattered was, when he roundhouse swung at me, I punched him and he went down. I should've thought about that when he said to me, "*I bet you're too scared to climb those stairs!*"

I looked at Steve and he just shook his head at both of us as Chris smiled.

I said, "*HA!*" and ran up the bare staircase of untreated wood, dodging all the hanging wires and cables.

When I reached the second floor I looked down through the unfinished roof of the first floor and waved to Chris and laughed. Not knowing yet what "*quit while you're ahead*" meant I then turned and jumped over a stack of 2x4s, tripped over a landing, and quickly fell through the unfinished roof. With both hands I desperately reached out, grabbed the ledge of the landing, and held on tight. I took a deep breath and in my five-year-old high-pitched voice I screamed, "*Chris! Steve! Help me!*"

My hands began to slip since they were both bleeding from the splintery wood I was grasping, and when I looked down I was amazed to see Chris and Steve running away. I sobbed, "*I need help! Doris! Clem! Is anybody there? Frr . . . Freddy!*"

Just then Clem ran up to the construction site having interrogated Chris and Steve about my whereabouts. He heard my sobs and ran to where I was hanging. I sobbed, "*Clem? Where are you?*"

Clem looked up and said, "*I'm right here, boy.*"

I choked back a breath and whispered, "*I can't hold on . . .*" and Clem said, "*Then . . . don't.*"

I looked down, then nodded to myself and let go, dropping into Clem's arms. Clem smiled at me and lowered me to the ground. I remember that I sighed with relief, but my relief was brief.

Clem walked us back to our Mid Lane home and walked me past Doris and my two sisters, Micki and Anne, who were sitting on the couch in the Television room/Den. He led me into his bedroom and into his closet where he kept his suits, ties, and, yes, his belts. I'd been there several times before and my eyes zoomed in on a thick black belt. In a calm voice, Clem said, "*You know which one it is. Let's have it.*"

I began to shake and sob again but this time no one was there to catch me. I saw Clem's strong face as he reached out to steady me and guide my hand to his favorite belt. I looked at him in fear, then struggled to deliver the belt to this huge man towering over me. I watched as he coiled the belt and I felt his hand turn me around. I sobbed and tried to move away but he held me tight. Then I heard the whoosh of his leather belt as he delivered it to my bare bottom.

YEOWWW! The tears began to flow and my scream filled the room. Yes, this kind of corporal punishment is frowned upon now and, yes, if I repeated what he'd warned me *not* to do, Clem would've nodded and instructed me to again hand him his favorite tool for punishment.

At that critical moment, I heard the Television turn on in the Den and heard the music theme to *Superman* as the announcer began his familiar opening, "*And now for another exciting episode in the adventures of Superman!*"

Even though Doris wore black Cat Eye glasses, she was still pretty smart and knew a reprieve when she saw one. She jumped up from the couch, where she'd been sitting with my older sisters, and hurried to Clem's dressing room.

She saw him raise up his belt to hit me again as I cowered against the wall. She was unaware that I had not followed Clem's warning but his face bore a look that, after 14 years of marriage, Doris recognized. In the den, over my sobs, the announcer continued, *"Faster than a speeding bullet, more powerful than a locomotive, able to leap tall buildings in a single bound..."*

Doris made a plea to her husband, the father of me, *"Clem, honey, I thought you and Kirk wanted to watch Superman! C'mon, it just started!"* Before Clem honey could reply, Doris swooped me up and, together, we flew to the Den. She placed me on the couch in my sister Micki's place (who tried to push me away). The voices of the TV crowd on the street said, *"Look! Up in the sky! It's a bird! It's a plane! It's Superman!"*

Clem followed us into the Den, sat down next to his briefcase at the other end of the couch and focused on the TV as the Announcer continued, *"Yes, it's Superman. Strange visitor from another planet who..."*

I was in the Doris safety zone, and I sneaked a peek around her at Clem. He looked distracted and that was good. The Announcer continued, *"...came to earth with powers and abilities far beyond those of mortal men. Superman! Who can change the course of mighty rivers... Bend steel in his bare hands... And who, disguised as..."*

I saw Clem pick up his briefcase which held a stack of legal papers that he began to read.

"...Clark Kent, mild-mannered reporter for a great metropolitan newspaper..."

I shifted my eyes back and forth between the TV and Clem, feeling safer as each second passed. Then I saw Clem's lips move in sync with the Announcer for his favorite line, *"...fights a never-ending battle for truth, justice, and the American way!"*

I saw Clem nod, then he looked down to continue reading his legal files... I was safe.

So as I share these episodes from my past, it should be obvious that Clem mesmerized me. I learned something new about him every day: how he loved his black Cadillac Coupe Deville with the huge tailfins; how he shared his philosophies with me without telling me what to think; how he loved his 16 gauge Remington Shotguns; how he loved his saved copies of Playboy magazine (me, too, once I discovered where he hid them); and how he loved hunting and fishing to bring game home so Doris could delight him with her Cook (good name) family recipes.

My sisters and I were in good hands

    To accurately portray Clem, he was a Christian who, with his three brothers and one sister, was taught to respect the Bible. Raised in the Bible belt in Fayetteville, Arkansas by his father, C. K. McClelland and his wife, Honey, Clem and the McClelland brood learned to fear God and love Jesus. When I was older and struggling to choose my calling, Clem shared with me that he had considered preaching as a worthwhile occupation, and it was a toss-up over that or the law.

    The first week he moved to Houston, Clem joined the First Presbyterian Church and in time became a Deacon in charge of overseeing the financial welfare of that huge church. He never bragged about this responsibility. He stayed behind the scenes as he exercised this power with pride and efficiency. He often discussed with me the *"value of proper monetary decision-making to sustain and maintain the word of God in a righteous setting."* When he spoke like that I just nodded, especially when I had no clue about the subject being discussed.

Due to how Clem was raised, our going to Sunday school was an automatic requirement for my sisters and me, and since we were different ages (they were two and four years older), we were in different classrooms at the church.

We were happy to go to church

I met my first Sunday school teacher, Mrs. Evans, and I remember how her eyes filled up as she told me about David and Goliath, or helped me to sing *"Jesus Loves Me."* She was especially attentive to me when I think back on my time with her, and I remember Doris telling me she'd lost a son about my age to pneumonia the year before.

One Sunday after my first month with Mrs. Evans, Clem (not Doris) came to pick me up from my Sunday school class. We had just discussed The Golden Rule and when Mrs. Evans saw Clem enter her room, she abruptly turned away and stumbled across the room to put away our hymnals. Clem looked at her and then he put his hand on my head asking, *"Hey, boy, learn any new songs today?"* I nodded and noticed that Mrs. Evans wasn't saying *hello* to Clem the way she did whenever Doris came to fetch me.

Several Sundays later I learned Mrs. Evans had a serious conflict with my father. She hated him due to an inheritance case similar to the one I'd seen in Clem's Courtroom between Mildred Henderson and her brother. Mrs. Evans's conflict was between her and her older sister. Doris shared with me that Mrs. Evans saw Clem smile at me with his wonderful love and affection and then when she saw him put his hand on my head, she simply lost it. In her mind this *"adorable child"* could never be related to *"that horrible judge."* When Doris finally spoke to her about Clem, Mrs. Evans confessed she'd *"cried her eyes out"* and given this situation *"a great deal of thought"* and prayed for forgiveness for having been such a *"terrible judge of character"* when it came to judging Clem.

I remember Clem's confident smile on that Sunday morning as we left Mrs. Evans's classroom behind.

He said, *"I hope that nice lady's teaching you how to be acceptable in His sight."*

I looked into his eyes and I said, *"Yes, sir, she is. And Amen, sir."*

Time to discuss more about Doris since she *was* the great woman behind my father:

Her full name was Doris Alma Cook. "Alma" was her mother's name and Doris was born in Mexia (pronounced /ma-heya/), Texas. In the mid-1800s her family raised tons of crops on one of the largest farms in Central Texas and after the Civil War all of their freed slaves decided to stay on at their farm because her family treated them like family.

My happiest memory of Doris was when she told me, in whispered secrecy, how she totally loved how close Clem and I were becoming. Her fulltime *"job"* she told me, was to keep Clem happy and that meant whatever Kirk wanted, Kirk got. She spoiled me rotten and I was too young to know how lucky I was. So my earliest memory of Doris was her giving me whatever I wanted whenever I wanted it.

8 mm Home Movie shot by Doris

I mention Doris here because of the incident with my Sunday school teacher. Mrs. Evans had no idea how her words concerning my Clem affected my Doris. It couldn't have been easy for my mother to hear derogatory gossip about *"her man."* It was probably more than just a little difficult for her to hear bad things said about him because she knew they just weren't true.

In my early years, I had no clue that Clem was anything other than Superman's best friend. This was because I thought Clem and Doris were totally in control and could handle everything. I never lost any sleep since I knew Doris was working hard to protect/love her children and her Clem in the McClelland home. So then, what about Doris McClelland? How'd *she* feel? Who was there to help *her* when she felt down and out? Years later when all hell broke loose, she and I had insightful discussions as she shared how her 3 children had helped her survive some tough nights and even tougher days. As time passed and troubles multiplied, Doris and I would spend hours discussing the many "why" questions: Why had trouble come looking for Clem (and the rest of us by association)? Why was Clem an easy target for the powers that would eventually attack him? Why did Clem make the choices he made when it came time for him to fight back? And the real kicker, why were the McClellands cursed with the likes of Frank Briscoe and a Texas law written back in 1876?

Clem McClelland   **Doris McClelland**
November 22, 1941 *"Marriage Announcement"* **Pics**

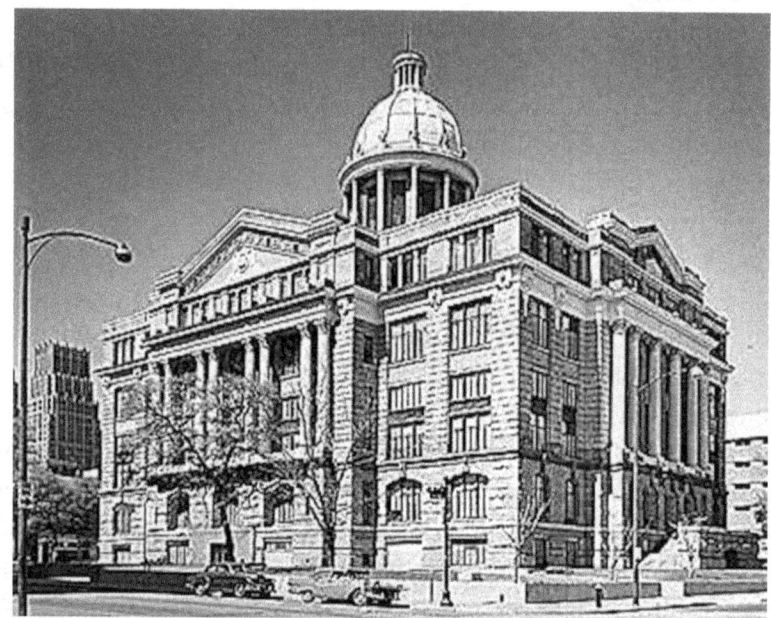

Harris County Courthouse--1955

Clem was sworn in by Judge Glenn Perry to become the youngest Harris County Judge

CHAPTER TWO

IT MAY HAPPEN HERE, 1955–1957

I was lucky to spend a lot of time with Clem. He was a judge, a Shriner, a husband, a Mason, and a Deacon. I remember he and I spent a lot of his free time together. He took me bass fishing, quail and duck and goose and dove hunting, and I remember him driving all around Houston in his black Cadillac as he shared with me his view of the world.

I was half past 6 years old, listening to him as he drove and he shared, "*. . . and your dad works every day to help people. It's what every good judge tries to do.*"

Then Clem swerved his Caddy into a strip mall and parked in front of a store with signs displaying record players and guitars and an assortment of electronic products. He smiled at me as he opened his Caddy door to step out, "*Let's go in here for a second.*"

We walked into the front door of **A-Z ELECTRONICS** and were greeted by a salesman, "*Hello, Judge. I've got it right here.*"

The salesman lifted what I'd soon learn was a *Tape Recorder* up onto a counter, then he plugged it in, picked up a Microphone, turned to me, and said, "*I'm gonna show you how this works, Judge junior, and then I want you to help me, okay?*"

The Recorder was a reel-to-reel and as it turned I was hypnotized by its lights and controls. The salesman surprised me when he started to sing **A WORRIED MAN**, "*Got myself a Cadillac, $30 down. Got myself a brand-new house, 5 miles out of town. Got myself a gal named . . .* (The salesman smiles at Clem) *. . . Doris, she treats me really fine. Yes, she's my lady, and I love her all the time.*" Then he pointed the Mic at me, "*Now you.*"

I knew the song, but no one had ever asked me to sing. I opened my mouth and, "*It takes a worried man to sing a worried song, I'm worried now but I won't be worried long.*" I looked at Clem and smiled timidly at the salesman who stopped the Recorder and told me, "*Very good!*"

Then he rewound the tape just a bit and said, "*Now, let's listen . . .*" The tape started playing and we heard him and then me singing, "*. . . Doris, she treats me* *really fine. Yes, she's my lady and I love her all the time . . . Now you. It takes a worried man to sing a worried song, I'm worried now but I won't be worried long."* Clem and I both laughed out loud and I clapped my hands. I couldn't believe that was *my* voice coming out of the Recorder's speakers! Clem patted the salesman on his back and said, *"It's perfect. We'll take it!"*

Clem and I drove away from the little mall and I sat in the front seat with the Tape Recorder (*my* Tape Recorder) sitting on the floor in front of me. As Clem discussed the wonders of electronics I couldn't stop smiling. This was my second electric present (my train was the first) and this one opened up all kinds of possibilities. I loved the songs my sisters played on their 45 rpm turntable but I began to imagine pointing the Microphone at my radio and recording **THE HIGH and MIGHTY,** Marilyn Monroe singing **RIVER of NO RETURN,** and Frank Sinatra singing **THREE COINS in the FOUNTAIN** (whenever Clem and Doris took us to the movies, I paid attention to all the film Soundtracks).

I also loved the **SUPERMAN** theme and the theme from **TOPPER, ZORRO,** and **THE HIGHWAY PATROL** so I imagined pointing my Mic at the Television, and recording those melodies, too. Clem was still driving when he looked into his rear-view mirror and said, *"Okay, what's this?"*

At that moment I heard a Police siren and I turned in my seat to see a Houston Police Car pulling up behind us with its lights flashing. The Police Officer double-tapped his siren to further announce his presence.

Clem in his pay-attention-I'm-teaching voice said, *"A safe driver pulls over quickly when a siren sounds . . ."*

The two cars pulled to the side of the road as traffic continued to pass us. I watched Clem's eyes and saw him thinking as I turned again to see the Police Officer exit his car and walk up to where Clem sat. Clem rolled down his window.

The young, overweight Officer removed his sunglasses and with a good ol' boy smile said, *"What makes you think you can drive this big Caddy so recklessly over my streets like it's some kinda tank? Are you one of those fruits who think you're better than everyone else?"*

I noticed that the Officer had a line of sweat on his face where his hat pressed against his head and, as I observed that unattractive aspect of his appearance, the Officer surprised both of us when he jammed his finger into Clem's chest and spit, *"Let me see your God damned driver's license!"*

I was shocked by the pitch of the man's voice as well as by how he spoke to Clem. I'd never seen anyone speak to him with such disrespect, so his outburst was amazing to me.

As the Officer opened his ticket book I stared at Clem, closely watching his calm face and noticing how steady his hands were. He reached inside his coat and pulled out his wallet from his inside jacket pocket.

I watched Clem flip the wallet open to reveal his judge's badge and his judge's credentials of what court he chaired in the Harris County Courthouse, and what term he was presently serving to prove his tenure as an officer of the Harris County justice system.

He held the Badge up to the Officer and I watched that man's mean face freeze up as he began to count all the mistakes he'd made in the last minute. Clem then proceeded to *put the Icing on the Cake*, one of his favorite platitudes, as he spoke, "*My name as you can see printed on this document is Judge Clem McClelland and I want you to repeat what you just said a little louder this time . . .*" he pointed to me " *. . . so my six-year-old son will be sure to hear all of it.*"

The Officer looked at me and looked at the Badge but he did not look again at Clem's face. He lowered his ticket book and stammered, "*I'm so . . . so sorry, Judge. I . . . I guess I misspoke.*"

Clem leaned toward the now very uncomfortable Officer and asked, "*What did you say?*"

I imitated Clem's body language and leaned toward them both. The unhappy Officer said, "*I . . . I'm . . . very . . .*" to which Clem said, "*Take your time, Officer, I've . . .*" He looked at me and smiled, " *. . . We've got all day . . .*"

After the Officer had apologized for the tenth time, Clem started up his *tank* and spoke no more to the Policeman. He drove away and began to talk to *me* since I guess he thought the episode could be a learning experience.

As I went about my job of growing-up, Clem sometimes used irritating and humorous clichés in order to teach me how to live and be successful. The first time I heard one of his top ten, it was okay since I was young and I was processing so much. So I tried to accept the annoying platitudes that Clem used such as *"Familiarity Breeds Contempt"* or *'Hard Work Always Pays Off"* or *"Great Minds Think Alike"* or *"Such Is Life"* or *"Time Heals All Wounds"* or *"After the Storm the Sun Will Always Shine."*

On that particular day I was open to hearing a Clem favorite since the Policeman had made such a huge impression on me, so when Clem said, "*Don't judge him too harshly. We're All in This Together"* it sounded okay.

Now, many years later, I smile with gratitude for how much of his time Clem devoted to me, but I have to work overtime to adopt his familiar *"words to live by."*

Next, a *word* about where we were driving . . .

Our new home at 4514 Ivanhoe had been finished a week before and, to Doris and Clem, the best way to celebrate its completion was to throw a party.

When Clem and I arrived home from buying my Tape Recorder *and* policing the Police, the sun was about to set. There was still plenty of light to easily see the beautifully majestic 2-story red brick house with a semi-circular driveway that, like the street in front of it, was full of cars. Clem and I parked, then disembarked from the Caddy and we snuck in a back door to the Master Bedroom. He smiled at me and said, *"I'm going to change clothes and take my insulin, so play with your new Recorder."*

He pulled down his trousers. Then he held up a syringe and a bottle of insulin, pushed the needle of the syringe into the bottle and withdrew 30 units. He then took a cotton swab, poured some alcohol on it, and cleaned off an area on his upper thigh. Finally he jabbed the needle into his thigh and injected the insulin.

I'd seen Clem do his diabetic drill before since he took two shots a day. There were times when he and I would be sitting in a deer blind or a duck blind or in a fishing boat and he'd have to inject his insulin so he could stay alive to catch more fish or shoot something. I was used to it but my sisters would scream and run away every time they saw him pull out his syringe.

He put his diabetic tools aside, put on his shirt and tie and his Fez that read *"Patrol Captain"* (I was reading better) and then he opened the door to the rest of the house and walked through it, with me and my Recorder following close behind.

To shouts of *"There he is!"* and *"Finally, the Master of the house!"* Clem entered the Den that was filled with Shriners wearing Fezzes standing next to the bar. Their wives all stood next to Doris and her piano in the Living Room. I carried my Recorder to the stairway (which led up to my room and my sisters' rooms) and I hooked up the Microphone cable in case the party opened up and gave me a reason to record something.

I looked at all the Fezzes and I was able to read, *"Divan" "Provost Guard" "Lancers"* and then I saw Bryson Martin who wore a *"Patrol"* Fez and Guy Price also wearing a *"Patrol"* Fez. I remembered those two men from Clem's Courtroom and, semi-spoiler alert, they both would play important roles in what would happen to Clem and the rest of us.

I moved from the stairway to the Den and I watched Clem joke and drink with his male guests. I noticed another group of Shriners who surrounded a man with *"Past Potentate"* on his Fez and I heard *"Say hello to Ben Jeffries"* as he was introduced by one Shriner to another.

I was still young and unsophisticated about social behavior but as I watched the two groups of men it seemed to me that Clem was more interested in Ben Jeffries' group than his own. He kept trying to get Mr. Jeffries' attention but Mr. Jeffries was busy telling fascinating tales to his followers and paid no attention to Clem. This was interesting. I looked again at Jeffries' Fez but I was still learning so I had no idea what the letters forming *"Past Potentate"* meant.

I wanted to point my new Recorder at something musical so I moved to the Living Room where Doris was holding court. I heard her say, *"Somebody go get Bryson to come play the piano. It's time for my performance!"*

BRING CLEM HOME

**8 MM Home Movies
Bryson Martin and Guy Price wore their Fezzes**

I laid the Recorder down on the floor behind one of two Wingback chairs and plugged it into the wall. A red "Power" light came on indicating I was ready to record. Then I put on the Headphones that came with the Recorder to check the *"levels"* of sound in the room. I heard adult voices talking and laughing and I heard my sisters, Micki and Anne, sitting on the piano bench trying to play **HEART AND SOUL**. I didn't record them due to a surplus of missed notes.

I saw Doris put on her special performance Cat Eye sunglasses and then she came to me, leaned down and asked, *"Did your father take his insulin?"*

I nodded to her, and she happily moved to the piano.

Micki looked up at her and asked, *"When do I get to sing, mama?"*

Doris replied, *"Soon. Now, take your places..."*

Micki rolled her eyes, then she and Anne stood and took their places at each end of the piano. Bryson and most of the other men came into the Living Room to join their wives and Bryson sat down at the piano as Doris turned and clapped her hands, *"It's time everyone! Let me present Bryson Martin at the piano, and my daughters Micki and Anne, my favorite page-turners!"*

Everyone applauded and moved closer to Doris who looked like she was in heaven: A new house, a handsome husband with 3 beautiful kids, her own piano player, and a captive audience.

I held up my Mic and Bryson started playing the opening to **BILL BAILEY** as Doris began to perform, first singing to Bryson, *"Won't you come home, Bill Bailey, won't you come home."* Then to her guests, *"I've moaned the whole night long."*

She danced away from the piano which made her guests take a few steps back. *"I'll do the cookin', honey, I'll pay the rent... I know I done you wrong."*

She smiled brightly as she sang and danced, *"You remember that rainy evenin' I threw you out... with nothin' but a fine tooth comb..."* Doris swayed with the music and she threw a smile at Bryson as she finished her lyric, *"I know I'm to blame, ain't it a cryin' shame... Bill Bailey won't you please come home!"*

Clem (he was still 6'4") marched into the room playing his Clarinet and he and Bryson began the instrumental bridge to **BILL BAILEY**. Everyone was surprised and everyone cheered as the music became more up tempo and louder. I laughed at my father's ability to hit perfect pitch on his horn and I adjusted the volume on my Recorder and tried to capture his great sound. I looked at Doris, and her face showed a trace of disappointment at being forgotten but then, just as he and Bryson ended the song with a loud fanfare, I saw Clem sashay over to her.

As everyone applauded, Clem took his lips off his Clarinet and put them on Doris's lips as their guests laughed.

My sisters and I watched this display of affection and we realized we'd just seen an image of our parents that would last forever. With their kiss, I also recognized that our new house had been properly baptized and converted into our new home. It was one of those happy memories that I mentioned the McClelland family would recall later when we'd need it.

Bryson kept playing the piano and Doris kept singing romantic songs like **MOONLIGHT BECOMES YOU** as Micki and Anne danced together. I saw Clem head for the bar so I turned off my Recorder, pushed it under the Wingchair, and in my best *Phantom* mode, I followed him. As he walked I saw him looking left and right and I heard Clem ask Guy Price, "*Have you seen Ben Jeffries?*" Mr. Price shook his head, "*No.*"

Clem sat down on one of several bar stools as he greeted his Bartender, Woodrow Freeman, "*Hey Woodrow, Jack it up please.*" Clem pointed to a Jack Daniels bottle in the well of the bar which Woodrow picked up and began to pour saying, "*Nice tootin' as usual, Mr. Mac.*" The bar in our new home's Den was designed by Clem and was fully stocked with first class liquor and liqueurs and he was proud to hear all his Shriner pals praise him saying, "*The judge is open for business, wow!*" and "*Nice collection, Clem!*"

I saw Woodrow place Clem's glass on the wooden bar top just as Ben Jeffries sat down on the bar stool next to him. As *The Phantom* I moved closer to where they sat by sliding up to where Woodrow stood next to the well. He smiled down on me and gave me his normal wink. Jeffries raised his glass to Clem and said, "*That was impressive, Judge.*"

Clem said, with relief, "*Hey, Ben. I'm glad you could make it.*"

Ben said, "*You've been on my mind for a while, so listen, Clem. I like what everyone tells me about you. We have a meeting next week to plan next year's Arabia Temple Circus and you know how important this event is . . . Care to join us?*"

I moved closer to Woodrow to hear better and I bumped into the well which made Woodrow drop the Jack Daniels bottle to the floor with a loud crash. Woodrow quickly pushed me away from the broken glass as he apologized to his employer, "*I'm so sorry, Mr. Clem.*"

I was suddenly very scared. I hid under the bar still in my *Phantom* mode.

Probably since Jeffries was watching him, I heard Clem laugh and say, "*No problem, Woodrow. Did you cut yourself?*"

Woodrow said, "*No sir, but I'm real sorry cause I know you loves your Jack.*"

Clem asked, "*Was that the 29 ounce bottle?*"

Woodrow wasn't sure where this was going, "*Yes, sir, it was.*"

I could hear Clem's smile, "*You know that drink is the Nectar of the Gods, don't you?*"

I could see the sweat on Woodrow's brow, "*Yes, sir, I do.*"

Then Clem said, "*Don't worry, Woodrow, I'll just dock your pay!*"

All three men laughed.

Woodrow nodded. "*Yes, sir, Mr. Clem, you sure is a funny man, yes sir, you is!*"

What a mess! And Woodrow was going to get "*docked*," whatever that meant! I looked at him cleaning up what I'd done and wondered if Clem would use his black belt on Woodrow or the new cowboy belt that Doris had bought for Clem the week before. Still hidden by the bar top, I reached over and touched Woodrow's leg in thanks, which caused him to look down at me and wink again. Another spoiler-alert: Years later Woodrow and his wife Josephine (Doris's housemaid and a good friend to my family) would be there with us on a very difficult day . . .

The Phantom hid behind the Bar
(*that's Clem and Ben in the mirror*)

My parents, my sisters, and I began to adjust to our new home. I'll share a quick description of how we ate dinner almost every night in the new McClelland household: First, Clem and I would hunt or fish, we'd bag our game, bring it home where I'd watch Clem clean the duck, goose, or fish. Then Doris would add her Cook recipe with breading or seasoning for the dish she'd prepare, and finally she'd use the grill in our kitchen to cook it.

Clem and I hunted and fished

When it was dinner time we'd all sit at our round kitchen table and listen to Clem's before-dinner prayer. Subjects covered by his brief sermons included the normal litany of Pride, Jealousy, Vanity, gratitude for the blessings we had, how we shouldn't covet our neighbor's ass (his words, not mine), and why we should fear God and love Jesus.

In my *Phantom* mode I'd bow my head solemnly but then I'd squint open my eyes just enough to see my sisters yawn and my mother smile at her man as she silently prayed he'd say "*Amen*" before her dinner got cold.

Dinner time was also important because, starting with Doris, we'd each take a few minutes to share "*something of interest*" for the other family members to enjoy and experience. This was a useful exercise since it gave us the chance to hear what juicy conflicts were going on in Clem's court or in Doris's Parent Teacher's Association meetings (where she kept being re-elected President of the PTA since all three of her children attended the same Elementary school).

Mealtime prayers/talks were valuable for learning about what each of us were doing, but more importantly it taught us how to express ourselves. My sisters would offer tidbits about new dresses and shoes that they wanted Doris to buy for them and I'd share how my sling shots and pea shooters were deadly accurate as my friends and I took aim at each other after school. The McClelland Nightly News gave all of us a chance to perform to a captive family audience and it was good practice to use our voices to convey information. Another alert: A day would come when I'd use this verbal skillset in an attempt to influence several important decision-makers.

Having discussed the early *family side* of Clem, the other side of his coin was his work. Clem had figured out that his life would be governed by the Law. He applied to the University of Arkansas and earned a Bachelor of Arts degree in Law. Then he traveled to Austin, Texas to attend the University of Texas Law School and graduated with a Master of Laws degree.

In 1941, the year he married Doris Cook and the year Clem decided to hang his lawyer shingle out in Houston, he wasn't sure what aspect of the law would be both enjoyable and profitable for him. In the beginning he tried real estate, he tried civil cases, but he never tried criminal law because he felt both the prosecutors and defense attorneys spent more time "*choreographing the truth*" than they did practicing law. The more he hung around the Harris County Courthouse, the more he learned there was another game that could challenge him and satisfy his need for legal conflicts, and that was *probate law*.

Houston had never required a full-time probate judge or a full-time probate court. Clem started taking cases (there were many) that were instead handled by a quasi-probate court. All probate cases in Harris County were processed through the office of County Judge Glenn Perry, a slick legal eagle whose workload was burdened with too many insanity cases. Ironically Judge Perry was a few years away from retirement, and when Clem met him, Perry was "*going crazy*." His *insanity* was due to the extra probate workload and all the family drama that went with it. So when Perry saw the positive energy displayed by the knowledgeable McClelland (as he ran around the courthouse) he reached out and made Clem a great offer, "*If you come and take this damn monkey off my back, someday when they create a real probate court I'll make sure you get the judgeship.*"

Clem was pretty cool about the shortage of Harris County legal opportunities and he appreciated the logic in Judge Perry's proposal . . . So what did Clem do?

A few years later, early one morning, Clem and I sat in a dark duck blind in Katy, Texas right before the sun came up. We listened as hundreds of geese flew over us and the Katy rice fields. The high volume of honking geese was amazing but Clem's voice in that darkness made a more solid impression on my mind, "*I desperately wanted to be Harris County's first probate judge. I'd have given up drinking Mr. Daniels to wear that robe.*" Using a small flashlight from our hunt satchel I watched his face as he fondly remembered shaking Judge Perry's hand to seal the deal.

Clem went to work for the County on December 1, 1947, as Judge Perry's probate assistant at a salary of $350 per month. The deal for them both was that Clem would not bother Perry with anything remotely probative.

Here's how Judge Perry laid down *his* law, "*If you don't understand something, read your law books. If you have a dispute you can't handle, handle it anyway. If I have to hold your hand, you have to give me your paycheck for that month. Are we clear about what I want?"*

Clem smiled at the memory, and I smiled because it was another inside story shared with me about *and by* my father.

Over the next few years Clem worked hard at being probate-savvy and at being a father/husband. He juggled the research he needed to do in order to keep his paycheck away from Judge Perry, and he juggled his wife, two daughters, and new-born son to keep Doris happy. He shared with me in several duck blind conversations that Doris was the real father/mother during that time, "*She was the true juggler of all things McClelland.*"

As for the probate cases, I think we were in a deer blind on another morning when Clem told me some of the horror stories that described the complicated cases that crossed his desk daily, "*I'll never understand how such small-minded people can cook up such hateful ways to steal money from the people they're supposed to love.* (I saw him smile) *I'd sure hate to be in line behind them on Judgement Day! I hope you and your sisters are up front with each other when it comes to being kind and giving. Never get greedy.*"

The more cases he took as a lawyer in his quasi-probate court, the more he realized that the sensitive decisions a probate judge had to make every day required both a sharp legal mind and a healthy temperament (remember he was a good Christian) for that Court to work.

When he talked to the people who were most affected by the Probative atrocities that existed, his awareness changed to rage at the injustice and apparent lack of concern for the large number of defenseless people. That's when Clem realized he was the right man to ultimately be the judge of this court. There was no question in his mind that fighting the Probative atrocities was God's plan for him.

Clem's research of probate courts around the country revealed cases which left heirs to many estates unprotected. He also discovered cases with victims of laughable theft by the very court that was appointed to prevent that theft.

Other less obvious outrages were caused by networks of thieving probate attorneys and guardianship groups who freely pilfered the pocketbooks of the elderly and defenseless. There were countless cases of wrongly seized possessions and split up estates at the behest of the probate judge.

He told me about one advocate for probate oversight who said, "*It's the deception of protection*" as she tried to expose lawless probate courts and their ability to abuse their power unchallenged.

It became Clem's mission to protect the probate court that he would help to create. With Judge Perry's blessing, he told the local politicos that he was a tireless, faithful Democrat and he was ready to serve the citizens of Houston, Texas as their new and capable probate judge. The men in power were skeptical at first, but Clement was very charming and determined to succeed.

The truth: the men in power didn't have the guts to say *"No"* to him.

So Doris went right to work creating posters for his campaign, *"McClelland Will Protect Your Wills!" "Clem McClelland's The One!" "Probe No More! McClelland for Probate Judge!"* and she began carrying her signs whenever she shopped at the **Weingarten's** grocery store or took her children to the park or went to **Mable's Able Hair Salon** to have her hair done.

Clem was a Shriner, devoted to the Arabia Temple, and a member of the Scottish Rite of Masons. These groups all had political juice and their leaders knew how to fuel Clem's rise to probate power. Houston was the perfect location for a man like Clem to gain power, and he proved it when he won on his first attempt. The first probate race wasn't close, probably due to those *"Probe No More"* posters.

In 1950 Clem became the first Judge of the new Harris County Probate Court, and he was the youngest Judge in the courthouse. He was thirty-three years old and would soon earn $8,250 per year.

Over several terms Republican opponents for his office would appear then disappear because Harris County was Democratic. They'd also disappear thanks to Clem's deep-rooted spot in Houston's political arena. Whenever an election rolled around, the Honorable Judge McClelland ran unopposed . . .

First Judge for the new Probate Court

The whole time that Clem was gaining his power, there were people standing in the political wings who were interested in his success. They watched and took note of the fact that the newly elected probate judge of Harris County was a wily character who chose his friends carefully and tended to side with men who wore those ridiculous Fezzes.

One of the men who looked on my Clem with disapproving eyes was careful to keep his opinions to himself. He was not in a position of political power at that time, but he understood the rule that whispered, *"Speak no ill of your fellow being, especially if he/she is a Democrat . . ."*

This man was Assistant District Attorney Frank Briscoe and he, too, hung around the courthouse to take its pulse and stay in touch with the many and varied soap operas that played there daily.

As previously mentioned, Frank was mean and hungry. When his eyes zoomed in on the face of Judge McClelland, Frank Briscoe was like a starved turkey buzzard to Clem's blissful possum trying to cross a busy highway . . .

ADA Frank Briscoe

It was early 1957 and Clem was in his Chambers on the third floor of the courthouse. His office was located in a corner space and according to Clem's secretary, Helen Smith, "*It has the best view and no harsh sunlight!*"

Inside Clem's Chamber were pictures and diplomas on the walls from the Universities of Arkansas and Texas as well as certificates from his Sigma Chi days and from his Chamber of Commerce, Arabia Temple, and Masonic affiliations. There was also me.

I lay asleep on Clem's couch, taking a nap, having risen early that day with Clem to shoot down some unlucky ducks. On that day Guy Price and Bryson Martin sat on comfortable leather chairs in front of Clem's big rosewood desk. On that day there were also two envelopes on Clem's desk, one thick and one thin.

As I lay there pretending to sleep, I went into my *Phantom* mode so I could listen.

Guy Price had the appearance and hair-style of a weasel whereas Bryson Martin was a tall and handsome ladies' man with a full watt smile that burned all the time. Clem pushed the two envelopes toward the two very different men and then looked down at a legal brief that covered the rest of the space on his desk.

Both men opened their respective packets and looked inside.

I heard Mr. Price snort at Mr. Martin and unhappily whine, *"You always get the big bass, Martin. All I get are the minnows."*

Bryson grinned and replied, *"Fisherman Price, as I've explained before . . . it's all a matter of how you use your wrists."* He demonstrated by flicking his wrists.

Guy continued to moan and blinked, *"I want the bass."*

Clem, with his eyes still looking down at the brief, said, *"Use better bait . . ."*

At that moment there was a knock on the Chamber door and Bryson quickly reached over and grabbed Guy's packet to hide both envelopes under a Newspaper he held in his other hand.

I sat up and waved at Helen Smith as she walked in wearing her usual grin. She said to Clem, *"Judge, Assistant DA Briscoe and that reporter from The Houston Press, Mr. Detrick, wish to see you."*

Clem shook his head impatiently, *"Helen, tell Mr. Briscoe I'm busy now, and then wait five minutes and send in Mr. Detrick."* Helen nodded, waved to me, and walked out the chamber's front door.

Guy and Bryson stood up and Clem pointed to the side door leading to his Courtroom, *"See you both later at the Temple."* and they left.

Clem stood and walked into his bathroom where he put on his black Judge's robe and checked himself in the mirror. He was sensible about his appearance especially with members of the press, and his take on Cap Detrick as an *"arrogant Pulitzer Prize wannabe"* forced Clem to comb and part his hair.

Clem sat down behind his desk just as Cap Detrick entered the Chamber. Cap was in his late twenties with Tab Hunter blonde hair and a smirk that Clem didn't like. I was sitting up on the couch when he walked in and Cap waved at me.

Clem returned his attention to the legal brief spread out on his desk and said, *"Yes, Mr. Detrick, what story are you pushing this week?"*

Cap's smirk changed to a smile, *"Straight to it as always, right Judge?"*

Clem looked up with his eyebrows raised and Cap hopped to it, *"We're doing a Sunday supplement on Houston leaders, their contributions to Houston's growth, and what they or YOU think of Houston's future."*

Clem replied, *"Use the notes from the last epic article you wrote. Quote **Judge Clem McClelland loves Houston** Unquote."*

Clem pointed at the door, *"As you go out, please send Mrs. Smith back in, will you?"*

Cap hesitated then kicked his heels ever so slightly in a mock salute and said, *"Sure, Judge. Always a pleasure."*

He waved and smiled at me again as he turned away to exit out the front door to the Chamber. I sat there and yawned as I thought about what I'd just seen and heard.

Cap did as the judge commanded and he told Helen, *"Hiz Honor asked me to send you back in."*

Helen nodded and said, *"Thank you, Mr. Detrick."*

Helen Smith was a smart lady and she decided to wait a moment before she went back in to see the judge. She and Frank Briscoe's secretary, Judy Wyatt, were best friends and they shared a lot of information with each other about their bosses.

Since Judy's boss was sitting in Clem's Waiting Room, Helen picked up her phone and acted like she was on an important call so she could monitor Frank Briscoe.

In Helen's words to me, "*Cap was on his way out the door when he noticed Briscoe's unhappy face. Cap stopped to introduce himself. He said, Mr. Briscoe? My name is Cap Detrick, reporter for The Houston Press. We met last week at your boss's Campaign Dinner.*"

Briscoe nodded. "*Yes, I remember, Mr. Detrick. Say, I've been waiting a long time to meet with the judge. How'd your meeting go?*"

Cap smirked and said, "*Some days he's available but today wasn't one of them. The nature of my business.*"

Helen said she watched Cap as she continued to pretend her phone call was urgent.

She saw Cap think, and listened as he continued,

"*From what I hear in the courthouse hallways, you're an aggressive prosecutor. I wonder if you have time for a quick interview . . .*"

Helen watched Briscoe as he asked, "*About?*" Cap answered, "*About where you think Houston is headed.*" Helen saw Frank rub his hand over his chin as his eyes came to life, "*Cap. May I call you that?*" Cap nodded as Frank continued, "*Cap, let's have lunch, whadaya say?*"

They shook hands and together they walked out of Clem's Front Office. Helen watched them leave and she made a note to share what she'd just heard with her friend Judy. Cap and Frank's meeting would not be good news for Clem, and soon there'd be other meets where their topic of discussion would shift from *The Future of Houston* to *The Future of Frank Briscoe* . . .

One night in June of 1957, Clem and 75 Shriners of the Arabia Temple were marching around the Temple parking lot preparing for a parade in Dallas. There were bells and cymbals and drums and car horns working overtime to make a lot of noise. Shriners loved parades because they could dress in their elaborate costumes, ride their mini Model Ts, and express their brotherly love while they raised funds for their Crippled Children's Hospital in Houston.

Shriner's Hospitals had been the focus of Shriners nationwide starting back in the early '20s. The hospitals (twenty-two at one time) helped children with polio, spinal cord injuries, burns, diseases, and birth defects and Clem's involvement in this crusade was a large part of who he was. His belief system demanded that he help other people, children in this case, with no restraints due to religion or race. If a child was under 18 years of age, suffered one of the problems listed above and could be treated, they'd be admitted to the Children's Hospital AT NO CHARGE.

Getting back to the Shriner parade rehearsal, Clem's Fez read *"General Chairman"* and I was 8 years old as I leaned against his cooler sitting on the hood of his black Cadillac Sedan Deville. I watched and listened to his directions as he choreographed his marching men and I was enjoying the Drum and Bugle Corps' brigade, the Motor Corps' mini-Model Ts and tricked-out motorcycles when Clem blew his whistle for all to take a break.

He walked over to me and opened the cooler to pull out a bottle of Jack Daniels.

Sweating, he swallowed straight from the bottle, and then he smiled at me as he asked, *"How's it look so far?" "Great, Dad." "Now don't be afraid to tell me if it looks bad, son." "It looks great, Clem." "You're not saying that so I'll buy you a chocolate sundae, are you?" "No, sir. But I think a sundae sounds good." "Think you and I can share one?" "Absolutely!" "Maybe we'll get one then."*

Clem and I had played the **Tell Me What You Really Think** game for as long as I could remember and on hot, humid Houston nights I'd tell him anything if it served me up a sundae.

A group of Shriners including Bryson, Guy, and Ben Jeffries walked over to us slapping each other's back, laughing, and obviously pleased with the rehearsal. Bryson came up to me, and as he gave me a hug, he said to Clem, *"Es Selamu Aleikum, Judge!"* Which translated means *"Peace be unto you, Judge!"*

Clem wiped his brow and responded, *"And to you, as well, Mr. Martin. Wa alaikum assalam wa rahmatu Allah!"*

Which translated means, *"May the peace, mercy, and blessings of Allah be with you, too!"*

Ben Jeffries approached Clem and the other Shriners stepped aside as he shook Clem's hand, *"If your Circus is half as good as your parade, we're going to sell some tickets, Judge."*

I watched my father be the Center of the Universe in that place at that time as he said, *"I'll make it twice as good, Ben. We leave tomorrow."*

Ben nodded confidently and said, *"Find some great acts, Clem."*

Ben patted Clem on his back and then he and several Shriners walked away.

Bryson and Guy opened Clem's cooler to remove two bottles of Lone Star beer, their favorite.

It was also my favorite because it had the words *"The National Beer of Texas"* on its label.

I was a proud Texan.

Guy was in a very thirsty mood that night and he downed his Lone Star in about 5 seconds. I watched him with interest because I'd seen him drink like this before and, when he drank heavily, he slipped into his normal weasel-mode. In that mode I'd seen him try to slip up on Clem and attack him verbally. I had seen Clem in his Courtroom, in our fishing boat, at Church, in our different blinds, and at our dinner table for his nightly sermons. He was the word master and better fitted to slay attackers than be slain by them. But on that night, after 4 or 5 beers, Guy was ready for battle. He blinked rapidly for several seconds then he confronted Clem, "*Are . . . are you still thinking about adding a Wild West Show to your Circus?*"

Clem had Guy's number before Guy had drunk his first beer so he smiled and answered, "*Yes, this will be the greatest Shrine Circus in Arabia Temple history . . .*"

Guy blinked. "*I don't know, Clem . . .*" to which Clem smiled and cleverly responded, "*Uh-huh.*"

Guy blinked rapidly. "*I don't think anyone will want to pay money to see it.*"

I looked at Bryson as his mouth, like mine, opened wide in surprise. The truth: Guy was about 8 inches shorter than Clem. The word "*diminutive*" comes to my mind now. The word "*little*" probably came to my mind then. Clem raised both of his big hands and put them on Guy's shoulders. He smiled and slowly said, "*Guy Price. Mr. Price. Guy. A question, GUY.*"

I saw Guy swallow as he blinked again. I felt sorry for him because I remembered how Clem could make *me* feel when his powerful gaze scrutinized me, "*How's your little girl doing?*"

Guy said, "*She's . . . She's doing fine, Judge. Thanks, uh, thanks for asking.*"

Clem slid his right arm around Guy's left shoulder and they began to walk.

Guy had no choice. He had to follow Clem's lead.

Clem with a concerned voice asked, "*So no problem with the adoption?*"

Guy walked carefully so he wouldn't trip, and he answered respectfully, "*No, sir. You made it happen and my wife and I will always be very grateful.*"

Clem stopped and turned Guy to face him so he could stare at his face, "*We did it, didn't we Mr. Minnow?*"

Guy blinked and nodded as Clem finished, "*Same thing here. Stay tuned.*"

Bryson raised his eyebrows at me and I realized that once again I'd been a witness to an adult confrontation that would stay with me forever.

I watched Clem walk away from Guy to pick up his Jack Daniels bottle and smoothly return it to his lips. I watched him drink a long drink before he wiped his mouth and smiled at me. I smiled back since, as usual, I was impressed by Clem. But remember that I was also an eight-year-old, motivated by thoughts of a cool sundae on a hot summer night . . .

I remember listening to a wonderful tape of Circus Music on my Tape Recorder the night Clem placed the last suitcase on top of our blue 1958 Chevy Station Wagon. My sisters and Doris were asleep in the house as Clem let me help him gather all the traveling items we'd need to take with us on our Circus trip.

This was going to be an adventure for me. We were going to travel across country to see Circus acts as they performed in different cities and towns and, if the acts passed muster, Clem would hire them for his Circus in Houston.

Clem had told my sisters and I, "*Doris and I want your opinion. If you see an act that you LOVE, tell us why you love it. If I'm about to sign an act you HATE you'd better tell me why you hate it or I might make the wrong decision and book them. Are we clear?*"

My sisters and I saluted him (equal to a thumbs up now) and we three joined his search party.

Early that morning as Clem pulled away from our house, Doris laid out our journey, "*We're going to Dallas, to St. Louis, Chicago, Kansas City, Santa Fe, Las Vegas, and finally Los Angeles.*"

I shut my eyes and visualized the different acts that Clem had shown me using brochures and his 8 mm film projector: Lion tamer Pat Anthony, High wire acts, Clowns, Horse acts, Acrobats, the Kelly Elephants, Tight rope walkers, the Wallendas, and The Flying Malkos.

With my eyes still closed I imagined Opening Night, and I knew it'd be a visual wonder . . .

Pat Anthony played with his Lions and Tigers

I learned a lot about the entertainment business as I watched Clem audition and interview various Circus elements. I watched him sign a dog or a horse act, a clown troupe or a ringmaster. I studied him as he spoke to the rigging pros who put the Big Top together so the ropes and wires would keep the Circus safe. Clem had a knack for choosing the best. He was the man with the plan and he was the only one who could make the Houston Shrine Circus shine.

As I studied him on that trip I learned how strong-willed and powerful he was. I knew how motivated he was to impress Ben Jeffries and the Shrine's Circus committee, but I learned he was truly inspired to create the best Circus possible so it would generate money and expand the services of Houston's Crippled Children's Hospital.

The next part of Clem's plan was his Wild West Show idea, and he knew he needed something special to pull it together. Before we took the Circus trip the McClellands watched RIN-TIN-TIN on ABC-TV every Friday night. It was the second-highest rated ABC-TV program of the late '50s, and Clem was not shy about lying down with dogs if it would sell tickets.

On our Circus trip our last stop was Los Angeles so Clem could meet with RIN-TIN-TIN's owner-trainer Frank Barnes. Mr. Barnes was the key to Clem's acquiring the entire RIN-TIN-TIN troupe including Lt. Rip Masters and Rusty since without the dog there would just be fleas. So when Mr. Barnes said "*Yes*" and shook Clem's hand, the Wild West Show had its star attraction.

Rin-Tin-Tin Cast

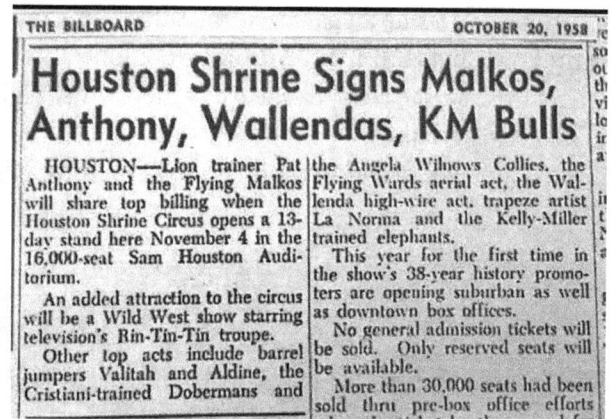

Circus Promotional

After meeting with Mr. Barnes, Clem drove our Wagon along one of the feeder streets to the main highway leading into Los Angeles. I'd seen Clem happy before but, probably due to his success with signing "*Rinty*," he sang **THE YELLOW ROSE OF TEXAS** with a vengeance.

Just as Clem had begun the third verse of **The Yellow Rose**, he and the rest of us suddenly saw a major jam-up ahead at the next intersection. Clem slowed down and when he saw that the traffic lights weren't working, he stopped our Station Wagon to evaluate the situation. The intersection was jammed with cars trying to move in all 4 directions as Clem opened his door and got out. Doris yelled, "*Clem! What are you doing? Don't leave us alone!*"

I jumped from the back seat into the driver's seat and pressed my face against the window to watch him. I saw Micki and Anne do the same in the back seat. We all saw Clem run from one car to another, talking animatedly, pointing in different directions.

He moved into the middle of the intersection, held his Harris County Badge high over his head for all of the frustrated drivers to see . . . and then he began directing traffic.

He put on quite a show and he kept his cool pointing at one line of cars going North (I guessed) and as he motioned them forward he motioned the cars opposite (that were facing South I guessed) to also move forward. Then he halted those two lines of traffic, pointed to the East and West-bound lanes and motioned them forward at the same time reminding the North and South lanes to be patient since everything was hunky-dory and okey-dokey.

There was nothing to fear. Judge Clem McClelland was on the job. I couldn't believe what I was watching. He was ready, willing, and able to make it work. The traffic started to move with Clem standing in the middle of the intersection waving at passing motorists who honked and waved their thanks to him for his effort.

I could tell he was having a great time as he unclogged the traffic jam, and I continued to listen to him as he exuberantly sang **The Yellow Rose** at an elevated volume. As he directed traffic I watched with pride as my dad saved the day.

The next chapter of our adventure was unknown to the rest of us. Clem had looked up information about some of the Game Shows that were on National Television and broadcast from Los Angeles. Knowing that **Truth or Consequences** was one of Doris's favorites he drove us into the parking lot at Hollywood Center Studios on Las Palmas Avenue in Hollywood. Doris looked around at all of the tall Royal Palm Trees surrounding these studios and asked, "*Why'd we stop here, Clem? I thought we were having lunch at* **THE BROWN DERBY** . . ." He smiled. "*Slight change in plans. Follow me . . .*"

He got out of the wagon and began to walk toward a line of people standing in front of the studio's doors where a sign read **Truth or Consequences Audience Entrance**. About midway to the sign Doris and my sisters began letting Clem know what they thought:

Doris, "*We came all the way to Los Angeles, through traffic jams, to see a quiz show?*"

Micki: (whining) "*I have to go to the bathroom!*" Anne, "*So do I!*"

What nonsense! Thanks to Clem's efforts we'd traveled across the country for days looking at Circus acts, meeting lots of new people, staying in a dozen or so motels and hotels, and NOW they all wanted to tell Clem where to go, what to do, and how to do it?

Clem firmly said, "*Settle down. We're here, let's see this.*"

End of protests, end of discussion. Clem was in charge.

The studio doors opened and the long line of people started moving inside. Clem saw that the moving line looked like a cattle call and he began to moo like a cow. All of the McClellands started to laugh. The rest of the herd didn't get it.

When we entered the studio I saw what looked like stadium bleachers leading down to a theater stage. There were lights everywhere and, as the herd moved down to fill the bleacher seats, I realized there were three men eyeing each audience member as we entered.

I found out later that this trio were "*Spotters*" for the show and when one of them saw Clem (he was still 6'4") he called out to him, "*Excuse me, sir. Yes, sir. You!*"

We stopped and waited as the Spotter came closer and looked favorably at Clem, *"Hello, sir, would you like to be a Contestant on today's show?"*

Clem shrugged like he could care less. I saw Doris pat down her hair and light up her brightest smile which she threw at the Spotter but his eyes were on Clem, *"What's your name, please?"*

Clem looked at the Spotter a long time, taking his measure before replying to him.

Then he answered, *"Judge Clem McClelland."*

The Spotter's eyes seemed to bug out of his head as he exclaimed, *"You're perfect!"*

He grabbed Clem and quickly escorted him away from us. We watched as he led Clem down a side ramp that curved behind the stage. Clem looked back at us and I saw a hint of a smile to let us know he was having a good time. I also noticed that the remaining Spotters were keeping their eyes open for more potential suck . . . uh, Contestants.

The rest of the McClellands found seats down in the middle, close to the stage. The place was packed due to the popularity of the show and also due to Los Angeles being a summertime destination for tourists. I saw Clem and two others standing center stage when the lights went down and an off-stage announcer's voice said, *"And now the National Broadcasting Company is proud to present* **Truth or Consequences***! And here is the star of our show, Bob Barker!"*

Signs with **APPLAUD** began to flash. The cattle cooperated as Bob pranced down the aisle from the back of the theater onto the stage waving a Revolutionary American flag.

Bob cried out, *"Happy Fourth of July to all of you! I'm glad you're watching today because we taped this show yesterday so we could take today off, too! And that's the truth!"*

The studio audience again cooperated with a burst of applause as Bob Barker continued, *"So let's start our revolution today with our first three contestants. This is Julie Hawes from Sacramento, Ned Dalton from Denver, and Clem McClelland from Houston."*

On cue, the audience applauded. I remember Bob asked Julie about what she did for a living, a secretary I think, and Ned was an insurance salesman, and then, *"And next, say hello to Clem McClelland."*

Clem smiled and waved to us in the middle row. Anne stood up and waved back as she cutely yelled out, *"Hi, Daddy!"* The audience laughed at her. I wanted to hide under the seats.

Bob looked down at his index card for Clem and said, *"Clem, it says here that you're a Judge, is that right?"*

Clem looked at the middle camera and smiled, *"Harris County, Texas* (Clem made a dumb face) **and that's the truth!"**

The audience burst out laughing as Clem stole Bob's line away. Bob increased the voltage on his smile, looked at the same middle camera, and said, "*Yes, Judge, but can you play by* our *rules and still win!*"

Clem smirked with his dumb face again and said, "**Only if I have to!**"

The audience laughed and Beulah the monkey pressed her buzzer twice, her way of showing she liked Clem . . . A brief story about Clem's dumb face: In the '40s and '50s there was a comic named Red Skelton who had several characters he played for laughs. One of those characters was *Clem Kadiddlehopper*, a country bumpkin who made a dumb face.

Clem McClelland mimicked Red Skelton whenever *he* wanted to be funny. The first time I saw my Clem impersonate Clem Kadiddlehopper I thought I'd never stop laughing. Whenever Clem did his funny bumpkin it wasn't his face or his performance. I laughed at *him*.

**Clem Kadiddlehopper
(Red Skelton)**

So when Clem made his dumb face, this time on National Television, Bob Barker laughed, too, and then he tried to regain control of his show saying, "*That buzzer you heard is from our own Beulah, so let's go over the rules of our game:*

I'll ask you a question and if your answer is wrong Beulah will hit her buzzer and you'll have to compete against each other in order to win the prize."

Clem raised his hand to get Bob's attention and he asked Bob, "What's the prize?"

Bob laughed, "*You judges always want all the facts up front! But wait. Before we can continue you have to hear the question first.*"

Clem repeated the dumb face while he pondered Bob's rule of play. He started to say something and then stopped. His timing was hilarious but he knew the show had to go on. He nodded as if everything was satisfying to him and he said, "*Okay, I'm ready.*"

The audience laughed again and this time Clem waved to everyone in the room. He was hilarious and having a good time. Clem stood in the middle of the other two (shorter) Contestants as Bob pulled out an index card and asked, "*Okay Contestants, here's your question: Why was the wife concerned that her husband was a light drinker?*"

Everyone looked at Clem as he considered an answer and then Beulah buzzed her buzzer. Bob said, "*Sorry, time's up! Why was the wife concerned that her husband was a light drinker? Because every night he'd drink until it got light!*"

The audience laughed and then Bob said, "*Since there was no Truth there must now be Consequences. So let's get ready to play!*"

Clem could be a clown   **Bob Barker liked that**

As he spoke, Bob's assistants lined up the 3 Contestants on the left side of the stage and began to tie their hands behind their backs. Clem didn't look too happy about his hands being laced up but he was very unhappy when the assistant placed a spoon into his mouth.

Bob spoke to Clem as he explained the rules, "*What you have to do here, Judge, is run across the stage . . .*"

His assistants placed an egg on each of the Contestant's spoons as he continued, "*. . . and not let the egg on your spoon fall off until you reach your basket on the other side.*" One of his assistants pointed to the three target baskets each individually labeled with the name "*Julie*" and "*Ned*" and "*Clem.*"

Bob continued, "*That's where you drop it in.*"

At that moment Ned dropped his egg and one of the assistants shook her finger at him to indicate that was unacceptable.

Bob continued, "*The first Contestant to drop 3 eggs into their basket, wins the prize.*"

Clem was struggling to say something but the spoon in his mouth made it impossible.

An assistant ran to Clem and removed the spoon and the egg.

Clem asked, again, "*What's the prize?*"

The audience again laughed. I think Clem could've performed the Alphabet and these heifers would have eaten it up.

The female assistant shook her finger at Clem, reinserted the spoon into Clem's mouth, and then re-laid his first egg onto his spoon.

By that time Bob was ready to start the contest and, very excited, he said, *"Okay! On your mark, get set, GO!"*

Clem took off running across the stage. He moved fast, and his look showed his determination. He was the first to cross and he carefully leaned over to drop his first egg into his basket.

Doris, Micki, Anne, and I were jumping up and down and yelling and screaming, *"Go, Clem, Go! Go, Clem, Go!"*

Clem rushed back to where his assistant waited and she put egg #2 onto his spoon.

At the basket end of the stage the other Contestants had run into each other and both had dropped their eggs. Ned slipped on the mess made and fell down amidst laughter and howls from the studio audience.

Clem was flawless and when he dropped his third egg into his basket, Beulah buzzed her buzzer. The audience applauded and laughed as Clem let the spoon fall from his mouth with a loud clanging sound. His face showed a big grin as his family shouted insanely. My final memory from that event was an image of an impressed Bob Barker patting Clem on his back...

We were again in our Station Wagon and making pretty good time as we headed toward the California/Arizona border town of Needles, California. As Clem drove, Doris was reading the Owner's Manual for the new Polaroid Camera that Clem had just won as his prize.

He shook his head and said, *"That's the best they could do?"*

Doris defended the prize, *"You LOVE cameras! Look at this wonderful picture of your darling children that I just took! This is amazing!"*

She handed Clem a picture she had just taken of the 3 of us sitting in the back seat and said, *"And we didn't have to wait but half a minute to see it!"*

Clem snatched the picture and held it away from his face so he could inspect it, *"Hmmm. I don't think it'll catch on . . ."*

Sister Micki peered over the front seat at Doris, *"Shouldn't we tell someone about Clem being on television tomorrow?"*

Doris shrieked, *"You're right!"*

She turned and grabbed Micki's arm, *"Bob did say it won't air until the fourth! That's tomorrow!"*

Did she just say *"Bob"*?

She touched Clem's arm, *"Pull over, Clement!"*

Clem shook his head and swerved the Station Wagon off the highway. I looked around and all I saw was desert, the Mojave Desert. Clem must have been reading my mind since he said with an inflection, *"You wantum me send up smoke signals?"*

We all laughed and then Doris tapped the side of her black Cat Eye sunglasses and said, *"I'm going to need a lot of quarters..."*

Clem continued to drive toward Needles and found a Gas Station where there was an outdoor phone booth in the shade of a palm tree.

Clem gave the owner/operator a twenty dollar bill for the quarters and Doris took out her black book, opened it in the booth, and started making calls:

"Hello, yes, it's Doris McClelland... Yes, hi. Now listen... Tomorrow Clem will be starring with Bob Barker on Truth or Consequences! That's right, the game show so you be sure to watch 'cause Clem's great! No, just check your TV Guide... Gotta go, more calls to make!"

While Doris spent all of her quarters, Clem sat in the front seat of the Station Wagon smiling and watching over the 3 exhausted McClelland children. We napped on the wagon's back seats as it sat underneath the Gas Station's overhang...

A month after we had returned to Houston from our magical circus tour I started playing Pop Warner Football. It was my first year and I remember the incredible feeling of putting on shoulder pads, thigh/hip/knee pads, a helmet and face mask for the first time.

I also remember that all that protective gear turned me into a different person, but I wasn't sure I'd be able to run straight or fast. As Clem helped me suit up that first time he said, *"You've watched it on television. Now let's see you do it!"*

I played in the Will Rogers Elementary School's division, and I was skinny. But I was also fast so Clem spoke to the coach of my team and told him I'd be perfect to run back kickoffs and to return punts. The coach was my third grade Art and Music teacher as well, and he proved he was a smart fellow by paying close attention to Clem's ruling (my coach/teacher was short).

Suddenly I was standing on the Football field waiting for my first encounter with Football.

I had watched my teammates get ready to play and I stretched like they stretched, I rubbed dirt on my face because I saw one or two of them do that, and then I noticed that the opposing players on the other team (Tanglewood Elementary) were all bigger than me and my teammates. I tried to stand taller but my growth spurt was still a few years off.

Clem drank from his JD flask and then he happily tapped my helmet with his finger to help me focus on the job at hand.

I looked up at his confident face and he coached me, *"Just remember all the times you ran like a gazelle at the Boy's Club. Same thing here. Just run like the wind and make me proud."*

He walked away from me to join the other parents on our side of the field and I noticed there were parents standing across the field on the Tanglewood's sideline.

Then I heard the referee blow his whistle and my heart started racing.

I saw Clem raise his flask.

I saw the Tanglewood kicker run up to and kick the ball, and then I ran to catch it . . . and I fumbled it.

The parents on our side of the field let out a collective groan.

How could I drop the ball?

For a second I looked down at that damn pigskin and then I picked it up and dodged two very large fellows whose sole mission in life was to hurt me. I ran a straight line across the field to their sideline, then I turned an immediate left and ran up their sideline scared to death that one of those larger players would catch me.

Potential pain was a great motivator and I ran like a cheetah (it's faster than a gazelle) to get away from any painful possibilities *and* to score my first touchdown.

The Will Rogers parents standing on my sideline cheered and then Clem laughed out loud as he raised his flask, "*Speed always works . . . That's my boy.*"

I liked pleasing Clem and just like that, I was hooked forever on playing Football . . .

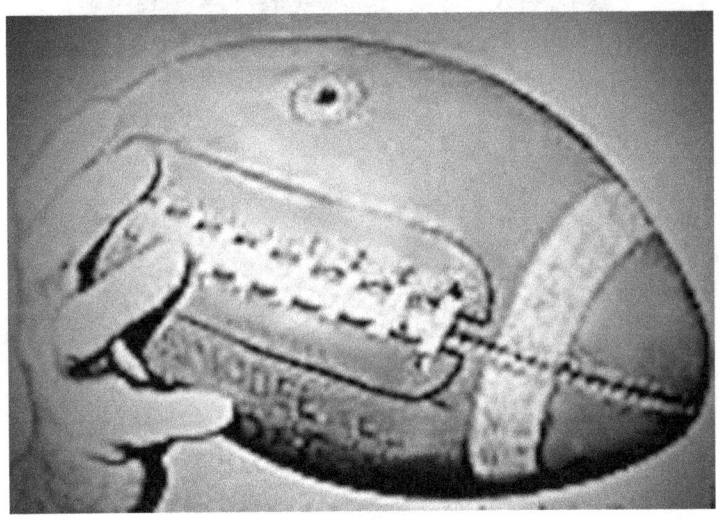

Pop Warner Football in the '50s

Doris and Clem planned a great Circus

I was a true Texan

CHAPTER THREE

IT WILL HAPPEN HERE, 1958–1960

In telling this story I've tried to avoid being too sunny or too gloomy. I've tried to share what took place back then using my green point of view. My choice of adjectives and cute phrases reflect who I was at that time: cute and light, with a gray center. But in the late '50s my world began to change to a darker hue because of the rumbling forces moving all around me.

Looking back I was fortunate to have one last chance to enjoy my youth: Clem's Circus was upon us and it was simply brilliant. The things that I learned from his event, in addition to the things that I saw, inspired me and created great memories of a happy time . . .

I was officially in the Fourth Grade at Will Rogers Elementary, and when I first met my new teacher for that year I thought that I'd seen her somewhere before. She was Mrs. Henderson. That's all I knew. Neither Clem nor Doris had any idea she was the same crazy lady who'd yelled at Clem and hit her brother with her purse in Clem's Courtroom four years before.

That's right, MILDRED Henderson.

On the first day of class that year I walked into her classroom for an early look at the seating arrangements. She gave me an unpleasant look that I misread as a welcome-to-my-class look. I was distracted at the time by a girl named Gracie Newland who had blue-eyes and blonde hair in pigtails, and I was trying to maneuver Gracie's pretty self to sit next to me when Mrs. Henderson put her hand on mine and said, *"Hello and welcome to my class Mr. McClelland. I've heard such nice things about you from your previous teachers. I'm looking forward to teaching you things your father probably hasn't taken the time to share with you."* Then she turned and walked away.

I was so preoccupied with Gracie's pigtails that I didn't really hear or care about what Mrs. Henderson had said. I would learn soon enough about her consuming hatred for Clem.

The Fourth Grade curriculum in every Texas elementary school always included a course on Texas History. As young Texans we were spoon-fed Sam Houston,

Mirabeau B. Lamar, James Bowie, William B. Travis, David Crockett, The Alamo Assault, the Goliad Massacre, Stephen F. Austin, James Fannin, Thomas Rusk, and Moses Bryan.

My teacher, Mildred Henderson, was a fanatic when it came to describing Texas History and she proved it during one of her early lessons. She had written on the blackboard the names of the men she called "*The Founding Fathers of Texas*" at the same time Gracie Newland had decided to pass me a note. Note passing in this classroom was risky. Mrs. Henderson would seize notes passed in her class and, after reading aloud whatever the note said, she'd send the pupil and the note to the principal's office where the offending student would sit for the rest of the day.

So Gracie took a chance unaware that Mildred already had me in her sights. My two best friends Chris Hale and Steve Taylor were both in Mrs. Henderson's class with me, and both had seen the note pass from Gracie's hand to mine. When I looked over at Chris he was shaking his head at my stirring a pot that was already boiling over. He had observed, "*Mac (both he and Steve called me "Mac") this teacher doesn't like you because of your dad. You better be careful.*"

I *was* careless, but I was also eight and a half years old and smitten by goldilocks.

Then Gracie, sitting behind me, made the mistake of whispering something to me just as Mrs. Henderson turned around from the blackboard. She had written "*The Goliad Massacre*" on the board and hearing Gracie, she bellowed, "*Mr. McClelland, please stand!*" I heard a group intake of breath from my other classmates.

Gracie whispered, "*Uh oh, not again . . .*"

I hesitated then slowly stood, still holding Gracie's note.

Mildred said, "*Mr. McClelland, we are talking today about the Mexican attack on the small Texas town of Goliad . . . where 350 Texican soldiers and injured prisoners were massacred so YOU'D be able to live in the greatest state in this country.*"

She continued, "*Goliad fell a week after the Alamo fell. Do you understand their sacrifice? Do you see how privileged you are to be a Texan?*"

I gulped, swallowed and said, "*Yes, ma'am . . .*"

She turned and I heard her chalk scratch more words that she wanted read. I watched Steve, Chris and Gracie as Mrs. Henderson wrote "*Colonel William Travis*" then "*Stephen F. Austin.*"

She kept chalking/talking, "*Are you honored to study the brave men who made this great state GREAT?*"

She continued to write "*General Sam Houston*" and "*David Crockett*" on the board.

I was getting more uncomfortable, but I said, "*Yes, ma'am.*"

She turned from the board and looked straight at me, breathing roughly, "*Young man, you can't learn what makes a great man great with your mouth open, or didn't your father, the great Judge Clem McClelland teach you that?*"

I shook my head, "*I don't get this, Mrs. Henderson. What did my father . . . ?*"

She cut in on me struggling for breath, "*He, like you, always has things his way, doesn't he?*" She pointed at me with her chalk. "*He always decides who wins and who loses, doesn't he?*"

I looked at her and closed my hand over Gracie's note so Mildred wouldn't have the chance to give me further punishment. She turned back to the blackboard and, with a flourish, she scratched "*Judge Clem McClelland*" on the board underneath the Texas heroes listed.

I quickly opened Gracie's crushed note in my hand to see written, "*I love Texas and Texans!*" and I smiled at her. I looked up at Mildred's blackboard.

Under my breath I said, "*His name looks pretty good up there.*"

Mildred turned angrily toward me and said, "*YOU will hold your tongue, sir!*"

She moved to her desk, opened a drawer and took out a thick ruler. The class recognized its purpose and again gasped. Clem's black belt came to mind as Mildred slapped the ruler against her palm and tried to control her breathing.

She said, "*You will pay better attention in my Court . . . uh . . . Classroom. Be seated.*"

My wide-eyed classmates looked at me and Mildred, and tried to understand our struggle . . .

The drama that took place in Mildred's classroom set the tone for future episodes with other people who thought they knew everything about my Clem. I learned early the real meaning of *judgmental* and I learned how certain people could make me feel uncomfortable about *everything*. I began to hate what Doris and I called *blatant stupidity* when someone thought bad thoughts about our Clem. I had no idea how bad it would get . . .

As the Circus play dates approached, Clem and Doris had an inspiration: Children loved Circuses. I was a child, so why not let me help promote Clem's Circus? When they first asked me if I'd be interested I didn't know what I could do or how I could help. And then Doris said, "*Kitirik . . . Kirk can go on her show and talk about the Circus and tell Houston why this Circus will be the best Circus Houston's ever seen.*"

I watched Clem as he considered her idea.

This was Doris's *brilliant marketing inspiration* and as Clem considered this I saw his eyes light up. Then he nodded and said, "*Set it up.*"

A little background on Kitirik: The ABC-TV affiliate in Houston was KTRK-TV, and it played on Channel 13.

Site of my television debut

To offset the negative vibes associated with the number 13 the owners of the Station decided to add a black cat to their logo. Their real inspiration though was to create an after-school program hosted by a nice lady dressed up in a black cat costume with whiskers painted on her face, who wore fishnet hose and black high heels.

The Station owners thought they were clever and took the letters of their Station, KTRK, and named their black cat lady KiTiRiK. Her real name was Bunny Orsak and her show owned the after-school time slot.

As for her helping Clem's Circus, Kitirik was more than willing and told Doris, "*I can't wait to meet your son. He sounds like he'll deliver your message eloquently!*"

She and Doris decided Kitirik would ask me agreed-upon questions and then let me do most of the talking.

The day of my television performance arrived and I sat at the kitchen table with Clem and Doris as I ate my favorite breakfast of pancakes and sausage. Doris handed me a note to give to Mrs. Henderson and said, "*Now, when you give this to Mrs. Henderson, explain to her that you have to leave early for your interview with Kitirik this afternoon. Be sure to thank her for me.*"

I nodded.

I had not told Doris nor Clem about who Mrs. Henderson really was and I hadn't shared her negative attitude toward all things McClelland. It was instinct but also fear of upsetting them with something I'd done, although I still didn't know what I'd done.

Then Clem smiled at me the same way he did whenever I played Football or ran a race, "*Let's talk about what you're gonna say and how you're gonna say it. Remember Kitirik will ask you questions and you need to answer her with the stuff we talked about. You got any problems with that?*" I shook my head.

Clem asked, "*Do you remember everything?*"

I had to assure him that his Circus was safe with me, "*Uh, yes sir.*"

He nodded, about to throw a curve, "*There's one other thing I want you to do, okay?*" I nodded and waited.

He took a deep breath, looked deeply into my eyes and said, "*I need you to think about all the crippled children who will benefit from the money this Circus will earn for* them. Think about the Hospital, the Doctors, and the Nurses. Think about all of the Circus acts we signed up to share with the people who'll buy tickets, and how much fun those people will have watching those acts, okay?"

I nodded, then he nodded and said, "*That's my boy.*"

When I went to school that day I was more apprehensive about handing Doris's note to Mrs. Henderson than I was about going on television that afternoon. Mildred took the note and held it away from her like it carried some foul-smelling disease.

After reading it, she said, "*What makes you so special that you get to go on television?*"

I said proudly, "*I'm doing it for my dad.*"

Her face reacted with my mentioning Clem, but just for a second.

She got herself under control and said, "*I'll let you go on this 'interview', but you have to write me a report on why Texas is called* **The Lone Star State**. *Turn in that report next Monday!*" I nodded.

Later that day Doris picked me up and drove us to the KTRK station. We went through the front entrance and a teenaged girl guided us through the lobby down a hall into a Dressing Room. I was seated and a make-up technician applied a flesh-colored cream to my face while one of the producers of the show walked me through how Kitirik's show worked. I didn't pay much attention to him since I was going through my own "*talking points*" as given by Clem. When the producer asked me if I had any questions I shook my head and smiled since I thought that would get him away from me. I knew I was ready. All I needed was a tall Pussycat.

The show started and Kitirik meowed and played with her studio audience for several minutes and then I was pulled out of my chair and led backstage to the entrance of the Interview area. Suddenly I was sitting in a chair in front of three large Cameras, surrounded by bright lights that hung down from the ceiling and smaller lights that sat on large stands with wheels.

Then this nice and totally sincere lady dressed in a black cat outfit complete with black tail cat-walked over to me. I sat there with my heart pounding a mile a minute.

I remember thinking that all I wanted on that day was to make Clem and Doris proud.

The Studio was full of kids sitting in bleachers with some of their parents visible, and I saw the three large Cameras were on some kind of rollers with three Cameramen behind them. I tried to swallow my fear and I smiled at Kitirik as she said, "*Hi there, Kirk. Thank you so much for being on my show today. I hear you have a Circus to talk about.*"

I hesitated, tongue-tied for a second, and Kitirik filled the gap by asking me, "*Is it true that you think this year's Circus is puuuuur-fect?*"

The kids and parents laughed and her humor loosened me up a little bit. I was still frozen.

She continued, *"I'm curious about how anyone puts together a big-time Circus. Did you and your family have to drive all over the country to see a lot of Circuses in order to find the best acts for this one?"*

Fortunately I thawed a bit, "Yes . . . uh, yes, Kitirik, we drove to Dallas and Chicago and even Los Angeles and we saw hundreds of Circus acts so we could "book" the finest acts for this year's Shrine Circus."

I smiled at the end of my speech. Kitirik realized she had a little ham sitting in front of her. She kept it going asking, *"What acts were your favorites?"*

I leaned forward toward her, "Just so you know, I love every one of the acts that Chairman Clem McClelland signed up for this year's Circus. We saw over 200 different acts in 30 different categories and I want to tell you these Circus people were all very professional and proud of what they do for a living. But what really impressed me was how all the Circus people we met were eager to help the Shriners sell tickets to raise money for the Crippled Children's Hospital here in Houston. That's why the Shrine Circus has so many acts that will thrill and amaze you!"

Kitirik gave me a huge smile and put her hand (paw) on mine. My heart beat a little faster.

Kitirik was like catnip to me

Kitirik was playing along, asking me the right questions in the right order. She helped me be successful and then she asked, *"Is there anything different about this Circus?"*

I smiled and said, "*Yes, Kitirik, this Shrine Circus is unlike any Circus anywhere. It DOES have clowns and elephants but it also has Cowboys and Indians! That's because it's not only a Circus, it also has a Wild West Show!*"

Clem had not told the staff at Channel 13 about the Wild West Show so it caught Kitirik by surprise. Her cute cat eyes opened wide and she said, "*A what?*"

Doris had rehearsed me, "*At every performance, our Circus will also have Lieutenant Rip Masters and Rusty and Rin Tin Tin defending their stockade and fighting off an Indian attack.*"

Kitirik didn't have a response so she just said, "*Wow . . . that sounds incredible!*"

I continued, "*And you know what's really neat?*"

She was delightful and said, "*I don't know how you can beat what you just said!*"

I shared, "*Rip Masters and Rusty are going to stay with us at our house while they're performing for the Circus! Rusty will be sleeping in my room!*"

Kititirk laughed and punctuated the interview with, "*That sounds wonderful!*"

With her signature cat-smile she played to her middle camera, "*Moms, Dads, boys and girls, the Shrine Circus will start November 4. Tickets are by reservation only, so get 'em while they're available at outlets all over Houston. I know for sure I'm buying mine today! Yo, Rinty!*" And that, was that.

Doris's interview idea had worked out. On our drive home she shared with me, "*If that doesn't sell tickets, nothing will. I hope your dad saw that. You did great!*"

I was happy. I wanted to help them and Doris told me that's what I'd done . . .

The next day I asked Clem if I could go with him to the Sam Houston Coliseum even though I knew Mrs. Henderson would scream.

It was the first day of "*rigging*" where all the Circus people arrive and begin the rough job of making their acts fit the available arena. He said "*Yes*" since I'd done him a favor by appearing on television and since I *was* going to let *Rusty* share my room.

When we arrived at the back entrance to the Coliseum, Clem parked his Cadillac and he pointed at a white Golf Cart with the Arabia Temple logo on both sides.

He smiled at me and said, "*This place is too large for us to walk around so I got us this ride to help. Wanna drive?*"

I said, "*This is neat! Thanks, Clem!*" and we saddled up.

I was suddenly the Chairman's chauffeur and I loved it. I flipped the Cart's control switch (that was located under my legs) to the *Drive* slot and we took off. It was *Wow* to the max.

Sam Houston Coliseum, 1958

Over the next few days as I drove Clem around (Doris sent another note to Mrs. Henderson describing what a useful learning experience the Circus was for me) I watched men and women work their hands to the bone to make the Sam Houston Coliseum their own. This would be a Three Ring Circus and it would be rigged from the ground up to the very highest point above the Coliseum floor.

When I think back on how I watched Clem's Circus begin to materialize I found myself looking *up* more than I'd expected. There were high-rope acrobats, trapeze artists, the Wallendas, the tight-rope walkers, the Flying Wards, and the Sway-Polers. Over the two week run of the show, some ticket holders would complain about the pain they suffered from having to constantly crane their necks *up* to watch all these talented high-in-the-sky Circus performers.

What impressed me was the incredible rigging: the higher these acts had to go, the more wires and ropes were needed to secure their equipment and protect the lives of the performers.

The Three Rings

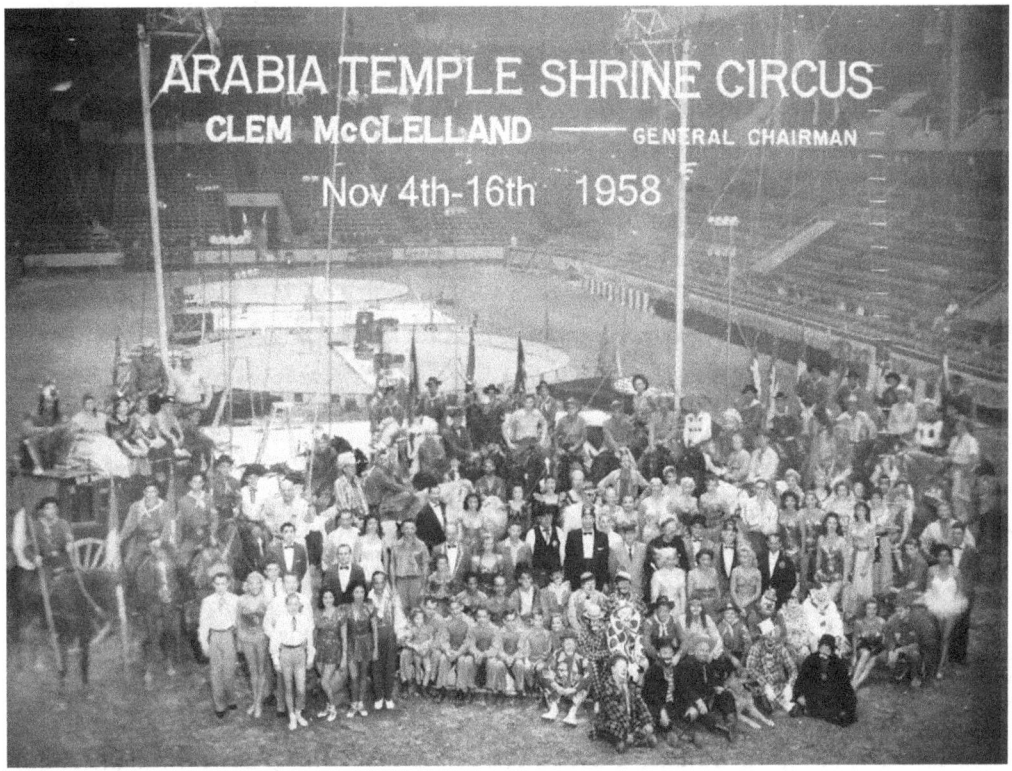

All the performers for Clem's Circus
(*Where's Clem?*)

It was awesome for me to watch the pieces of Clem's Circus puzzle as they came together.

One other puzzle item was the wild animals: the lions, the bears, the tigers, the elephants, and all the horses that would be used to stage the Wild West Show. These animals had to be fed and that meant food and bales of hay and water as well as the muckers to clean up after them.

Finally, two days before the Circus opened, I heard Clem's Cadillac honk in front of our Ivanhoe home and when I opened the front door there was Clem, James Brown aka Rip Masters, his wife, Betty, and Lee Aaker aka Rusty.

I shook their hands and helped move their luggage into their rooms: James and Betty to the downstairs Guest Room and Lee upstairs to my room. Lee looked around the upstairs area and rightly concluded that 2 of the 3 bedrooms belonged to "*two females*" which intrigued him.

We shared nothing more when he sniffed at having to have a roommate. I guessed I hadn't told him how impressed I was with his acting. I should have mentioned I remembered his neat moment when he ran into Gary Cooper in ***HIGH NOON*** and how I loved his work in ***HONDO*** with John Wayne and Geraldine

Page. But when I look back on my Rin Tin Tin experience, I would have preferred sleeping with the dog.

We went downstairs for a dinner feast that Doris had set in the Dining Room (which we never used unless we meant to impress). Doris introduced our maid, Josephine Freeman (Woodrow's heavyset, amusing wife and Doris's best friend) as she helped Doris serve everyone.

When all the plates were in front of our house guests, Josephine took over, "*Hey, y'all, as Miss Doris tol' ya, I'm Josephine. Miss Doris 'n' Mistah Clem wants you all to know that if you needs anything to jus holla, and I'll be sure to ask Master Kirk to get it for ya.*"

Our guests thought this was hilarious. Josephine had about ten running gags and they always worked because, after saying one of them, Josephine would laugh like there was no tomorrow.

Clem thanked his guests for coming and for their willingness to help the Children's Hospital, "*When I first joined the Arabia Temple eighteen years ago I envisioned being called to handle the huge responsibility of our annual Circus, to make it not just good but great. You will make it great and I thank you for being here.*"

I liked his speech and was relieved there was no need for a sermon-prayer since it was clear there were no sinners sitting at our table that night . . .

It was exciting to watch the Dress Rehearsal that took place on the afternoon of the first performance on November 4. At the first night's show, as Clem and I watched, we saw thousands of customers enter the Main Entrance of the Coliseum surrounded by various Vendors hawking their pricey Shrine Circus souvenirs.

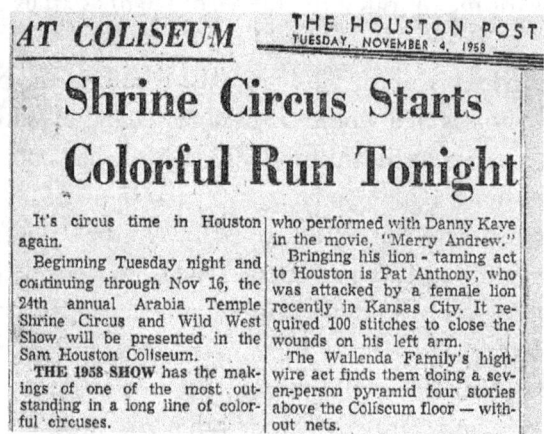

The Houston Media was helpful

I remember the music that Clem chose to greet the public each night as they entered and it was perfect. I'd been listening to the Circus standards for months and I knew the cuts that went with horse acts, with trapeze acts, with clowns, with acrobatics and with the Opening Parade. Clem's Music band director, William Pruym, was an expert on historical Circus classics dating back to the time of Buffalo Bill's Wild West Show. His music fit the flavor of Clem's Circus so well that the paying customers would sometimes begin clapping and stomping their feet without a thought.

In the Opening Parade the curtains over the main entrance separated to reveal Kelly-Miller's wonderful marching elephants and behind them came all the acts and entertainers that would perform. It was The Greatest Show on Earth "Texas-style" with Horses, Cowboys, and Indians riding around the arena alongside Clowns, Jugglers, and Acrobats. Clem had carefully watched all the parades we'd seen the previous summer, and he'd stolen the best visual styles and made them his own. It was an eyeful and the most dazzling Opening Parade to be found anywhere.

Every audience member received a program with all the acts and entertainers listed in the order of their performance. Clem and Doris had spent many hours designing the program and selling ads that were placed inside. Thanks to Doris the program generated a lot of revenue for the Shriners and the Children's Hospital . . .

The Circus program entertained/informed

As I mentioned before, close scrutiny of the program revealed the careful staggering of the aerial and the Three Ring acts so the ticket-buying patrons had less chance of whiplash from looking up too much at one time. It was sensibly planned by my Clem so that the boring performances (the dog acts) were only permitted to have the play time it took for the rigging crews to break down the previous impressive act and set up the next stupendous act.

Another great act that Clem used to help the rigging crews have the necessary between-acts rig time, was Norbu the Purse-Stealing Gorilla. Norbu was a very funny Chinese man who dressed up in a Gorilla suit and then ran up into the grandstands, scaring the customers, and making them laugh as he made them scream. Norbu's job was to find a woman with a purse (his real life wife) and then steal it from her. But when this *Gorilla* grabbed her and stole her purse, instead of acting afraid she began yelling at him and hitting him over his head with her purse as she chased him out of the arena. It was a guaranteed crowd-pleaser that everyone loved to watch, especially the riggers who'd used that time to set up special rigging for the next complicated aerial act.

Norbu was one of Clem's favorites

Next came The Great Wallendas. I remembered seeing their stunning 7 person Pyramid when we saw them in Chicago, and I'd enjoyed watching Clem and Doris watch *them*. They both had held their breaths as the 7 tight rope walkers walked across those ropes in sync so that all 7 survived the crossing.

I watched Clem sign Karl Wallenda who said, "*I love performing at Shrine Circuses . . . Your work crews make me and my family feel safer.*" The Wallendas were amazing and thrilling.

The Great Wallendas

Halfway through the performance just when people were expecting a break, the curtains opened and we heard a piercing war cry as a party of ferocious Indians (about 15) came riding into the arena followed by the Cavalry led by Rip Masters (with the appropriate buglers bugling).

The Shriners had dressed up as Indians (Guy Price was one of the Indians) and Bryson Martin and 10 other Shriners dressed up as Cavalrymen riding next to Rip as they pursued those very loud and savage devils. They all rode hell-bent-for-leather around the arena shooting and yelling, and it was great fun if you didn't mind stereotyping those darn injuns.

As predicted, after riding around the arena five or six or ten times, Rip and his Cavalry took care of them injuns and then he somehow found a microphone so he could sing a song about a **WHITE BUFFALO**. When he hit the emotional part of the song a wounded injun from the previous fight (that the audience had been watching for three verses) tried to sneak up and scalp him. Yep, pardner, just as that dern injun was about to rip into poor Rip, Rusty and Rinty came out of nowhere to warn Rip and capture that no-good injun. Yo Rinty!

Clem, Doris, The Flying Malkos

My favorite act was The Flying Malkos, a Ukranian trapeze troupe who fit the tone of Clem's Circus better than any of the other performers. They were fearless and so skilled that as I watched them I held *my* breath. Every night before a show I stared at them as they prepped their trapeze riggings and their gear like all the other artists. The difference was their checking process included actual swinging and flying to be sure their split second timing was perfect.

They were solid professionals AND they had a sense of humor. Clem made an agreement with them to perform a nightly skit.

Just as their act neared the end Clem would walk to the Center Ring wearing his best suit and his Arabia Temple Fez. He'd hold a white envelope up for all to see and a spotlight would shine on him as the Ringmaster announced, "*The Flying Malkos, which you have been watching, are world famous for their incredible triple flip. Standing in the Center Ring is General Chairman Clem McClelland of the Shriner's Arabia Temple and he holds an envelope with ten one-hundred dollar bills inside of it. If The Malkos are successful in completing their triple flip tonight, Chairman McClelland will hand them this envelope. Let's wish them Good Luck!*"

The spotlight on Clem went dark and the arena sounds faded until it was completely quiet.

The catcher, Mike Malko, and the flyer, Tony Steele, began swinging back and forth. Then Malko clapped his hands to signal he was ready and Steele began to swing faster.

With each swing he gained more speed and momentum swinging higher and higher until he almost touched the roof of the Coliseum. The audience held its breath and the only sounds heard were the stretching of the swings, the breathing of Tony Steele as he pushed his trapeze higher, and a single drum roll from the Band. Then Steele released his trapeze and began turning and turning and falling until Mike Malko grabbed his arms, and the Triple Flip was completed. Every night it was an amazing feat.

The Malko troupe slid down their ropes and met Clem in the Center Ring, the Circus Band played triumphant music, and Clem handed Mike Malko the white envelope as the loudest and longest applause of the entire Circus was heard.

I was backstage that night and I watched Clem as he walked back through the curtains. Suddenly he was surrounded by a large group of Shriners, one of whom was a surprise. The Grand Imperial Potentate, George Stringfellow, dressed completely in white, approached Clem. Stringfellow shook Clem's hand and said, "*Congrats, Clem. Your Arabia Temple has done a fine job! And abiding by our age-old ritual, my hat's off to you!*"

Stringfellow held up a new Fez with "*Potentate*" engraved on it and he handed it to Clem. The surrounding Shriners, some still dressed as Indians or Cavalrymen, began to clap their hands and they slapped Clem on his back as they placed his new Fez on top of his head.

It was a significant moment for Clem in this organization, and giving him that Fez was a serious gesture by the man in charge. After all of the hard work it had taken him to create the Circus, at that instant Clem reached his pinnacle. I watched his face and saw a great man being appreciated for his greatness.

The Shriners continued to congratulate Clem as Mike Malko pushed his way through them and handed Clem the white envelope. Speaking with his Ukranian accent and smiling his Ukranian smile he said, "*For you my illustrious Clement for the next time. Oh, and to make sure you are knowing, it was empty as usual . . .*"

The Shriners laughed, the Imperial Potentate smiled, and Clem, on top of his world, took off his new Fez to gaze at his new title.

Clem and Doris all dressed-up   **Clem's new Fez**

As Clem's Circus continued to rev up its engines, something else was brewing in Houston.

The brew master was Assistant DA Frank Briscoe. As I mentioned earlier, Frank had a sweet and very pretty secretary named Judy Wyatt and she and Clem's secretary, Helen, were best friends.

**Judy Wyatt shared
her bad news**

When Frank's bad feelings for Clem (that had been *brewing* for years) started to creep to the surface, it was Judy who made Helen aware of her boss' hatred for Clem. Helen shared this with me (what Judy told her in their "*girl talks*") as I watched Helen cut out Newspaper stories about the Circus. Helen had chosen various publicity pictures to supplement this *Newspaper File* of clippings so she could surprise Clem and give him his own personal Circus scrapbook.

When I saw the different stories before, during, and after the Circus, I realized there was a lot of positive Press, "*McClelland Promises 'The Greatest Show, 'A delightful variety of performances,*' and '*the Wild West Show is WILD!*'"

There were many other stories and many humorous pictures as well as a picture of Judge Clem sitting on a huge Kelly-Miller elephant underneath the headline: ***Shrine Circus Shines as Houstonians Applaud with CASH!***

Clem & Doris dressed up again ...   **and again**

Where do I sign, Chairman Clem?

Clem and Doris clowned around

Rip "*Masters*" a dance with Doris   **Clem sang "*Smile*"**

Helen looked at the wonderful scrapbook and remarked under her breath, "*Judy's boss isn't going to like any of this...*"

Her whispered statement seemed to come from left field to me, so I looked at her and said, "*What did you say? What are you talking about?*"

Helen shushed me with her finger to her lips and then she whispered to me that the man who would be the future district attorney, "*... is jealous of Clem, and Judy thinks all this positive publicity about Clem's Circus will just make it worse.*" I had no idea what she was talking about so I shut my mouth and listened. She told *me* that Judy had told *her* it wasn't that Clem's publicity would hurt Frank, it was that Clem, in Frank's eyes, didn't deserve all the favorable attention.

In Frank's eyes, "*Clem is a bad Judge who'd lucked into being a Judge in the first place.*"

And, "*Clem's decade of power is an insult to Frank who's never had any luck in his life.*"

Helen said Judy had said, "*Frank can't stand how Harris County politicians tolerate a Judge who wears a Fez!*"

Then Helen whispered to me, "*You're not going to believe this, but innocent and clueless Judy saw Guy Price sneak into Frank's office through his back door one day, and when Guy left, again through the back, Judy heard Frank happily singing* **Dixie** *inside his office.*"

Helen also whispered that Judy had heard her boss tell one of his assistant DAs, "*It'd be wonderful if one of McClelland's high-wire acts slipped and fell to a grisly death.*"

When Helen shared that one I laughed out loud. How bizarre! Guy Price? High wired death? Who *was* this guy? I'd learn soon enough that *this guy* was a mean-spirited predator who, based on what he ultimately achieved, had carefully planned how he would surround, then hurt, and finally destroy Judge Clem McClelland...

They Will Try the Triple Somersault At Shrine Circus -- And May Make It

SATURDAY, NOV. 10, 1956 *The Houston Press*

THE LEAP... ...THE TURN... ....AND THE CATCH

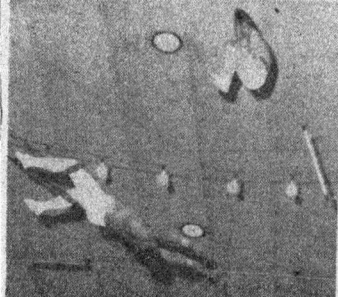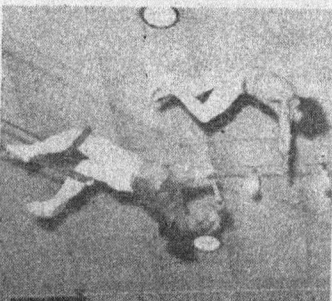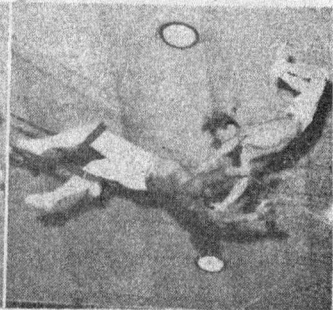

THEY DO THE FAMED TRIPLE SOMERSAULT AT THE SHRINE CIRCUS!
Tony Steele leaps into space... He completes his second turn... Then over again and into Mike Malko's arms!

The Malkos worked every night for Clem's envelope

December 8, 1958
Houston Crowds Reach 120,000

HOUSTON—Houston's Shrine Circus played to 120,000 people in its run early last month. Judge Clem McClelland, chairman, said this was 20,000 more than last year and that it represented several straw houses in Sam Houston Coliseum.

Shrine committee produced the show, while Bob Atterbury was equestrian director, Charles Basile was assistant and William Pruym was band director.

Performance included Pat Anthony's Lions, the Great Wallenda Family, Norbu, Flying Malkos, Flying Wards, and the "Rin Tin Tin" troupe from television. Latter included Lt. Rip Masters, Corporal Rusty, and Rin Tin Tin in old time Wild West action climaxed by an Indiana attack on the stockade and rescue by the Cavalry.

Circus Review

I'd learned a lot of useful things thanks to Clem's Circus. For instance, with every good event in life there might be some not-so-good side effects. Even though I'd experienced a major event in my life, my school work had taken a major hit during the first weeks of November.

I'd also suffered the resentment of Mrs. Henderson who told me, "*You think because you're the judge's son that the regular rules shouldn't apply to you. Well, I wonder if a "D" on your Report Card for Texas History will get the judge's attention!*"

Mildred Henderson was scary

Uh, oh.

I'd just begun to qualify for the Honor Roll at my school and a "D" wouldn't help that effort.

Yet, when I took the Report Card home I was more concerned about telling Clem and Doris the truth about Mildred, than telling them about the "D."

I sat them both down at the dinner table and said, "*I've got something to tell you about school. My teacher's mad at me for the time I spent at the Circus and she's kept me off the Honor Roll.*"

Doris, "*Mrs. Henderson wouldn't do that! I know her and she's a nice lady!*"

I looked at her and then softly said, "*No, she's not.*"

Clem, "*What about her isn't nice, boy?*"

Kirk, "*Everything. I haven't told you about her . . . Do you remember the problem we had with Mrs. Evans?*"

Clem and Doris, "*Yes.*"

Kirk, "*Well, Mrs. Henderson has the same problem with you, Dad, only 10 times worse.*" Clem, "*Was she involved with my Court?*"

Kirk, "*Yeah, she had a fight with a man the day I visited your Courtroom four years ago.*" Doris, "*I remember.* (She looked at Clem) *She hit her brother with her purse because you gave him what their father told you in his will to give him. And she's blaming you?*"

Clem, "*A lot of people do. They think I'm choosing instead of following what their parents or their relatives wanted.*"

Doris, "*What are these people thinking?*"

Kirk, "*Nobody likes to get the short end of the stick, right Clem?*"

Clem, "*You're right, boy. But now we need to fix this "D" problem.*"

I was watching them both and I hated what Mrs. Henderson was doing to *them*.

Doris, *"I'll go see Miss Thompson* (the Principal) *tomorrow and we'll have her put you in a different class with a different teacher."*

Kirk, *"That's no good. My friends are all in Mrs. Henderson's class."*

So here was my second taste of conflict associated with Clem's being a Judge.

As I look back and try to measure the experience honestly, the "D" was also *my* fault because I loved being around the Circus and hanging with the people I met there.

So I chose to live with the "D."

I know Doris discussed my situation with the Principal and Mrs. Henderson and I told her I appreciated her help. But when I rejoined my classmates in Mildred's menagerie, I found that my seat had been moved to the front row, next to Mildred's desk.

She said, *"I want you close to me so I can help you avoid getting any more Ds! For your mother's sake!"*

I looked around the classroom and Steve and Chris happily waved at me while Gracie, in the back row, looked at me with sad eyes . . .

The bottom line: In spite of any teacher conflicts, Clem still mesmerized me. He still surprised me with how he chose to do business. He still was tall and he still had the *authority attitude* whenever he entered a room. But after his Circus he seemed a bit taller to me and more focused. He'd morphed into a more confidant man, more sure of himself.

The downside was he suddenly became more distant. I'm not sure what happened. It could have been that I was growing up and spending extra time playing Football and Baseball and, a new sport, Basketball. It could've been we didn't hunt or fish together as often. It seemed to me that Clem spent additional time with his Shriner friends while I spent additional time with my friends on the weekends playing touch Football/Baseball/Basketball.

Things changed, as they always do. I remember one big difference was how we all used to talk and share stories at the dinner table. Clem didn't seem to have any interest in sharing courthouse gossip, and as a result I started to withhold stories I could've shared because I didn't think Clem would have any interest. If I could go back to one of those dinners, I'd say, *"Hey, Clem, do me a favor and share one of your favorite platitudes like With Great Power Comes Great Responsibility or Everything Works Out in the End."* I sometimes think about that last tired expression whenever I analyze the changes I felt were happening to Clem and me. Yes, he was stronger, and yes, he still loved Doris and his family, but we stopped going to Church as often as we used to. We all had other things to do on Sunday like play touch Football or Basketball or Baseball . . . And then, my sisters asked Clem if we could have a dog.

It'd been a while since our last dog died. Doris and Micki and Anne were in the Kitchen fixing courses for a nice breaded veal cutlet dinner with vegetables and scalloped potatoes, and I was in the Den watching television. Then Clem came home to his family. He walked in through the Kitchen door and he carried two dogs, one under each arm. They both barked.

He put them down onto the Kitchen floor and my sisters started screaming with delight, "*Clem, Clem, you kept your promise! Thank you, Cleeeeem! Thank you, Cleeeeeem!*"

I ran in from the Den and I started screaming, too, and I think I also jumped up and down a few times. Doris clapped her hands and joined her children as the four of us madly pet the new pets, a Dachshund and a Cocker Spaniel.

Clem stood there and watched his family in the throes of ecstasy, and I hope he knew how wonderful his gesture was for all of us.

I tallied up all the things I'd seen my father contribute: He'd given to the Circus, to the Shriners and Crippled Children, and to his probate homework (he came home every night with a briefcase full of files).

The puppies represented his love for us. This was Clem-gives-to-his-family time.

I smiled my distinct Kirk-to-Clem smile and asked him, "*What are their names?*"

He pointed to the Dachshund and said, "*Oscar.*"

He pointed to the gold-colored Cocker Spaniel and said, "*Gigi.*"

And then he held his right hand at waist height and said, "*SIT!*" My sisters and I instantly complied leaving the dogs and Doris still standing. We all laughed. It's a good memory.

Oscar, me, and Gigi

My sisters started to scream again and hugged both dogs who kept wagging their tails. I saw Clem look at Doris who had tears in her eyes as she rushed to hug him, "*You did good, Daddy!*"

He looked down at her and said, "*Daddy? I thought my name was CLEEEEEEEEEM!*"

Doris laughed and wiped her eyes as she pushed him away. Clem folded his arms and cocked his head as he inquired, "*Did they deliver it?*"

Doris shrugged and acted like she had no idea what his question referred to, but before she could answer I said, "*Yes, they did!*"

Doris shook her finger at me for being so easy.

I ran to the glassed Back Porch just off the Den.

Clem quickly followed me onto the Back Porch and when he saw the new Pool Table with the Cue Ball and the balls racked, ready and waiting, he started to jump up and down and he began screaming, "*Oh, Doris, Doris, you kept your promise!*" But what was really funny was the way he ran around and around the table which was fun to watch since he was still 6'4" tall.

He whispered, "*Thank you, thank you, Doris! You kept your promise!*"

Then he ran his hand over the green felt of the table as he walked around it. I saw him walk to the Stick Rack that Doris and I had put up that afternoon and he chose a smooth Cue Stick. Then he said to the universe, "*Once upon a time this was called The Back Porch. From now on it's The Billiard Room . . .*" He grabbed the Cue Ball and rolled it gently across the table.

I heard him whisper, "*Yeah . . .*"

I asked, "*Nice, huh?*"

He looked at me and said, "*Who could ask for anything more?*"

And then we both laughed as he hit the Cue Ball perfectly and the 7 ball went into the corner pocket and the 5 ball went into the side pocket...

It was Friday night and I remember watching the Opening sequence of RIN-TIN-TIN on TV with the whole family, when (after the Opening) a Commercial began. It showed Frank Briscoe campaigning to be the next DA of Houston and to my eyes it was pretty good for a local spot.

As it started, out of the corner of my eye, I saw Clem shake his head. The Commercial began with a Medium shot of Briscoe as he looked at the Camera and said, "*Hello. I'm Assistant District Attorney Frank Briscoe and I'm running for District Attorney here in Harris County.*"

I turned my head to see Clem down a healthy shot of JD in a gulp. The TV Camera moved in for a Close-Up of Frank, "*As you probably know, I stand for crime prevention.*"

Suddenly we were seeing a Montage of 1950s still shots of Houston policemen on the job as we heard Frank speak voice-over, "*I believe that by convicting the corrupt officials in our society . . .*"

We then saw perp shots of convicted criminals in jail.

"... *and putting them behind bars for as long as legally possible, the good citizens of Houston, Texas can sleep safely at night.*"

I watched Clem stand up and walk over to his bar. He shook his head as he poured another.

I watched Briscoe again in Close-Up for his finish, "*Please join my crusade to fight crime with your vote next Tuesday. Together we'll fully prosecute and put every last criminal where they belong . . . In jail!*"

The Commercial ended with a Freeze Frame of Briscoe which was pretty slick for a local political ad in those days.

As the picture faded out it faded up on a new episode of RIN-TIN-TIN...

So this was the first time I'd ever seen or heard this DA wannabe who believed a high wire performer who fell to his/her death would be a blessing. And then I heard him discuss putting *criminals* in jail. I wondered if he'd save a nice cell for himself...

I was worried about Clem, maybe more than usual due to our disconnection in recent months. So I paid attention to him and listened to him and Doris (in my *Phantom* mode) after lights out. It was midnight and I'd gone down to the Kitchen to make peanut butter and crackers to go with a late night glass of milk when I heard them talking behind their bedroom door. It was dark all through the house and I made myself invisible as I crept slowly to their closed door.

I heard Doris, "*What does he want from you? I don't get it.*"

Clem, "*He's a lowlife lawyer with a mediocre education and no Courtroom charisma. This is his way of elevating his status so he can get himself elected to DA.*"

Doris, "*But what does he have that can get you into trouble?*"

Clem, "*C'mon Doris, I'm good at my job but I've done this long enough to've made enemies. Look at Kirk's teacher, Henderson. That's the world I live in. It's not always squeaky clean.*"

I thought about what I heard them say. I felt guilty eavesdropping on them but I kept listening. Like the youngster I was, I thought there might be something I could do to help them. Doris, "*So what happens next?*"

Clem, "*Either he wakes up and leaves me alone, or he comes after me and we go to war.*" Doris started crying. I heard the mattress squeak as if Clem had moved close to comfort her. Clem, "*Let's say a prayer and hope he realizes he's made a big mistake. Then he can make his rep by going after somebody else.*"

I heard Doris continue to cry. I crept away, being careful not to spill my crackers and milk . . .

It was close to Christmas in 1960, and unfortunately Clem celebrated the holiday season with a whole lot of nothing in his stocking since a month earlier Frank Briscoe had become the newly elected District Attorney.

I was eleven years old then, and in the sixth grade.

Mrs. Campbell was my teacher and she was prewired to love my McClelland wit since she had taught both of my sisters before she had the pleasure of teaching me. She was an Honor Roll enthusiast and she shared with me some good rules for how to make good grades. She was also the first teacher to ever mention the word *Valedictorian* to me. I remember a lot from that year but at the time I was unaware of the forces beginning to surround Clem.

I thought that with the addition of dogs and a Pool Table we'd return to normal, but it wasn't meant to be. The weatherman wasn't cooperating and heavy thunderstorms were about to rain down on our parade.

Clem's secretary, Helen Smith, described to me the day things changed: She was sitting at her desk eating lunch while Clem took his regular one to two o'clock nap inside his Chamber. She looked up at her clock and it was 1:33 when Briscoe's secretary, Judy Wyatt, walked up.

Helen said, "*Hi Judy.*"

Judy nodded to Helen, handed her a note, and then walked away quickly.

Helen called out, "*Judy, what's wrong?*" but Judy kept walking. Helen picked up the note and as she read it her breath caught.

She stood up and looked at the clock: 1:35. She moved to Clem's Chamber door and read the note again. She didn't want to disturb Clem's nap but she knew she had to . . . She knocked.

Clem answered and she regretfully handed him the note.

It said, "*Frank's going after your judge!*"

It was on that day that the distancing I'd noticed between me and Clem began to change noticeably. He and I started talking again, and about a month later he shared with me how difficult it had been for him to drive home that night after work. Yes, he had a new black 1962 Cadillac Deville and yes, it was fun to drive, but that night he told me, "*When I saw Judy's note I had no room in my mind for recreational thoughts.*"

He recalled how fast he'd driven down Westheimer Road, and how he kept looking at himself in the rearview mirror and drumming his fingers on the steering wheel. He shared with me his painful thoughts for how he'd handle this very real threat. I watched his face and his kind but worried eyes as he recalled the last part of Frank Briscoe's TV commercial, "*Please join my crusade to fight crime with your vote next Tuesday. Together we'll fully prosecute and put every last criminal where they belong . . . In jail!*"

Clem struggled on that horrible night and tried to calculate what went wrong and what he could do to make things right. I was playing a noisy game of pool on his Pool Table with my sisters when Doris suddenly stepped out into The Billiard Room. We all noticed there was something different about her and our loud bickering stopped. She said, "*Come with me.*"

We followed her into the Living Room where she pointed to the couch. We sat down in unison and we all looked at Clem who sat on the piano bench in front of the piano. He held a full glass of Jack Daniels and he drained it as Doris, still standing, said, *"Starting today, things are going to change. Your father will explain."*

She joined us on the couch, and sat next to me. There was a 29 ounce bottle of JD sitting on the piano. Clem refilled his glass and then he started talking, *"Micki . . . Anne . . . Kirk. You are about to hear a lot of . . . stuff . . . about your dad. Most of it, probably all of it, isn't true."*

The three of us were frozen. We didn't move an inch as Clem continued, *"But know this. Everything will be fine. Nothing's going to change."* Clem drank until he was looking at the bottom of his glass, *"There is nothing for Mr. Briscoe to find."*

We looked at Clem then turned our heads to look at Doris, white as a sheet, saying nothing.

Clem finished with, *"Just remember, America has the greatest justice system in the world."*

I remember it rained the next morning when I went outside to collect The Houston Post newspaper from our front lawn. I carried the paper under the eaves and removed the transparent rain-protector to see the headline as raindrops splattered on it:

Judge McClelland under Investigation—DA Briscoe on the Hunt . . .

I looked around the neighborhood and saw the same Newspaper resting on all the other wet front lawns and I told myself, *"Things are gonna change."*

Almost overnight all three of the Houston papers began to run stories inside their Local News sections that suggested something was rotten in Houston's Probate Court system.

All the stories mentioned that investigations would soon follow. Within these stories were innuendos and rumors. Within these stories DA Frank Briscoe expressed his concern about improprieties in the handling of many estates. He announced that Judge Clem McClelland was under the microscope. There were also a few discussions about Clem awarding his favorite lawyers with regular probative work, and there were some discussions that those same lawyers had offered bribes to ensure they'd remain in his inner circle . . .

Clem and I posed June 1, 1962 for a positive Shrine publicity photo

District Attorney Frank Briscoe

McClelland's Court Under Fire; Briscoe Digs Into 60 Estates

The Houston Press headline on June 5, 1962

A Media-Driven Prosecution?

HEADLINE	NEWSPAPER	DATE
District Attorney Tells New Data In McClelland Probe	The Houston Post	June 7, 1962
Probate Court's Estate Handling To Be Probed	The Baytown Sun	June 8, 1962
Judge Is Linked To Fee Splitting	The Daily Texan	June 16, 1962
McClelland Inquiry -- Forgery To Estate Document Charged	Corpus Christi Caller Times	June 21, 1962

MORE HEADLINES:

McClelland Bank Book Probed by Grand Jury ...Secretary Quizzed
Figures in Probate Court Probe — County Employee Was Threatened

McClelland Court Probe May Involve Over $20 Million

DA Swamped By Complaints About Estate Handling

CHAPTER FOUR

IT'S HAPPENING NOW, 1962

So allow me to Fast Forward to the present for one short paragraph: I've researched case files from the '60s to be sure I told this story truthfully. I've struggled to include anything that made Clem look guilty, even though to this day I think he was innocent. But as Oscar Wilde or Shakespeare or maybe Woody Allen said, "*It is what it is. If you have a story to tell, just tell it.*"

Clem was a great man. How great depends on which side of the aisle you sat on, and whether or not you believed the bad guy or you believed the good guy. The News Media had a field day smearing Clem's name on their front pages and using his name/title and rumored transgressions as their lead story for the 6 and 10 o'clock TV News. This was a City Editor's and a News Director's dream come true: A sitting Judge being accused of dirty dealings in his own Courtroom and allegedly taking money from the Estates he'd been entrusted to protect in order to line his own pocket. Hell, if I'd sat on the City Desk at the Post or the Chronicle or the Press, I can guarantee what my big story would be for my reporters and Newspaper to cover: Judge Clem McClelland!

And yet, Clem had told us nothing was going to change. Hmmm. That wasn't true.

Monday morning I remember I looked in the mirror to comb my hair as I prepared to go to my Junior High School, T.H. Rogers.

I took a deep breath and admitted it would be a difficult exercise for me to move through the hallways as if nothing new had happened in my life. I was suddenly self-aware and uncomfortable because I knew everyone would be talking about my father, and me by association. I imagined hundreds of fingers pointing their judgments at me.

I imagined hands being held in front of mouths to shield classmates/teachers as they talked about my father and me. I felt I had done something wrong but I couldn't remember what it was.

I feared I was going to feel that way every day for a long time.

I parked my new black Moped (that Clem and Doris had given me for Christmas) in the T.H. Rogers parking lot. I walked through the doors of the main building and headed for my locker located next to my homeroom. As I turned the corner I saw Chris, Steve and Betsy waiting at my locker. I stutter-stepped and tried to control my breathing to appear normal . . . It was just another school day . . . No big deal. And then Chris and Steve patted me on the back and Betsy put her sweet lips on my cheek. (Betsy was my new girlfriend and to demonstrate my maturity I had already told her I'd marry her one day) It was hard for me to keep it together so I used a technique I'd seen Clem use when something got emotional: I laughed and I asked, "*Is it my birthday?*" I looked at Betsy, "*Is it our anniversary?*" They all laughed with me, and then Chris asked, "*How's Clem, Mac? Has this been hard on him?*"

I said, "*Of course. Harder than anything he's ever had to face.*"

Betsy asked, "*Kirk, is any of this true?*"

I looked at her sweet face and saw concern, not accusation, and I suddenly relaxed. These people were my friends. All they wanted was to know what was going on, and what they could do to help me handle this new weight. I told Betsy, "*I asked both of my parents what this was about. Clem swore to me he'd done nothing wrong and that all of this would go away. They both said this Briscoe-jerk is big-time jealous of Clem* (I bravely smiled) *because Clem's so tall and good-looking. There is no evidence of misconduct except in the mind of the new DA.*"

Steve gave me a big smile, "*It sounds like this DA just needs somebody to hug him, Mac!*"

I said, "*Don't look at me. I prefer someone I can talk to afterward.*"

This was one of our running gags and we all laughed. I realized how lucky I was to have that trio of friends and I focused again so I wouldn't lose it.

We were about to walk into our homeroom when a recurring problem walked around the corner headed in my direction. I sucked in a deep breath to help me handle a completely different emotion. His name was Larry Klump and he and I were on Rogers' Football team. I was a thin Split End and he was a huge Left Tackle. He outweighed me by about 60 pounds, he looked and sounded like a grunting pig, and he was a bully. Proof of that: He always put his hands on people and squeezed their arms or their hands until they hurt. Also, he was always flanked by his two co-bullies, Greg and Doug.

He pushed past me, grabbed Betsy's arm and said to her, "*Good morning, Betsy!*"

She, as usual, pushed back and fiercely scratched his hands with her fingernails to free herself. He cried out and laughed at the same time. She shuffled past the grunting pig, and gave me another kiss on my cheek, "*See ya inside . . .*" and walked away. Chris and Steve nodded, admiring her bravado.

Larry proceeded to move closer to me and, in my face, he loudly said, "*Hey McClelland! I saw your old man on TV Saturday night! Doesn't look too good for the McClelland family does it?*"

He turned to his bullyguards and they all laughed together as they walked away.

Chris and Steve huddled close to me and Steve calmly said, *"Don't worry, Mac"*— he looked at Klump walking away—*"we know Clem's the best."*

I nodded at them as they turned and went through the door into our homeroom. I stood there for a moment and evaluated my first *be-sure-to-defend-Clem* encounter. I hadn't done A+ work. I knew there would be more times when I'd be up against it but as I thought about it, I remember I told myself to avoid useless self-pity and just put up my dukes. It was Clem and Doris who needed protecting. They were the ones who needed assurance that everything would be all right. I walked into my homeroom and promised myself from that moment on I'd do whatever I could to defend and protect them . . .

Larry Klump was hard to take

It was evening and I stood in my front yard at 4514 Ivanhoe Street just as our paper boy pedaled past me. I took off running as he threw our paper to me, and that night I caught it.

He saluted me and pedaled away. I opened the paper, The Houston Press, and its headline read: ***Judge McClelland on Hot Seat!***

Under the headline was ***Written by Cap Detrick*** with a picture of Clem surrounded by reporters as he perp-walked down the front steps of the courthouse.

I strolled into our home and into the Den, where Doris and my sisters were watching TV.

I saw the same shot of Clem walking the steps but this was a moving image on 16 mm film. Anne was crying and Micki's arms were crossed, her way of building a wall to hide behind. Doris watched the TV shot of her husband entering his black Caddy parked in front of the courthouse, and she silently suffered the outrage of another blindsided attack on her family.

The TV News Anchor, Dave Webb, said, "*KTRK TV requested an interview with Judge McClelland but so far he's declined to speak. District Attorney Frank Briscoe however was happy to oblige.*"

The TV picture changed to Briscoe and his Assistant DA Pete Moore as Briscoe said, "*During my campaign I stated that I believe the best way to prevent crime is to jail criminals. We are confident that when the public sees what this Judge has been doing for all of these years, they will demand justice!*"

I reached over to turn off the television. I looked at Doris and I muttered something like, "*This man is a Devil . . .*"

Doris stood up and went into the Kitchen. Anne continued to cry. Micki and I stared at the blank screen of the TV set and I'm sure we both wondered what new surprises lay ahead . . .

The next morning I got an answer. Overnight our front yard had been filled with hate signs.

I was the early riser in our house and I walked out in semi-darkness to find sentiments such as, "*You're a thief!*" "*Rot in Hell, Judge!*" "*Judges will be Judged!*" and "*See ya in Jail, Judge!*"

I gave myself a moment as I tried to understand these ridiculous messages, and I realized that I'd never be able to process them.

I ran around the yard, collected all the signs, ran to the back of the house, and stuffed them into our garbage cans. Doris was making breakfast and saw me through the Kitchen window. She stuck her head out the Kitchen door, "*Kirk, what are you doing out there?*"

I answered her, "*Just cleaning up some trash . . .*"

I remember that I tried to put myself in Briscoe's shoes to guess what the Devil would do next, but I was totally oblivious. I didn't know if he or his Winged Monkeys had any proof on my Clem. I did know that if his Monkeys were like those in **THE WIZARD OF OZ** they could swoop down and wreak havoc without warning. That's what troubled me. I imagined DA Briscoe arresting Clem on our front lawn, or at our Church, or at one of my Football games. I envisioned Clem being led away in handcuffs, with Larry Klump and his bullyboy guards on the sidelines laughing it up.

I wished I could ask Clem what would happen next, but it seemed all he could do was react to Briscoe's assaults. And after the events of the past week I figured correctly that the assaults would continue. I thought back to what Judy had told Helen about Briscoe's obsession to go after Clem. Who knew what this lying Devil had up his slightly curved talons?

I began to imagine what it must have been like for Clem at the courthouse or for Doris at her weekly Church meetings. It had to be difficult for them the same way it was hard for my sisters and for me in our surroundings. The difference with Clem's situation was he had to continue doing his job without the trust of the public (who expected him to help them), without the respect of other judges, and with hostile lawyers who greeted every day (and now him) with adversarial minds. No picnic, no way. It must have been hell for him to deal with people judging every move he made, while all he could do was hope the truth would suddenly appear and set him free.

As Clem and Doris fought their private (excuse me) *public* demons, I began a campaign of my own. I set my alarm so every morning at 5 a.m. I'd wake up, quietly go downstairs and out the Kitchen door to check the front and side yards, and then I'd dispose of the hateful reminders that our world was populated by mean and crazy people. The signs were there every day. Sometimes these concerned citizens would dump garbage on our driveway to send a useful message to the judge. He didn't get their message cause I made sure it disappeared. I also disposed of the morning paper. That day's headline: ***Judge McClelland's Old Cases Besieged***.

My taking out the garbage became a daily routine and I began wondering when Clem would take a stand and say, "*Enough . . . No more!*" and retaliate against Briscoe and his Flying Monkeys. I imagined what I'd have had Clem say, "*The citizens of Houston shouldn't have to operate on innuendo or insufficient data or the vivid imagination of the District Attorney.*"

"*I've kept silent up to now because I wanted Mr. Briscoe to show me his cards and, let me tell you, he has none. There is no proof that I used my office for personal gain!*"

Why didn't Clem get off the bench and tell it like it was, "*I am innocent of any wrongdoing and I ask the citizens of Houston for their patience. Give me time to defend myself!*"

What was the value of sitting back and letting this man ride rough-shod over the McClelland name? I didn't get it.

A week later we were sitting at our Kitchen dinner table eating, when father Clem was re-establishing he was the father of my older sister, Micki. He said, "*If I say he's too old for you to go out with, then guess what? He's too old.*"

She was out of her league as she debated with her father, the judge. She tried logic, "*But he's captain of the Football team!*"

Clem, "*Is that an argument for or against not letting you go out with him?*"

Micki bit her lip, "*It's . . . uh . . . I don't know! You always do this whenever I want something!*"

The phone next to the dinner table began to ring and since Anne was closest, she answered it. She said in a soft voice, "*Hello, this is the McClelland residence!*"

The rest of us waited to see who was calling. Anne's face changed to a bright red and then to a deep purple and then she screamed, "*How can you say that? It's not true! Stop saying that!*"

She threw down the phone and ran out of the Kitchen.

Micki ran after her as Clem picked up the phone, "*This is Clem McClelland. Who is this?*"

I watched as Clem's face changed to the same dark purple shade that sister Anne had displayed, and then he spoke in a low and softer volume, "*Where would you like us to meet? How about the corner of Fifth and Main? Yes, I'll be there in ten minutes, you shit-kicker!*"

Clem calmly replaced the phone on the Kitchen sideboard, and as he moved toward the Kitchen door, Doris jumped up and grabbed both sets of car keys that hung from a key hanger next to the Kitchen's backdoor. Then she turned to face him, "*No, Clement, don't do this!*"

He kept moving toward her and gently took the keys out of her hand. As I witnessed this scene I told myself, "*Now is the time to protect . . .*"

I stood up, ran to his side and grabbed his hand that held the keys. I looked up and said, "*Clem, please stay . . .*"

So there we were, three McClellands locked in a struggle that made no sense due to some idiot with a phone, a warped agenda, and a miniscule intelligence. Clem looked at both of us. Doris looked up at him with a beautiful, sweet face full of love and confusion.

I did my James Dean impersonation from "**GIANT**" by sweeping my hands in front of me like an umpire ruling "*Safe.*" Clem remembered the scene and laughed.

And then the phone rang again. I said, "*I'll get it.*" and I jumped to where it sat on the counter.

I picked the phone off its cradle and said, "*Hello?*"

Whoever was on the line said, "*The judge is a BIG thief! Someday he'll rot in prison!*"

I replied, "*Yes, yes, and thanks for calling. I'll be sure to tell her.*" And I hung up.

Clem and Doris looked at me and I explained, "*It was Andy Griffith calling from Mayberry!*" They looked at me like I was crazy.

I continued, "*He wants Doris to take over as Aunt Bee on his show!*"

They both looked at me and laughed. I nodded as if it were true, and then I repeated my James Dean impersonation sweeping my hands in front of me, suggesting we were all "*Safe.*"

Clem smiled and said, "*That's my boy!*"

I've tried to make fun of it but the phone attack on our household was no joke. We received as many calls as we did hate letters in the mail and hate signs on the lawn. At first I thought our best defense was to take the phone off the hook, but then I dreamt up a different strategy . . .

After a week of these attacks Clem and I were sitting in the Den as he read his legal briefs and I did my homework. I'd had a late Football practice and I was trying to wind down when the phone rang. Clem and I looked at each other, wondering if the call was legit, when Doris picked up the Kitchen phone, "*Hello . . . What? How can you say—*" She caught her breath and we heard her voice break. "*You've got the wrong number!*" And then she hung up.

We heard her crying softly in the Kitchen and Clem moved quickly to join her and give her his shoulder. I decided I'd had enough with the phone. My parents were in shock and obviously paralyzed by what was happening on so many fronts. This phone attack, however, was too much: They shouldn't have to fight multiple unseen enemies.

So I suggested to Clem that, in the evenings, I'd play the part of designated phone man. I would answer and talk or not talk with every caller, friendly or not so friendly. That way (I suggested) Clem-Doris-Micki-Anne would not feel like they were being held hostage in their own home. When I asked his permission, he gave me his usual nod and smiled as he said, "*You're my hunting partner, and now, you're my hero!*"

Then, with his hands, he did an impersonation of my impersonation, "*Safe.*"

It was a good gesture since that was exactly how I wanted him to feel . . .

Later that night I was upstairs in my room.

I had moved the Kitchen phone to my nightstand next to my bed and that's where I planned to field calls from the Houstonians in need of serious therapy. Over the weeks and months that followed, depending on what the Houston Media was reporting, I received and learned to handle several dysfunctional layers of Houston's underbelly.

As I think back on those telephonic confrontations, I'm amused at how I interacted.

When the phone rang my game plan was to answer with a cordial "*Good Evening, McClelland residence,*" listen to their rant, thank them for sharing, and hang up. Then they could go open another beer or mix a vodka Collins and return to whatever nightly show on TV they normally used for their healing.

I'd sometimes had fun with these loonies just because I could, and on Halloween night when the phone rang, I answered, "*Merry Christmas!*"

A very scary voice retorted, "*Pretty funny, sonny. Are you studying to be a comedian someday or do you plan to be a thief like your father?*"

Usually that was my cue to hang up, but the tone of his voice and his low key look-out-I'm-coming attitude indicated that there was something else going on with this one. I let him talk. He breathed a low volume growl, "*The DA's going to get your father. You're a clever boy. You know he'll get the judge, and I know it gives you nightmares when you think about it . . .*"

I heard him breathe deeply and then he snarled, "*Doesn't it?*"

I tried to steady my voice to sound cool and collected instead of creeped out.

I said, "*Do they let you out every Halloween?*"

He sighed, then he chuckled softly and led me down a different path, "*It must be hard to have to defend your father every day. Are you tired of it yet?*"

I answered, "*Is that your best shot? I've heard a lot better, so listen: You be sure to have a good night.*"

And then I hung up.

Suddenly I no longer wanted to be the designated telephonic protector.

Maybe I was in over my head.

I knew I wanted to insulate my family but I had no clue for how to deal with people who weren't crazy. Give me a looney tune and I was fine.

But give me a real live ghoul, and I wanted to call in sick.

All the drama that took place over the next year simply felt wrong to me. It seemed dishonest and immoral and lame. To start with, there was no *legitimate* excuse for the Media attacks that Clem had to suffer. My family was being smothered by the Houston Chronicle, the Houston Post, and the Houston Press. Every day when I woke up I realized that all of us were locked in and we couldn't get away from our situation. We had no escape.

But that was only the beginning. Clem was about to learn that Briscoe and his Winged Monkeys had found a new way to attack him that was both incredible and unbelievable.

I found out about this new *attack* when I returned to my *Phantom* mode and eavesdropped again on Clem and Doris . . . I'd been fielding insane phone calls up until midnight while I caught up on a book report for school, and I took a break to make myself the perfect peanut butter sandwich. I crept quietly down the stairs and I heard them talking behind their bedroom door.

I mentally slipped into my invisible suit as I moved unseen to their door, and I overheard:

Doris, "*But this isn't legal, Clement! How can they do this?*"

Clem, "*They can pretty much do whatever they want, honey. You need to understand that.*

But I did ask Bryson to search the Texas law codes to see what he could find. He said it's a law from 1876 that's been used only a few times before . . ."

Doris, "*By who? For what?*"

Clem, "*Whenever a district attorney in Texas gets frustrated because his minions can't find their asses, he employs what is best described as an end run to bypass regular procedure.*"

Doris began to raise her voice, "*But how is that legal?*"

Clem lowered his voice, trying to lower hers, "*Because of this 1876 law. It's a convenient way to go fishing without using bait or a hook. All they have to do is throw out a line . . .*"

Doris began to cry, "*But it's so unfair!*"

Clem tried to soothe her, "*We'll figure it out. Don't worry . . .*"

I slipped away from their door and went to the Kitchen. Doris's use of the word *unfair* pretty much summed up my feelings about everything. The Media assault, the murmurings at school, Larry Klump, late night phone calls, early morning lawn signs. It was all unfair.

And now we had to deal with a law from 1876 which also sounded unfair. Didn't Clem mention something about our having the *greatest legal system in the world*? In Houston, at that point in time? I didn't think so.

So what was this 1876 law that favored the prosecutorial arm of the justice system? It was called "*The Court of Inquiry*," and it allowed the District Attorney to ignore a suspect's basic rights as he investigated anything/everything the suspect had ever thought or said or done. All in the name of the law. It's a serious example of the timeless struggle between personal freedom and governmental power. Clem's conflict was essentially about the American Dream and his absolute right to pursue happiness without bowing to the government on his bended knee.

As for the Court of Inquiry, it had a notorious history in Texican affairs since it *favored* prosecution. It legalized any suspect in Frank Briscoe's eyes to be *Guilty Until Proven Innocent*.

As I look back and try to understand his state of mind I'm guessing Briscoe was *that* desperate to take down the *corrupt official* that he'd decided years before to take down. It was unfair.

STRATEGY HUDDLE—The two investigators who have worked doggedly day and night for almost a month digging into records of estates in the probate court investigation hold a strategy conference in Briscoe's office with the district attorney and his first assistant. Dally and Zgourides now are delving deep into the bank records of the key figures in the probe while an expanding staff of investigators interviews witnesses in preparation for next week's court of inquiry.

D.A. FRANK BRISCOE   SAM ROBERTSON   GUS ZGOURIDES   CARL DALLY

Frank Briscoe/Sam Robertson/Gus Zgourides/Carl Dally

The truth: The Court of Inquiry that Briscoe would convene would draw conclusions based on arbitrary suggestions instead of fair facts. The Court of Inquiry would ignore Clem's right to *not* answer questions since it was certain it could *inquire*, and sure it could do so with impunity. Ultimately this court would be so convoluted that no one could've survived its onslaught.

Here's how it would work: The individuals who were the subject of the "*Inquiry*" would have to take an oath and then take the witness stand. They'd be asked questions and not be allowed to consult with their lawyers during proceedings. So without legal counsel they couldn't defend themselves, nor cross-examine or confront witnesses that accused them, and they couldn't call witnesses on their behalf or rebut the prosecution's evidence.

I imagined how *Friendly Frank, your favorite DA,* would have put it, "*Yes,*" said Friendly Frank, "*you're allowed to put up a fight, but only after I tie both of your hands behind your back, put a hood over your head to cover your eyes, and then plug up your ears.*"

That sounds fair, doesn't it?

From the very beginning Frank Briscoe only cared about depriving Clem of his rights so he could make Clem *look* guilty. Then Frank would be able to stand in front of a Grand Jury and expand his lies and continue to create indictments against Clem until all the cows came home.

In a nutshell that's exactly what he planned to do.

Let me repeat: Clem and the witnesses subpoenaed by Briscoe couldn't consult with their lawyers as they were questioned. Clem et al couldn't cross-examine those who'd accused them of wrong-doing . . . It was so unfair, it was disgusting. This crazy law allowed this elected bully to roam the schoolyard freely with no consequence whenever he knocked someone down. To make things worse, over those first few months, Briscoe had generated a ton of press about the rules of law and how his Court of Inquiry would " . . . *get to the bottom of all the Probative corruption.*"

So on June 5 of 1962, District Attorney Frank Briscoe filed a "*Petition for a Court of Inquiry*" with Justice of the Peace W. C. Ragan to examine "*the processing of various estates by the probate court.*" In his petition Briscoe stated, "*I have cause to believe that criminal offenses have been committed against the laws of Texas.*"

He asked that witnesses be called and used Article 886 (which states) "*If a Justice of the Peace has good cause to believe that an offense against the laws of the State has been or is about to be committed, he may summon and examine any witness in relation thereto.*"

On the same day, June 5, Justice Ragan entered his order reciting he had good cause to believe that offenses *had* been committed against the laws of Texas and he desired to **inquire** into matters set forth in the petition filed. The order set the hearing for June 14 at 10:00 a.m.

Officially, Clem was in big trouble. He and his attorneys had never heard such nonsense and here was a District Attorney and a Justice of the Peace (I thought they did Weddings) requiring him to come into a court of law, be sworn in, and answer any questions these guys wanted to ask with no protection for Clem as afforded by our wonderful Bill of Rights. Clem would be deprived of **all** his rights and privileges that were guaranteed by the law of the land.

That's why Clem finally let himself be interviewed by the Media. It was too late and too little but at least he stood up at home plate and took a swing. Later, when Clem's attorneys appealed his having to participate in that Court of Nonsense, the Appellate Court stated that Justice Regan would've been derelict of the duty imposed on him by Article 886 if he *hadn't* proceeded, since he had good cause to believe criminal offenses *had* been committed. And there it was. What was the *good cause* quoted by the Appellate Court? Was it tangible evidence documented by an unimpeachable paper trail? No, it wasn't. Was it reliable testimony from a person of high honor, like, say, The President of the United States? No, it wasn't. Judge Ragan had been convinced by **Frank Briscoe** telling Ragan that *criminal offenses* had been committed in the probate court of Harris County, Texas. Frankly speaking, it all came from Frank.

It was Frank who'd convinced Ragan to convene this horrible court so that they would "*bring the corrupt officials to justice!*" The final straw was Frank telling Ragan, "*Legally we're okay. This is purely an investigatory proceeding. I have a high volume of cases being handled by my Grand Jury, and I need to use the Court of Inquiry to lessen their load. The good News, unlike with the Grand Jury deliberations, we can go public with this one!*" What? He wanted The Court of Inquiry so he could expose Clem's history PUBLICLY?

McClelland Loses Plea for Injunction To Block Inquiry

The Houston Press headline on June 10, 1962

So there it was again: Frank's hidden agenda! He wanted to embarrass and bring Clem down, and he persuaded the Justice of the Peace to initiate the Court of Inquiry by "*swearing*" to Justice Ragan that he had good cause to believe many offenses against Texas law had been committed. Being a very bad guy, Frank had lied well under oath.

One other little twist, courtesy of The Court of Inquiry law of 1876: If a witness refused to appear and testify, the Justice of the Peace could fine the witness and/or imprison the witness until he/she testified. And there it was, with no one questioning this obvious abuse of power.

I have considered this question many times over my lifetime: Which is more important, protecting society or protecting an individual's rights? One of the Appellate judges who carefully reviewed this fiasco stated that the 1876 law was essentially unfair and was not a wise exercise of the powers of government. Why? Because this Court of Nonsense abandoned the incredibly important aspects of Due Process.

What's Due Process? In our Fifth and Fourteenth Amendments to the Constitution there is a Due Process Clause that provides safeguards for each of us. In Clem's case the safeguard that was ignored was a *procedural* safeguard arbitrarily denying Clem his rights in a civil or criminal proceeding. He couldn't cross-examine? He was forced to testify? If he refused to testify, he could be jailed AND fined? He couldn't confront the jerks saying bad things about him? What happened to that phrase we've all heard in movies and on TV when someone didn't want to answer a question? ***I plead the fifth!*** Briscoe said, that in his Court of Nonsense, no witness could plead the fifth since no one was under arrest. Frank was so good at splitting hairs he should have opened a chain of barber shops. Briscoe and his Winged Monkeys had indeed found the key to open the door to a room full of faux facts that, before the Court of Inquiry Law of 1876, would not have been available to them.

Briscoe, McClelland Square Off in First Court Test of Probe

The Houston Press headline on June 13, 1962

Having suffered countless *Newspaper* attacks, the Houston *Television* media suddenly became the enemy. Clem sat us all down at the dinner table one night and explained, "*This Court of Nonsense will be broadcast LIVE on KTRK Channel 13. The date for this soap operatic event is June 14 and it will be difficult for you. It will be hard on me, too, because I know what you all have to deal with at your schools and with your friends. Like I said before, there's nothing to worry about. Keep your heads on straight and trust in the Lord that He'll get us through this. Please bow your heads . . . (We did.) . . . Dear Most Heavenly Father, please let your divine grace protect us as we face another round of lies leveled against me. Please surround us with your abiding love, and guide Edwin Smith and Jack Rawitscher as they defend and protect all of us. In your son Jesus' name . . . Amen.."*

Judge Clem McClelland/Jack Rawitscher/J. Edwin Smith
Harris County Probate Judge with attorneys at today's hearing, June 12, 1962

Ed Smith and Jack Rawitscher (pronounced Rah-wits-her) were Clem's attorneys. They were chosen even though Doris and I wanted Clem to hire Percy Foreman, a trial lawyer with an impressive reputation for winning. But to Clem, his hiring Percy Foreman was equal to his admitting he was guilty. To Clem, Percy was a high priced, high profile lawyer with a reputation for success due to his skill as a master tactician, not due to his clients being innocent. To me, Percy would've been perfect but Clem was convinced the public would look skeptically on him if he stacked the deck with a Joker in *his* hand. I understood what Clem was saying but I'd watched the McClelland name get dragged through the mud for too long. I was eager for Clem to attack Briscoe and his Monkeys with no holds barred and with no mercy. Percy was like an attack dog on a leash and would have been the perfect lawyer, but Clem decided he wanted to play poker with the DA Monkeys. The difference: If they lost, they'd go home to dinner with their wives. If Clem lost, he'd go to prison.

So why hire Edwin Smith? The main reason was Smith's superior understanding of the Constitution and his wide-ranging experience using that knowledge to defend clients whose rights had been ignored. So instead of an attack dog, Clem decided to go with an intellectual dog who believed he could communicate the merits of a case to any judge/jury and convince them his client was innocent. My question, *"How do you fight a vicious, hungry predator like the Briscoe-Devil with "words?"* Clem had made a choice that would prove to be devastating . . .

It was summer so I was able to watch the Court of Inquiry as it was broadcast on KTRK, Channel 13, starting at 10:00 a.m. on June 14. It was a live feed from the courthouse using three monochromatic cameras that sent their broadcast signals to a Camera Control Unit (CCU) located back at the station.

On the subject of broadcasting, Briscoe's kangaroo-court's timing was unfortunate for Clem. KTRK had just purchased state of the art broadcasting equipment and they were eager to test it. When Briscoe contacted the owner of the station, the owner was thrilled at having the opportunity to take his new equipment into a courtroom and broadcast live images of a real court case to his viewing audience. As far as he knew, it had never been done before.

I sat in front of our black and white TV entranced by the sights and sounds of this court as it mounted a blatant attack on Clem.

Hour after hour I watched and listened as the Devil pursued his innocent prey in a court of law and it hurt for me to see/hear Clem and Bryson and others as they tried to dismantle Briscoe's evil contrivance.

On the third day the reporter from Channel 13 stood on the front steps of the courthouse with his microphone pointed at his smirking face. He reported, *"For the past three days, District Attorney Frank Briscoe has been conducting this Court of Inquiry to investigate what he calls 'malfeasance in our Justice System'. Witness after witness has revealed the inner workings of the probate court of Judge Clem McClelland here in Harris County, Texas."*

The reporter's name was Dave Webb and he was pretty good. He'd done his homework, didn't refer to his notes, and thereby kept good eye contact with the home audience.

As he kept speaking his face dissolved into a highlight reel of the most notable visuals from the previous days. There were many, many shots of Clem and Bryson talking and yelling at Briscoe (who the Cameras didn't capture since the shots were Medium Close-Ups on Clem and Bryson). The District Attorney had obviously instructed the Cameramen and Channel 13's Director to stay on the Witnesses' angry faces for maximum negative impact.

As the reporter Dave Webb described the past days' events and the process, it looked like whoever sat on the stand (in the Witness Box) was guilty as sin. Dave said, Voice-Over, *"As we've learned through this proceeding, a Court of Inquiry is nothing like a normal Grand Jury investigation."* I saw Bryson Martin on the stand and he was mad as hell. It was a good visual for Briscoe and Channel 13 when Bryson rose up out of the Witness Box. It looked like Bryson was about to inflict bodily harm on the Devil-Buzzard, but then, due to a large Bailiff standing nearby, he sat back down. Seething. Frustrated. But not beaten.

Dave continued, "*In this proceeding the District Attorney can ask anyONE, anyTHING without benefit of counsel, AND with no chance to cross-examine witnesses who testify against them. I remember from my High School Civics or my History class that there are certain procedures that must be followed. Here's an interesting moment that occurred this morning . . .*"

I saw and heard Bryson on the Witness Stand as he turned to look at Justice Ragan and said, "*Your Honor, this is a ridiculous fishing expedition and I refuse to answer any more questions without MY attorney present!*"

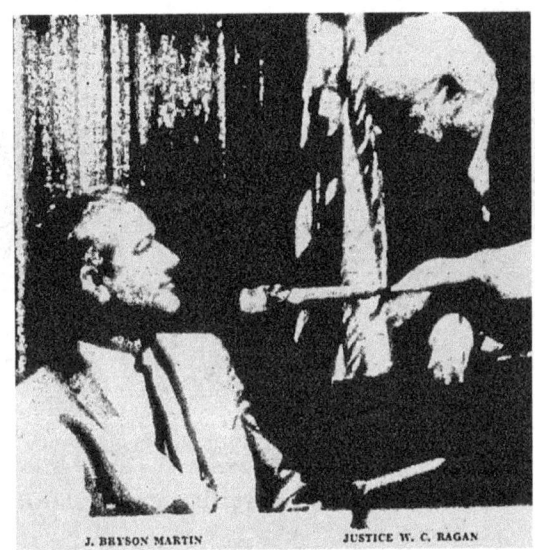

Bryson Martin battled Justice W.C. Ragan

The TV camera pulled back to a two-shot of Bryson and Justice Ragan.

The judge firmly said, "*I'm tired of your lecturing me about the law Mr. Martin. You WILL answer, or I will find you in contempt of this court!*"

Bryson smiled but it wasn't a friendly smile, "*Good! I'm totally in CONTEMPT of this court! It's ILLEGAL!*"

Ragan turned to his Bailiff and said, "*Bailiff, remove Mr. Martin from my courtroom, and levy a fine against him for $1,000!*"

The Camera went back to a shot of Dave Webb standing on the courthouse steps, "*Whoa! The thought of $1,000 leaving MY wallet would be pretty contemptible!*"

Dave laughed and finished his report with, "*The DA's next move will be to take the facts he's gathered from these proceedings and hand them over to the Grand Jury . . . This is Dave Webb. Back to you guys in the studio!*"

Atty. Smith & Judge Clem

TV Cameramen worked as overflow crowd showed up

I felt I'd had enough courtroom soap opera and I turned the volume down on the television.

I was obsessed with the American Civil War and I was reading my latest book on that war. This book supported my opinion that economics not slavery had caused that extremely complex conflict and I had a good notion concerning how the contentious tariff issues in 1860 had led to Southern secession. Then I heard the phone ring.

The phone was on a side table next to the couch in the Den so I picked it up and said, "*Hello, McClelland residence . . .*" I heard a familiar creepy voice say, "*Hello, Kirk. Your dad doesn't look happy when I see him on the TV. Why is that?*"

I reached down inside of myself for the courage I needed to talk to this scary man and after a deep breath I said, "*He thinks that the public, tha . . . that's you, will misinterpret and presume him guilty when he's simply being victimized.*"

I suddenly realized that I needed to assign this voice a name. I'd heard Clem and Doris talking about their life insurance policies the night before and *The Underwriter* popped into my head. So that was his new name.

The Underwriter asked me, "*Do you think someone should remove the high and mighty Mr. Briscoe from this drama?*"

Because sometimes I tended to respond too quickly, I countered, "*Are you offering your services?*"

Holy moly! I knew the moment I said it that I'd crossed over an important line, especially when Mr. Underwriter said, "*You never know . . . Go read your book, Kirk . . .*"

And then he hung up. Double holy moly!

Who was this guy? Why was I talking to him instead of hanging up?

It was like playing Steve Allen's **The Answer Man** game. The answer, "*You get burned!*" The question, "*What happens if an assassin lights a match under your ass?*"

The real question: To share or not to share? Should I tell Clem about The Underwriter phone caller? Clem was already surrounded by enough creeps, so . . . I didn't.

As Clem and his attorneys tried to prepare for whatever happened next they rightfully noted Briscoe's perverse use of the Justice system to obtain what he wanted: Clem's head!

The Houston Press headline on June 16, 1962

To Fast Forward for one paragraph, it's interesting to note that after 4 days of grueling testimony, with questions asked by Briscoe and his Monkeys, and answers given by Clem and the men who he worked with, none of the material obtained by the DA in this kangaroo court would ever be used in future trials.

It was obvious that all Frank Briscoe wanted to do was vilify Clem's image.

To quote an Appellate Judge, "*The bad publicity engendered by a Court of Inquiry is the fallout from any evidence discovered, since the individual loses his right to protect himself against false accusations and rumors which cause harm to that individual . . . This 1876 law is essentially unfair and not a wise exercise of government . . . In my opinion the Harris County Court of Inquiry was used purely for the sake of "humiliating exposure," and that is not constitutionally permissible.*"

This is why Clem and his attorneys were working to predict Briscoe's next move. For Clem the Justice System in Harris County had become a maze of swamps with poisonous snakes and quicksand waiting to drag Clem down and drown him. There was no safe haven. Since everything was at the DA's whim, Harris County was treacherous territory for my Clem.

Then the unthinkable happened: After months of speculation and skilled (?) analysis in the Media, Clem was indicted . . .

The Houston Press headline on June 20, 1962

The Houston Press story was written by Cap Detrick and included a perp-walk picture of Clem being led into the Justice Building so he could be photographed and finger-printed. He shared with me that he'd never felt lower at any time in his life.

INDICTED — Probate judge Clem McClelland of Houston, Tex., has been indicted on nine counts of conversion of funds of estates, felony theft

The Judge,

my Father,

suffered a new low

Just like that, my family was in mourning. What had died was our faith in the Justice System, the definition of the word "*fair*," and finally, the definition of the word "*hope*."

We weren't happy campers. Going to school and having to put on/keep a brave face was hard for me and my sisters. Going to Church was easier for Doris because people there weren't as judgmental (but it was still hard). After making bail, going to work was impossible for Clem but he sallied forth bravely.

Helen Smith told me, "*Kirk, you'd be pleased to see how your father's handling all of this. He still wears his robe proudly and works hard on every case I put in front of him.* (She cried)

He's really something . . ."

At night when Clem came home to his 2-story fortress, to what was *supposed* to be his refuge, Clem found the Newspaper reporters and Television station trucks parked in front of his house. It felt like we were all locked in with no relief in sight . . .

The next day I was about to talk to Betsy at my locker when Larry Klump rolled up to make my life more miserable. With his ugly smile he spoke loudly, "*Hey, McClelland, your dad's in it up to his neck! 9 indictments! How many years does that equal to in the big house? The answer? Way too many!*"

He moved close and slammed his hand hard on the locker next to me. I didn't flinch. He'd tried to shock me with that tactic before and it hadn't worked then either. He laughed and then he rolled away. I relaxed a little bit and then I noticed how Betsy was looking at me. I gave her my brave smile but she still looked uncomfortable. And then she smiled her sad smile and said, "*My parents told me to tell you we can't go out this Friday. Or any Friday. I'm sorry but we have to break up.*" I flinched. I hadn't seen that one coming.

"*C'mon, Betsy, Clem's my father. He's not the boogeyman. You do know that all of this is baloney, right?*"

She leaned toward me and kissed my cheek, "*I know . . .*"

She turned and walked into our homeroom as Velma Brennan, my homeroom teacher, came through her door to fetch me.

Velma Brennan was in her fifties with a kindness in her face and the positive attitude of a Norman Rockwell painting of a schoolteacher. Velma shook her head and gave me her usual I'll-be-there-to-support-you look. She and I had been tight from the start and, as Clem's situation fell farther, she and I grew closer. She said, "*Methinks the lady's parents doth protest too much.*" She put her arm around me, "*Mr. McClelland, would you care to chat about this, or uh, anything else?*"

I said, "*Thanks, Mrs. Brennan, but No.*"

The homeroom bell rang and then I changed my answer, "*On second thought, Yes.*"

I took her arm, we walked to the door, and I asked, "*What do you do when everything is perfect, and then suddenly it all falls apart?*"

We walked into her classroom and she whispered to me, "*Buy some glue . . .*"

The Media siege had begun. It was an ugly invasion of our privacy with no recourse for us. A dozen reporters were camped out in the street in front of the house and as the sun came up the photographers and film cameramen set up their respective cameras to click and shoot. The early morning paper boy for the Houston Post pedaled by as usual and he threw our paper on our lawn. The Houston Post Reporter and Photographer both applauded him and he waved back as he pedaled away. It would probably be the highlight of both their mornings and they both knew it.

Inside our house in the living room Doris sat on the couch as Clem looked outside from the window. I sat at the piano playing my old warm-up exercise of the do-re-mi tonal scale in a weak attempt to lighten the mood.

Doris said to Clem, "*Go talk to them.*"

Clem, "*It's not going to happen.*"

Doris, "*How can we live with these jerks on our doorstep watching our every move?*"

Clem, "*Stay tuned. We'll wait 'em out.*"

Clem pointed out the window and said, "*The thousand dollar iceman cometh . . .*"

He moved from the window toward the Kitchen back door in an instant.

I moved to the window in time to see Bryson Martin park his Cadillac Fleetwood and walk past the reporters to reach our house.

The reporters recognized him and yelled out questions, "*Mr. Martin, could you give us your take on The Court of Inquiry?*" and, "*Hey Bryson, how'd that thousand dollar hit make you feel?*"

He ignored them, walked around to the Carport to reach the Kitchen door. Clem was there and let him inside. I peeked around the corner in my *Phantom* mode as they huddled and talked, and then Bryson waved at me, shook Clem's hand, and left without saying another word.

Clem closed the Kitchen door and turned to me, "*Come with me, Kirk. I need your help.*"

I moved to the Kitchen, "*What's up?*"

Clem smiled at me, "*We're gonna walk the dogs . . .*"

We went out The Billiard Room backdoor, past the dogs in the back yard, and we walked to the garage, which was really Clem's workshop and storage area for his filing cabinets.

He had all the homeowner's tools neatly organized and arranged on one wall overlooking his workbench, and two large steel filing cabinets on the opposite wall in a corner. Clem unlocked the cabinets and he opened every drawer. He then walked over to several large bags of dog food and began to open them. My job was to go back outside and bring the dogs, Gigi and Oscar, into the garage. I grabbed both of our high-spirited dogs by their collars and led them inside.

I saw Clem pouring dog food and water into their dog dishes. When Clem finished doing that he patted both dogs to show them that he loved them, and then we left them in the garage and locked the door. As we walked back to the house both dogs started barking and scratching the door in their plea to be let out. Clem walked back to the door and commanded, "*OSCAR! GIGI! SHUT YOUR MOUTHS!*"

And then he added in a normal voice, "*. . . after you finish eating!*" We listened and there were no more complaints.

That was a Friday.

On Saturday afternoon Cap Detrick wrote, and The Houston Press published, an op-ed article that read like a page from Frank Briscoe's "**SMEAR CLEM**" playbook. It included all of Briscoe's one-sided catch-phrases and called The Court of Inquiry "*sensational*" when, at best, the court was unfair and, according to Bryson, illegal. The most interesting line in Cap's dogmatic diatribe was "***Judge McClelland, at the very least, should arrange a leave of absence from duty.***" Was it a prediction by Cap, or an insider's awareness of things yet to come?

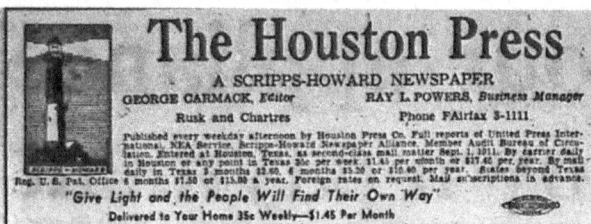

McClelland Should Get Off Bench---Or Be Put Off

Whatever else the sensational court of inquiry has disclosed, it has shown clearly Probate Judge Clem McClelland chose Tierra Grande Inc. over tierra firma.

He admits he accepted the payment of personal bills plus the use and joint registration of ownership of a Cadillac from a private firm. DA Frank Briscoe's statement that Tierra Grande's funds to pay for this were subscribed by men regularly appointed to handle estates under the jurisdiction of Judge McClelland's court, of course, makes matters look much worse.

However, the bald and admitted fact of acceptance of such gifts by a judge from a private firm is a shocking revelation of how Judge McClelland looked upon his obligation to the people.

• • •

Here was a personable young man who began working in the Court House on probate matters in 1947 at a salary of $350 per month.

In 1949, the new elective office of Probate Court Judge was created by the Texas Legislature with a salary of $8250, and was given by appointment to Judge McClelland. The circumstances considered, you might say it was created especially for him. By 1961, his salary had been increased to $17,200 — four times what he started for—and retirement-insurance benefits for his court as well as other judgeships had been expanded considerably.

He never has had an opponent. This is an amazing record. He was appointed July 21, 1949, nominated by the Democrats, then elected, in 1950, 1952, 1954 and 1956. He was renominated without an opponent in the May 5 Democratic primary in a race in which there was no Republican candidate. In other words, he was due to be re-elected to another four-year term, again without opposition.

Have the people in any way failed to support and provide for Judge McClelland as an elected official? We think not. From the above record, it appears they gave him their trust completely.

• • •

Another point in Judge McClelland's own testimony in the now recessed court of inquiry throws some light on his attitude toward his job.

He said he has followed the practice of splitting up any residue left in estates where there were no heirs between those who had handled the affairs of the estate.

A basic principle is that if anything—money, land or anything else of value—becomes ownerless, it reverts to the state under the law of escheat. Judge McClelland, therefore, by his own admission was handing out to those he chose things of value that belonged to the people of Texas as a whole in defiance of the people's law.

Such an attitude could only grow from the feeling he personally owned the office and all its powers, not that the office belonged to the people and that they trusted him to occupy it, conditioned always on good performance.

Regardless of the legality—or illegality—attached to his other acts in later proceedings, Judge Clem McClelland clearly and wilfully has betrayed the trust of the public in accepting the favors of Tierra Grande and in ignoring the basic law of public ownership implicit in the principle of escheat.

• • •

Judge McClelland has said he will not resign under fire. His lawyer, J. Edwin Smith, has made much of the fact Judge McClelland has continued to conduct his court—and has forecast that even should Judge McClelland be indicted on criminal charges he still would continue to hold onto his job.

The question here is not what Judge McClelland and Lawyer Smith want but what the people want. Do the people want Judge McClelland to continue to serve while—to put it mildly—he is under such a cloud?

Judge McClelland has six months more to serve and no accredited opponent for re-election. Will he be permitted to serve without challenge by those qualified to bring such a challenge—the members of his own profession? The matters revealed in the current court of inquiry probably will move slowly through the mills of justice.

• • •

Getting the affairs of the Probate Court removed completely from any such high-flung connection as Tierra Grande and back onto solid earth—tierra firma—is of vital importance to the public welfare, in our opinion.

Judge McClelland at the very least should arrange a leave of absence from duty.

If he fails to do this, the Houston-Harris County Bar Association should take whatever steps are necessary to suspend him from conducting that court until the testimony in the court of inquiry has been passed upon under due process.

Cap and The Houston Press had Clem in their sights

A day later I looked out the front windows to see if the reporters were still camped there. Over the past 24 hours I'd seen Vans drive up or drive away as shifts changed and reporters went home to drive their wives crazy instead of us. The paper boys continued to deliver papers, photographers yawned, and the McClelland household showed no signs of newsworthy activity.

Then a brand new blue Buick drove up and into our driveway. Two men got out and walked to our front door. Their names were Assistant DA Pete Moore and Assistant DA Fred Drury. They knocked on the door and Doris answered. I stood by her side to offer moral support as these winged Assistants revealed their mission, *"Good morning, Mrs. McClelland, I'm Pete and this is Fred."*

He handed her a Search Warrant, *"This is a Search Warrant that allows us to enter your home to discover any documents or correspondence that might be germane to your husband's legal problems. We hope we can do this quickly and without conflict."*

Doris invited them in but Mr. Moore said, *"Thank you, ma'am, but it's the rear building that the District Attorney wants us to inspect."*

They nodded to us and then walked around through the carport to the garage. The reporters watched them with heightened interest and the photographers snapped dozens of pictures.

The KTRK film cameraman, I learned his name was Jeff, ran to the side yard with his Camera handheld to film the Monkeys as they knocked on and then entered the garage door.

Gigi and Oscar, still inside, went berserk and barked wildly.

I couldn't see the commotion but I heard, *"Son-of-a-bitch! Goddamn it, get off me!"*

I saw the two Monkeys quickly back out of the garage with Clem's ferocious dogs showing their teeth, biting and jumping all over both men.

Jeff had a grin on his face as he happily filmed their dance, *"Yeah, yeah! This is good!"*

I ran out of the house as the dogs continued to bite and bark. I grabbed both of them by their collars and hooked them to their leashes which were tied to their magnolia tree in the backyard.

The Flying Monkeys took a breath, nodded their thanks to me, and then they reentered the garage. I heard a commotion as they squealed, *"Oh, my god, Pete . . . watch your step!" "Oh, no Fred! Holy shit!"*

Jeff the Cameraman was giggling. He kept filming the screaming Monkeys as they stepped back out of the garage and wiped their shoes on the backyard grass. I was down on my knees next to the dogs trying to calm them as the Monkeys shouted, *"Goddamn! There's dog shit and piss all over the place in there!"*

I was pleased that Clem (with Bryson's help) had fought back using the weapons they had available. I kept patting his puppies as I watched Briscoe's unhappy Assistants hop around.

I told them, *"Good dogs."*

GUS ZGOURIDES   CARL DALLY   DIST. ATTY. FRANK BRISCOE
District Attorney and aides prepare argument in McClelland hearing.

Frank worked overtime to smear Clem

MORE HEADLINES:

'Obviously Politics,' McClelland Says

The Houston Press THURSDAY, JUNE 7, 1962

McClelland Probers Dig Up New Facts

Indicted Judge Ouster Sought

Lawyer Paid McClelland $2800; O'Brien Collected Fees For Non-Existent Attorneys

The Houston Press headline on June 15th, 1962

McClelland Quits As Dem Nominee In Probate Race

CLEM McCLELLAND
Ends Candidacy

Candidate Left Up To Party

The Houston Chronicle headline on July 22, 1962

CHAPTER FIVE

DID IT HAPPEN HERE? 1962–1963

To say the probate court in Houston, Texas was a *mess* is an understatement. Citizens made formal complaints that their cases were being handled by a lawbreaker/thief/criminal and they were not pleased. Who could blame them? Frank Briscoe had smeared Clem's reputation with his Media brush and there was no doubt in anyone's mind that Clem was guilty.

The powers that be, The Harris County Bar Association, decided to suspend Judge Clem and replace him with a squeaky clean magistrate (what they called a temporary substitute) so the world could continue to spin. It wasn't that easy, though, since no one wanted to get their hands dirty if suddenly the Honorable Judge Clem McClelland was shown to be innocent of all charges.

The Houston Bar Association took on the responsibility, and I found an old 1962 videotape in the Houston Public Library archives of a Press Conference film where the President of the Bar urged all members to attend a voting session. At that session the members voted to select a temporary replacement while Clem dealt with the charges against him.

Channel 13's Cameraman, Jeff Wilson, also filmed Clem as he said the following, "*I hope that the Bar association will select a fine man who is well versed in probate law. I know he will have the support of the Bar and the public when he has been thus chosen.*"

This sound bite was obviously filmed for Channel 13's Nightly News and Clem looked and sounded like a man who had no choice but to participate. He was up against the wall with no room for dodging bullets. I will say that he looked damn good on Camera (probably due to good lighting by Jeff) but his handsome face was tainted by his unhappy situation. He'd suffered disgrace and humiliation of the worst kind. He no longer had an office and no longer had a job. Helen Smith would become secretary to Judge Arthur C. Lesher, Clem's replacement.

It was on that day that my Clem suffered a major insulin shock, a diabetic's worst nightmare. By definition an insulin shock occurs when a diabetic takes too much insulin and doesn't consume enough food to balance the insulin and stabilize his/her blood sugar. The problem with an insulin shock: It short circuits the brain so it no longer functions normally. My guess was that the stress of his suspension contributed to or caused his instability and it made his bad insulin shock that much worse.

He was driving back to our home in his black Caddy. As he drove on Westheimer Road he began to lose control of his mind. The insulin that diabetics depend on to stay alive started to work against him and it shut down his ability to understand reality. It shut down his ability to think and make choices. In other words, he blacked out. According to witnesses in the cars around him, Clem's head simply slid down the car seat until he was no longer visible. Then, since the Caddy was moving, it rolled to the side of the road at about 30 mph and ran into three parked cars which luckily had no one in them. Because Clem was already unconscious he wasn't hurt. His body wasn't rigid and it just rolled with the punch as his Caddy came to a very abrupt stop.

When the Police showed up they pulled Clem's wallet out of his pocket, saw who he was and read his "I'M A DIABETIC" card and called for an ambulance since he was unconscious. I could say it wasn't a good day because his insurance premium rose a bit, but he wasn't hurt. That made it a good day.

When I asked him to describe to me what a *black out* was or felt like, he said, *"My only memory of the shock was it felt like I was sliding into a dream, and then nothing until I woke up here with this IV dripping sugar fluid into my arm. It was strange to be awake one second and passed out the next. Diabetes and insulin are risky realities."*

A black out was a pretty scary proposition but I worried that the high stress level connected to Clem's situation might cause him to have more major shocks. As for his stress level coming down, Frank Briscoe would prove to be no help. The Devil's next move was obvious, and we all knew there'd be no relief. Clem was out of a job, but he wasn't out of the woods.

It was time for Clem's attorneys to update him on their game plan. We knew the Devil was having a hard time choosing which of the 9 indictments he was going to prosecute. Finding an unhappy citizen who lost out on an inheritance was no challenge. Finding a case where Clem actually broke the law would prove to be difficult if not impossible, at least according to Clem.

When the doorbell rang I answered it and let Ed Smith and Jack Rawitzcher in. I shook their hands and led them to the Dining Room table that I had cleared for the meeting.

I'd asked Clem if I could listen in on this discussion and, much to Ed's and Jack's surprise, Clem said yes. I'd told him I was old enough and smart enough to analyze and separate *tactics* from *strategy* and since he was trying to get something positive out of this nonsense he agreed that, if Ed and Jack agreed, I could sit in.

I looked at them carefully. Ed was in his fifties and looked like a college professor who'd earned tenure years before. He had well-groomed grey hair and he dressed in a dark blue suit with a thin dark blue necktie. This is what I saw him wear whenever I saw him.

Jack was in his late thirties and it was obvious to me that he loved working in the law because no matter what clothing was on his body, he always wore a sincere and happy smile. That night Jack wore a Texas University T-shirt and a UT baseball cap. These guys were complete opposites and I hoped that would prove to be a successful formula for Clem.

Doris came into the Dining Room and shook both of their hands.

To Clem she said, "*Clem, Percy Foreman called again.*"

She smiled at the rest of us and continued, "*He's very persistent.*"

Clem looked at the two lawyers in front of him and went to work putting out the fire Doris had just ignited, "*Don't worry, gentlemen. He's been chasing me for a month now and sometimes I chat with him just to stay sharp about my choices.*"

Ed said, "*You don't have to explain, Clem. Jack and I appreciate your situation and we know you're standing on top of an anthill.*"

Doris kissed Clem and left us alone. She'd made her plea for Percy so I'm sure she felt her work on that issue was done.

Clem turned to Ed and Jack, "*So what's my best move here?*"

Jack chuckled and said, "*Trust in the law and in us. We've spent a lot of time calculating the odds that a jury will pay attention and side with you, against a man whose apparent political ambitions are his only reason for being.*"

Clem, "*Okay. Same question. What's my best move?*"

Ed said, "*Jack and I have different opinions, Judge, and I apologize for that, but it's one of the things we wanted to discuss tonight. We've never had a disagreement this severe.*"

I watched Clem steeple his fingers in the likeness of a church. I could tell that bit of information troubled him.

He said, "*Tell me.*"

Ed said, "*I think you should let us defend you on Constitutional grounds, and Jack thinks you should engage in an alley fight and use Briscoe's lack of evidence as your Defense.*"

Jack jumped in and tried to sell Clem saying, "*Judge, you're being railroaded by a District Attorney whose political ambitions have made him more than a little crazy.*"

Clem, "*The voters here like him, Mr. Rawitscher.*"

Jack nodded. "*Which is why, no matter which strategy you choose, we'll ask for a change of venue . . .*"

A change of venue meant asking a District Judge to move Clem's trial away from Houston due to all the adverse publicity here about Clem's case. Jack pulled out a file and opened it. At least a hundred Newspaper clippings with "*McClelland*" written in each headline spilled out onto the table. Most of the clippings were published by The Houston Press.

Jack, "*Thanks to Mr. Briscoe's use of the Media, especially The Houston Press and their reporter Cap Detrick, you've been on the front burner now for too many months.*"

Jack took a deep breath and said, "*It's time for you to get the hell out of Dodge . . .*"

Clem used one of his poker techniques designed to surprise other players. He *called* and then he *raised* as he asked, "*What do you think about Percy Foreman defending me?*"

Both Attorneys smiled, and Ed said, "*You're putting us through the wringer here, Judge. If we say he's no good, you know we're not telling the truth. If we say he's wonderful, you'll fire us and hire him!*"

Ed put on his glasses from his glasses case, and stared at Clem with a scholarly look, "*I'm confident we can convince any jury anywhere that your rights as a citizen of the United States have been severely abused. It's time for you to kick Mr. Briscoe in the balls and shove our country's Bill of Rights up his left nostril.*"

Clem and Jack and I all laughed at the conservative Ed Smith's sudden passion and I really enjoyed his *nose* reference. Clem thought for a moment and rubbed his hand over his lower chin as he said, "*I'm fond of the kicking-Briscoe-in-the-balls image.*"

He stood and put out his hand for both men to shake as he said, "*Let's turn this around, Gentlemen.*" They both stood and shook Clem's hand. To me they all looked confident. A Clem platitude (rephrased), "*Where There's a Lawyer, There's Hope.*"

When the Devil finally chose which case he'd prosecute, Ed Smith and Jack Rawitscher went before Judge Gaylord at the Harris County Courthouse to plead their change of venue case. The courtroom was empty except for the judge's staff, Clem, and Cap Detrick. Clem described to me what took place: Ed and Jack stood together and it was Jack who spoke to the judge. After outlining the enormous amount of bad Publicity as the cause, Jack said, "*. . . and for those reasons Your Honor, the defendant requests a change in venue for all future proceedings. Thank you.*"

Ed and Jack sat down next to Clem. According to Clem's description, Judge Earl Gaylord was similar to Clem's mentor, Judge Glenn Perry. Same crusty persona, same manner of swiftly getting to the crux of every issue before him and then stating his position clearly.

After clearing his sixty-year-old throat, Judge Gaylord spoke, "*Thank you, Mr. Rawitscher. I agree with your take on the ridiculous Media blitz that's taken place here over the last few months. I've never seen anything like The Houston Press except in my worst nightmares.*" Judge Gaylord looked over at Cap Detrick, smiled at Briscoe's pet snake, and then blew his honorable nose on his honorable hanky (Clem's words, not mine).

Judge Gaylord, "*Therefore, your request for a change in venue is granted.*"

The Judge nodded to his Legal Assistant. "*I'll now ask my Assistant to hold up a box that contains index cards with the names of towns at least 150 miles away from our Media-stained city of Houston, Texas.*"

He turned to his Assistant who held up the box. He reached into the box and as he pulled out a white card he held it up so everyone could see it and then he said, "*Congratulations, Gentlemen. You've won an all-expenses paid trip, to be paid by your client, to the beautiful town of . . .* (He paused to see the name again) *. . . Belton, Texas. I pray it gives you everything you need to find Justice.* (He banged his gavel) *My court is dismissed.*"

Clem and I sat in front of the TV again, him drinking while I did homework. Clem sat staring at the television and, after glancing over at the clock, he turned it on. On the screen we saw Frank Briscoe telling Channel 13's Dave Webb details of the upcoming trial.

Briscoe, "*That's why I chose this case to prosecute. My office will punish those who steal funds from defenseless people, in this case, defenseless children.*"

Clem turned it off. He paced back and forth in front of the TV and he said, "*Jesus . . .*" as he paced. Then he sat back down. I saw how upset Clem was and I walked to the bar to make him a drink. I reached into the well and found the Jack Daniels bottle.

I poured a drink, neat, into a glass and took it to Clem who had a distant look in his eye.

He took the glass, "*Thanks, boy. Mr. Daniels is a close friend of mine.*"

The phone rang and we looked at each other with dread. I was the telephonic phone man so I moved quickly into the Kitchen. I hesitated for a second, I took a breath and I picked up. I said, "*McClelland residence . . .*"

The next voice I heard was a choir of angels from heaven above.

Betsy said, "*Hello, sweet boy.*" I tried to contain myself but it was impossible. I was enamored by Betsy and I replied:

"*Hello, my turtle dove. It's . . . It's an unexpected pleasure to hear your lovely voice.*"

I heard real concern as she asked, "*How's your dad doing? How are YOU doing?*"

I lied and said, "*We're both doing fine . . . How about you?*"

She laughed, "*Listen to us. Splendid small talk, Kirk. I never thought we'd play this game.*"

I said, "*I'll play whatever game you want. Speaking of which, how're your folks?*"

She laughed and said, "*Oh, Kirk. I . . . I miss talking to you. I just wanted you to know I still love you.*"

Oh my . . . There are no nicer words to hear than "*I love you*" when your father's the DA's target. Betsy had no idea what a relief she was to me at that time. To pay her back I said, "*So that's why you called! Your wish is my command!* (I cleared my throat and then I began to sing "**Moonlight Becomes You**" to her)

"Moonlight becomes you, it goes with your hair. You certainly know the right things to wear. Moonlight becomes you, I'm thrilled at the sight. And I could get so romantic, tonight." I heard Betsy softly sigh and I peeked into the Den to see Clem smiling as I continued to croon, *"You're all dressed up to go dreamin', tell me if I'm wrong. What a night to go dreamin', mind if I tag along?"*

As part of our ritual I stopped singing so I could ask her, *"Are you ready?"* and like she always did, she answered, *"Am I ever!"*

Then came my wrap-up of this love song *"If I say I love you* [I loudly hiccupped], *I want you to know. It's not just because there's Moonlight, although* [I hiccupped again], *Moonlight becomes you so!"* I finished with a loud *"HIC-CUP,"* and Betsy laughed.

She was still giggling as she said, *"You always make me laugh! I miss that . . . and you."*

I said, *"Call this number anytime for Your Favorite Laugh Tunes."* I hiccupped again and she giggled again. I heard a knock in her background as Betsy whispered, *"Oops, gotta go!"* and she quickly hung up. When I heard her dial tone it was like a death to me. Damn.

I walked back to the Den and sat down close to Clem. He was looking deep into his JD glass.

He asked, *"Was that Miss Betsy?"* I said, *"Yes, sir."*

Clem, *"How's her family doing?"* I said, *"Who cares?"* We both laughed and Clem said, *"I enjoyed your singing. Does she know it's in the genes from which you spring?"*

I happily said, *"She does indeed."*

Clem, *"That's good."*

The telephone started to ring again. I ran into the Kitchen thinking it was Betsy and when I picked up the phone I said, *"Your concert wish is my command!"*

Instead of hearing the angels sing I heard a voice from my past as it said, *"Your father is a thief! I hate how he stole money from me and gave it to my brother! He's a no good thief!"* I wasn't sure if I was right but it sure sounded like . . .

She continued, *"I know you're answering the phone, Kirk! I've called before and listened to your smart wisecrackin' mouth. You always have a line so you can make people feel guilty for calling, don't you? Well, now the judge can feel guilty for a change! It's his turn! Judge Clem McClelland will finally get what HE deserves!"*

I couldn't believe my ears. What had Clem done to this woman to make her so unreasonable?

I hesitated for a moment and, when I heard her about to continue her rant, I interrupted her.

I said, *"Mrs. Henderson? Is that you, Mrs. Henderson?"* Her response was silence on the line.

Then I heard a click as Mildred hung up . . .

I continued to wake early to handle the *"hate sign detail"* and I continued to get out of bed at midnight for my peanut butter fixes. As we moved closer to Clem's trial date, I began to run into Clem doing his own nighttime kitchen run. I guess it was a genetic affection for Jiffy Extra Crunchy, but no matter what it was it gave me quality sharing time with him.

During our midnight talks I learned the degree of pressure my father was suffering. Clem told me things and then punctuated the shared information with, "*. . . and don't bother your mother or your sisters with what I just told you. This is between you and me.*"

So as we talked and we shared, I again became his hunting partner. The difference was I longed to hear the ducks and honking geese flying over our duck blind in the darkness.

I was constantly reminded that my family was at war with the imperfection of the Harris County (for lack of a better description) *Justice System*, and it was clear that my whole family suffered shell shock daily.

The truth: It still felt good to have Clem back home. He and I started planting bushes in the front flower bed, and trees in the backyard next to the garage. And then Clem said, "*You're too old to have to live upstairs with your sisters. Let's turn the garage into your new stronghold. How does that sound?*" Well gee, Clem, hot damn!

For the next month we cleared out boxes of old receipts and income tax records. And then, suddenly, the Cuban Missile Crisis happened. All the space he and I had cleared, started to fill up with cans of meat, fruit, vegetables and water. Clem and Doris and everyone else were certain the world would blow up. Our stockpile of bomb shelter food grew, and Clem instructed, "*Think safe with canned goods. If you have a bad feeling about any food-can, toss it.*" The good news: When the 13 days of October passed, we didn't have to shop as often as before.

Getting back to remodeling the garage: I watched and learned as Clem taught me how to install a toilet. Clem was a skilled plumber and electrician and he plumbed and wired up my *new stronghold* so I could be independent. We also installed a window air conditioner/heater unit. When we moved my dressers and bed in, the stronghold was mine.

As days and nights passed I grew accustomed to my new setting and it became my home. I had my own phone and could talk to Betsy whenever I wanted, and I did. Suddenly I was getting older, faster. I was making straight A's, I wrote better reports and I increased my vocabulary in the process. It was easier for me to juggle Football/Basketball and Track because I was becoming my own man. I felt it and I started to realize that Clem and Doris had given me my own transportation with my Moped, and then they'd given me my own house so I could be self-sufficient and free. I realized that, with all the other things they'd given me, I was the luckiest lad in the world.

But I still had one constant ache: How could we save Clem?

He was meeting almost daily with Ed and Jack to finalize their presentation of his Defense. I didn't join them for their meetings because I had homework and I thought I'd get in the way. But I did go into the house to pay my respects since these men were trying to get Clem out of this mess. It seemed to me a formidable task and I noticed that Ed was growing more grey hair and Jack was growing a beard.

And then Doris had an inspiration . . . We waited one evening for Clem to come home from a Shriners meeting. When he parked his Caddy and came into the house via the Kitchen door I put my arm around him and greeted him with, "*Hey, Clem. How was your day?*" Clem was no dummy and with no expression he took note of my youthful grin, he grabbed my left arm and he asked, "*Okay, sonny-boy, what's up?*"

I felt like an unlucky duck caught in Clem's shotgun sights so I removed my arm and tried to be mysterious, "*Hey! I've got a surprise for you! Wanna take a guess?*"

He tried not to show any sign of emotion but sister Micki had observed that when Clem tried not to laugh his nose got bigger. Sure enough his nose started to inflate and to contain it he said, "*What's up . . . KIRK?*"

I stammered, "*Well, we asked Josephine to stay over tonight and cook us dinner.*"

His nose had stopped growing and he said, "*Okay. Last chance, partner.*"

I quickly explained, "*So you and Doris can go out and spend an evening alone!*"

He laughed, gave me his "*That's my boy*" smile and asked, "*What's your mother think about this?*"

I said, "*She's already dressed and ready to go! Doesn't that sound cool?*"

Clem nodded and said, "*You're gonna be a fine young man . . .*" He put his arm around me and finished his sentence, "*. . . SOMEDAY!*"

As if on cue here came Doris, Micki, Anne, and Josephine all laughing and celebrating the parents-taking-a-deserved-night-out, saying, "*You guys are going to have fun!*" and "*I love where you're going for dinner! Lucky you!*" and "*First dibs on the leftovers!*"

And then it was time for Josephine, "*I'm so glad to see you two goin' out Mistah Clem! But do us all a favor and take yo time comin' back home!*" It was a standing joke and we all laughed. A good moment.

After the parents left I sat at the round dinner table eating Josephine's cooked meal of fried chicken ala collard greens and chitlins. Yum. I think. To add to the taste treat, I had the added pleasure of eating inside the house for a change so I could share dinnertime repartee with three, uh, very interesting and different women. Micki said, "*I love Tab Hunter! He's got the longest eyelashes!*"

Anne as usual followed her lead and said, "*Yes, he does! I love him, too!*"

Josephine was part of our family and a huge contributor to every discussion. It didn't matter if she had or didn't have any firsthand experience with the subject matter. She said, "*Eyelashes? Huh! Back when I was yo age . . .*"

I piped in, "*A hundred years ago!*"

She wagged her finger at me and said to the sisters, "*We judged a boy by how fas' he cud run from the PO-lice . . . not by his purty eyes!*"

That got a laugh from all of us. Josephine stood up from the table, carrying plates. I stood to help her and met her in the Kitchen where she was putting yummy scraps onto a plate.

I asked her, "*Is that for Oscar and Gigi?*" She nodded.

I said, "*I'll take it out to 'em.*" She shook her head and made it clear, "*I got this, Master Kirk, thank ya!*"

She stepped lively out of the Kitchen and walked through The Billiard Room to open the door to the backyard where the dogs were always tied to their magnolia tree. The yard lights were lit and when she looked out into the yard she began to scream, "*Oh no, oh no! Where'd they go? Where'd they go? Help, Master Kirk, come help me!*"

My sisters and I ran out into the yard to see Josephine standing there on the upside down scrap plate, holding the empty dog leashes.

She was yelling, "*They gone! Oscar, Gigi, they gone!*"

I tried to calm her down, "*It's all right, Josephine. We'll find them, it's all right.*"

She shook her head, "*No, sir, Master Kirk. Someone's snatched them!*"

Micki was crying, "*What should we do?*" Anne cried, "*Find them!*"

Josephine ran out of the backyard and into the front. I chased after her as we both frantically searched for a sign of Clem's puppies.

Josephine cried out, "*Oscar! Gigi! Where are you? Mistah Clem is gonna go crazy!*" Then she turned and grabbed me with her eyes blazing, "*Wait, Master Kirk, I knows who can help! Mistah Hopkins!*"

We both started running across the street and two doors down.

Josephine was still yelling, "*Oscar! Gigi!*" as we ran to the only house in the neighborhood with lights showing through the front windows. Fortunately, it was the Hopkins' house.

I ran up to the front door with Josephine still yelling behind me, "*Oh my Lord! Oscar, Gigi! Come home, right now!*"

Her screams had apparently been heard by Mr. Hopkins since he was opening his door just as we reached it. Mr. Hopkins was in his 60s and looked ready, willing, and eager to help anyone in any emergency. He was already my friend because he had a basketball hoop at the perfect height over his garage, and he let me come over and use it whenever I wanted. Nice neighbor.

Mr. Hopkins greeted me with a handshake and asked, "*What's the trouble here, Kirk?*"

Josephine jumped in front of me and hysterically said, "*Mistah Hopkins, you gots ta help us!*"

Mr. Hopkins said, "*Hello, uh, Josephine, right?*" I nodded.

She continued, "*Little Oscar and Miss Gigi are gone!*"

He was visibly shaken by that and said, "*Oh my God, that's terrible! Please come in!*"

He beckoned us inside his house and kept asking questions, *"How did this happen?"*

We didn't answer since we didn't know the answer, and we followed him to his front parlor where he picked up his phone and dialed the Police. He said into the phone, *"Yes, hello! Yes, we . . . we have an emergency here!"*

He listened and then continued, *"Yes, Oscar and Gigi have disappeared!"*

He listened as we watched him. Josephine had begun to sob gently and she sat down on a couch to put her head into her hands. I felt sorry for her but I needed to focus on Mr. Hopkins' conversation with the Police.

Mr. Hopkins said, *"Yes, let me get that for you . . ."*

He looked at Josephine not at me which I thought was interesting. I guess he thought she was the dog whisperer since she was crying her eyes out.

He asked her, *"They need a description. First of all, how old are they?"*

Josephine was still terrified but she answered him, *"I'm not sure, Mistah Hopkins! I guess six or seven!"*

Hopkins spoke into the phone, *"They're six or seven . . . Yes."*

He listened and then asked Josephine, *"One's a boy, the other's a girl?"*

It was all she could do to hold it together, *"Oh, yessuh! Oh, help us please!"*

Mr. Hopkins confirmed the information to the Police, as Josephine moaned to me, *"Oh, Master Kirk, Miz Doris will never forgive me for losin' 'em! And Mistah Clem! What will he think of me?"*

Then Mr. Hopkins said to the Police, *"That's right. I'll see . . ."*

He asked Josephine, *"How were they dressed?"*

Josephine was confused as she answered, *"How were they dressed? Why they were dressed like DOGS, Mistah Hopkins! Oh my Lawd . . ."*

Josephine was crying as she kept apologizing, *"I'm so sorry Miz Doris, Mistah Clem! . . ."*

Mr. Hopkins spoke softly to the Police, *"Yes, my apologies, officer . . . Yes, thank you anyway."*

He hung up, and turned to me, *"You led me on there a bit, didn't you Kirk?"*

I shrugged and shared my reality with him, *"Screaming sisters, screaming Josephine. I was willing to try anything to bring 'em home, sir."*

Mr. Hopkins nodded. Then he winked at the bereft Miz Josephine and said, *"You know, I've got a dog whistle that might help . . ."*

Clem and Doris met at The Steakhouse in the Sky

While the three of us searched for dogs, Clem and Doris sat in a restaurant many stories high. ***The Steakhouse in the Sky*** was one of their favorites because Clem was an ardent steak and potatoes man, and Doris loved to look out the windows at the Houston skyline as the restaurant revolved.

I was able to find out what they discussed over dinner, this time from Doris . . .

She told me how disgusted Clem was with the whole Briscoe fiasco, and how Briscoe had convinced everyone at the courthouse that Clem was taking advantage of his position. He was sick with how Briscoe had smeared Clem's name by saying Clem played favorites whenever he assigned his probate cases, *"He justifies going after me by saying he's protecting the citizens of Houston. He justifies stepping on me as a "corrupt official," but all he's doing is using me to lift himself up so he can run for and win a seat in Congress someday."*

According to Clem, Doris said, the Briscoe-Devil was also afraid of falling flat on his face.

He knew that the negative publicity he and Cap Detrick had directed toward Clem would be a career-ending mistake if he didn't convict Clem. But since he *WAS* a Devil, he worked tirelessly to protect his ass while he kept stoking the flame of Clem's guilt.

Doris also said that Clem was not confident that Belton, Texas would prove to be beneficial.

He'd told Doris that he'd carefully studied the population size of 10,000 people, with 2025 households, and a demographic composed of 71 percent White, 8 percent Black, and 16 percent Hispanic. The projected median age of jury members in that small town was between 50 and 60 years old.

As for his lawyers, Doris reminded Clem again that she would have preferred Percy Foreman and Clem smiled as he shook his head, "*Percy would not play well in Belton, Texas. Ed and Jack will. They're not arrogant or presuming. They both dress tastefully and both look moral and upright. To a small town crowd Ed and Jack will create a positive impression that will help their presentation of the facts be more easily believed and understood. I wasn't sure they'd be able to step up, but now I am.*"

Doris told me that she looked hard at her Clem and as he smiled confidently at her, she suddenly flashbacked to when they'd met there over twenty years before:

They were at a Shriners' function designed to introduce new members like Clem to single women like Doris (who was part of a secretarial pool working at the City Hall). She was a fast typist with a cute smile for every tall man who looked her way.

She was an obvious *catch* but when she met Clem her eyes never looked at another. He was perfect, she told me, in every way. After they'd gone on several dates Doris said she initiated their first kiss while at a ground level restaurant eating steak and potatoes. She said she gently grabbed Clem's face into her hands and, between bites, she "*kissed him like there was no tomorrow*" (her exact words) . . .

As they ate dinner that night at **The Steakhouse in the Sky** she reminded Clem of the first time he ever told her he loved her, and how her breath caught and she started to cough "*like there'd be no tomorrow.*" Clem slapped her on the back for a minute, she settled down, and then he kissed her the way the tall man of her dreams was supposed to.

This night at their **Steakhouse** date she told me that Clem kissed her the same way he had when he'd first kissed her. Fortunately on this date, she told me, she didn't cough in his face . . .

As Clem and Doris kissed, I continually blew Mr. Hopkins' dog whistle. I couldn't hear a sound since the whistle was high-pitched, and I had my head out the passenger window of his car as he drove up and down the streets close to the Highland Village Shopping Center.

When I asked Mr. Hopkins why we were looking for the dogs in that neighborhood, he said, "*Your Oscar and Gigi are not big dogs. That means their little legs won't take them far away. So I'm guessing they'll go somewhere close, somewhere they've been to before . . .*"

What he said made sense. Half a mile from our front door was the **HIGHLAND VILLAGE PET STORE** where Doris and I bought their food, their collars, their leashes and their toys.

As Mr. Hopkins drove his car up to that store he told me, "*Now blow that whistle like you really mean it!*"

I took a deep breath and then I blew and blew his whistle until I was blue in the face. I kept blowing. Josephine watched me with tears in her eyes and, I'm sure, a prayer in her heart. The thought of disappointing my parents, because of her not doing her job, was unbearable to her.

So as I blew, Josephine began to yell, "*Oscar! Gigi! Oscar! Gigi! Come on home, puppies! We gots left-overs! So come 'n get 'em!*" After a minute of blowing and yelling we heard familiar barking and suddenly, there they were, wagging their tails behind them. Whew!

Obviously Josephine was beside herself, crying more with relief than she had when the dogs were lost. She knew the timing of this incident, if it had turned out badly, would've hurt my family on many levels.

I shook Mr. Hopkins' hand and thanked him when he drove us to our driveway to let us out. Josephine held Oscar and I held Gigi and we laughed as he honked his horn to say goodbye to us. His honking horn alerted my sisters of our return and they ran out the Kitchen door to greet us. Their high-pitched screams of joy filled the night air.

Oscar and Gigi were home.

And then it was time to pack our bags and travel to Belton for Clem's trial. I'd asked Clem and Doris if they'd let me take time off from school to go with them so I could attend the estimated 5 day event.

I was more than curious. I wanted to see Briscoe in action and see for myself if he had anything to justify his numerous allegations against my father.

Doris wanted me to go so she'd have me to sit next to her in a strange courtroom. Clem wanted me to go because I was his hunting partner and my being there would keep him focused and sharp.

Our plan was for my sisters to stay in Houston and go to school. Then on Friday they'd drive to Belton to be present for closing arguments and the verdict. Josephine and Woodrow would look after the house and the dogs while we were gone.

Belton was a three-hour drive west-northwest from Houston. On our drive to Belton our journey started on a four-lane highway and after two hours we rolled down a two-lane highway peppered with bluebonnets and butterflies. I noticed a lot of farms and a number of pickup trucks driving along the highway. Lotsa cows in the meadows, and lotsa barns next to the farmhouses.

The Texas signage dissolved from BELTON 60 to BELTON 30 to the BELTON CITY LIMITS and we entered the small Texas town. We drove to the center of town and saw a square.

There sat the courthouse where my dad would fight the fight of his life. My heart beat a little faster as I considered what he was about to face. It felt like an out-of-town Football game where he'd be playing against a favored team. I had a pit in my stomach that I'd feel all week.

Bell County Courthouse in Belton, Texas

There were pickup trucks galore around the square because that first day was pick-the-jury day. Clem found a parking space behind the courthouse for his black Caddy and squeezed it in beside an elderly John Deere tractor doubling on that occasion as a transport to jury duty. We all exited the Caddy and began our slow walk to the courthouse.

I noticed almost immediately that we were the center of attention, and it was probably due to our clothes. Yep, we were too well-dressed. I should've worn blue jeans and Clem should have left his $1000 suit in his closet at home. Doris fit right in with a no collar dress, a one button jacket and low heels.

We entered the building and walked into the court lobby where we saw on its interior walls several impressive murals of fields and farms and streams which the artist probably had wished actually adorned the Bell County community.

Outside the door to the ground floor courtroom stood Edwin and Jack awaiting our arrival. We all said hello and shook hands and then walked into the courtroom belonging to the Honorable Judge James K. Evetts of the Twenty-Seventh District Court of Bell County, Texas. He was the judge who would preside at Clem's trial, and his court would be the field of play for the first battle between Frank Briscoe and Clem McClelland.

The change of venue to Belton was not as simple or as easy as it sounded. Clem and his attorneys had been forced to work in uncomfortable pretrial locations such as the Belton coffee shop and the Belton Public Library, any place where the three of them could study their massive files and try to predict Briscoe's *Attack Strategy*.

Their prep work was to logically plan their responses and build a solid Defense. From the outset it was clear to them that the Devil would not play fair. His agenda was self-serving, and to quote the **Texas Observer**, "*Frank Briscoe's one of the most vicious prosecutors in Houston's history.*"

Clem's team knew Briscoe would do whatever it took to win. His motive for winning: To use the resultant upbeat publicity to help him win the next Congressional race for Houston's Seventh District. An interesting footnote: In 1966 Frank Briscoe would run against George H.W. Bush, our forty-first president, as George made an attempt to hold his first public office . . .

On day 1 Briscoe and his favorite High-Flying Monkey, Wallace *Pete* Moore, entered the courtroom and occupied the prosecutor's table. They wore different shades of grey suits that were not too flashy. They were very professional-looking in how they carried themselves and their suits had enough style to show they meant business.

DA Briscoe and ADA Moore

On the defense side of the room Jack wore a lawyer suit and tie to disguise the rebel that he really was, and Ed wore his predictable dark blue everything. As I watched Ed and Jack set up their files on the defense table and on the floor around the defense table, it was clear to me that Ed seemed more than a bit strained. His face was gaunt and full of exhaustion. Hmm . . .

"GUILTY UNTIL PROVEN INNOCENT"

JUDGE ARRIVES FOR TRIAL—Former Houston Probate Judge Clem McClelland, center, flanked by his attorneys, J. Ed Smith, left, and Jack Rawitscher

An important memorandum to the players on Clem's team:

My T. H. Rogers football coach at that time was Don Wilson and Coach Wilson always gave top priority to positive body language when it came to playing what he called the *"game of life."* Coach Wilson's philosophy was *"If you want to win, be sure you show it!"* That meant have a positive attitude when you suit up, and leave all the negative bullshit in your locker. **Be Positive** was my mantra every day at practice and every Friday Night when we played that week's game.

So if I could just take Ed Smith for a walk I'd explain to him the importance of positivity. But I held my tongue. I was 14 years old and he was 61. I knew what he needed to project to this future jury that would decide Clem's fate, but there was no way he'd listen to me.

It would be hard for me to quietly sit the bench . . .

As I looked over the room I saw potential jurors who respected the law enough to wear their Sunday best, but I also saw a few coveralls that implied they'd come here straight from milking. My radar picked up other courtroom hints on day 1.

For instance, the crowd of potential jurors had already filled all the seats in the room and when Clem and his attorneys first entered, the potential jury pool neither nodded nor smiled. When Frank and Pete entered, I saw several potential jurors point at Briscoe and talk to each other with nodding heads and smiles of support.

From the start, if our jury deck *was* as stacked as it looked to me, it would prove to be a long week for my Clem.

Suspended Judge Clem McClelland and wife, of Houston, spend a long week in Belton during his trial

(Front Page: *The Belton Journal, November 22, 1962*)
Clem and Doris wore long faces during the long week

There was a round dark-brown Meridian clock above the judge's bench in the court and there was a court clerk / court reporter of sixty-odd years ready and waiting to serve. As the clock's arms hit 9:00 a.m. the judge opened his chamber's door and entered.

His Bailiff, a tall and elderly black man named Isaac, called order by saying, "*All rise!* (We did) *The Twenty-Seventh District Court, Criminal Division, is now in session, the Honorable James K. Evetts presiding.*"

The Honorable Judge James K. Evetts

Judge Evetts looked out over his courtroom with a smile and he first acknowledged his constituents (prospective jurors) saying,

"*I want to thank you gentlemen* (there were women in the courtroom but none were present that day for jury duty) *for giving up your morning to be with us here today. I respect your hardship and I want you to know how much I appreciate your willingness to help me in the matter before my court. You may be seated.*"

He then turned to Frank and Pete and said, "*Good morning, counselors.*"

Frank and Pete nodded at His Honor.

Judge Evetts then turned to the defendant's table and said, "*Good morning to the defendant and his attorneys.*"

Ed and Jack and Clem politely nodded. I noticed that Judge Evetts gave an extra nod to Clem. It was probably a Judge courtesy thing.

The judge continued, "*I hope everyone is prepared to carry on. If there are any motions that will slow down or halt this trial, let me hear them now.*"

No motions were offered by either side. I noted that Cap Detrick sat in a row full of reporters from Houston and other Texas newspapers in an assigned section designated, "*News Only.*"

As I analyzed the flavor of Judge Evetts's court I noted the confident manner with which he conducted business. Evetts had been Judge of this court since 1952 but the bad news was he had also been the District Attorney for this District from 1936 to 1942 (he'd served in the war until 1946 and he'd won a Bronze Star and a Purple Heart) and then he returned to his District Attorney position from 1946 to 1952. I wondered if Frank knew how much he and Judge Evetts had in common. I also wondered if the judge's time as a District Attorney would improperly influence how he ran this trial.

Judge Evetts went right to work. He had his Bailiff help the first twelve men move from their courtroom seats to seats in the jury Box. He instructed the other hundred men-in-waiting to move one-at-a-time from their seats whenever a prospective juror was excused from the Box. The judge directed all prospective jurors to, *"Please move quickly and quietly so we can all get through this process efficiently."*

Then it was Frank's turn. He introduced himself, *"My name is Frank Briscoe, and I'm Houston's District Attorney. It will be my job to ask you questions so I can be sure you're in the right state of mind to help us find justice in this case."*

He stood in front of the Box and starting with juror no. 1, he asked questions like, *"Have you ever been personally worried, either for yourself or a close family member, about the outcome of a criminal case?"*

If any juror answered *"Yes"* to that kind of question they were automatically dismissed.

If their Uncle or Brother or Husband or Best Friend had ever been on trial, they'd most likely be sympathetic to the defense and hostile toward the prosecution. Not always, but they would definitely have bad feelings toward one side or the other. That's why this screening process was important: The stated goal of *voir dire* (*to tell the truth*) was to impanel an *impartial* jury.

I heard the phrase "*a level playing field*" said many times and it always referred to *fairness* in how the trial was conducted. If the Devil wanted to use his position to make a power play and it was blatantly obvious, it was Judge Evetts's job to level the playing field by sustaining any objections raised by the defense. For instance, if Frank tried to use his innuendo weapons on a prospective juror, the judge had to stop it.

Frank asked one juror, *"How do you feel about a Public Servant who steals funds from everyday citizens?"*

Ed and Jack AND Clem all said, *"Objection!"* at the same time since Frank had crossed the line between fair and unfair.

Frank asked another juror, *"Could you find someone guilty if evidence indicated that he'd misused his position and betrayed the public's trust?"*

Ed, *"Objection!"* Judge Evetts, *"Sustained."*

This exercise continued for the rest of the day. It was both dull and fascinating and it was completely necessary. Briscoe and his hired Monkey tried to sneak in hints of guilt whenever they thought the defense team was sleeping, and a few times the prospective juror answered before an Objection could be raised. For the majority of assaults Ed and Jack held their own.

The choosing of an acceptable jury took all of day 1 and all of day 2. Farmer after farmer had had a close relative involved in one form of debauchery or another. None of them involved pigs or sheep but I was amazed by how many of the agrarians were a bit short of what I'd refer to as "*good Christian ethics.*" Crops were pilfered, equipment filched, cattle rustled, gas siphoned, scrap metal was stolen, and even tractor batteries were lifted by their relatives.

At the end of day 2, when the round clock above the judge showed 4:10, the jury had finally been chosen. All the Houston papers as well as papers from Waco, Dallas, Corpus Christi and Austin began their coverage and I met a Staff reporter from the Houston Post named John Moore who'd show Cap Detrick how to report fairly and still be interesting.

McClelland Trial Jury Picked

The Houston Post headline November 13, 1962

At 5:30, after the jury was chosen, the prosecution followed the standard court protocol and read the indictment. Briscoe also shared the formal arraignment of the defendant to the jury. Then when the District Attorney looked at Clem and asked him to enter his plea Clem stood up, looked at Frank and then he turned toward the new jury. I didn't expect this procedure and I swiveled my head to scan the entire courtroom. I remember that the Bell County Courtroom was void of all sound as Clem used his deep and firm voice to declare, *"I am not now, nor have I ever been guilty!"*

Clem nodded to the jury and then sat down with no acknowledgement of Briscoe's presence.

Judge Evetts nodded and thanked the jurors as he said, *"I appreciate all of you and your willingness to see this trial through. Being judged by a jury of your peers is a fundamental right that we must always protect by being willing members when our chance to serve comes up. This trial begins tomorrow morning at 9:00 a.m. sharp. See you then!"*

I watched the twelve jurors and two alternate jurors stand and move out of the courtroom . . .

On day 3 Clem had chosen a less expensive suit to illustrate he was just like the twelve men who'd pass judgement on him. I wore blue jeans and my Rogers Football letter shirt to illustrate I could be counted on if anyone wanted to play ball. Doris wore a summer dress with a different jacket and her cute blue Cat Eye sunglasses.

The courtroom was filled with the faces of many interested citizens. I noticed that Clem held his head high and I watched the impaneled jury take note of his confidence. I watched Doris and I was proud of her ability to act confident when I knew she felt otherwise.

Doris listened and hoped . . .

I listened as Ed and Jack renewed their objection to the presence of newspaper and television cameras in the courtroom. Judge Evetts denied their motion and allowed the cameras to remain, "*. . . so long as the photographers stay behind the rails and not use flashbulbs and not make any unnecessary noise. If I hear any sort of ruckus, I'll order you to leave!*"

One other interesting journalistic footnote: I noticed that Cap Detrick had moved to sit behind Briscoe and Pete Moore's table. Cap looked at Clem with an unfeeling smile on his face and as he gazed at Clem, he shook his head as if he knew something Clem didn't. I understood better why Clem didn't like anything about him.

At the stroke of 9 a.m. Judge Evetts banged his gavel and said, "*Gentlemen* (He looked at Doris and she gave him a big grin) *and Lady. I hope everyone got up early and finished their milking, because we'll be here for the rest of the day! Let's hear your Opening Statements . . .*"

McClelland Testimony Set Today

Jury Selected In Conversion Case of Ex-Probate Judge

By JOHN MOORE
POST STAFF CORRESPONDENT

BELTON — Testimony will begin at 9 AM today in the case of Clem McClelland, the suspended probate judge of Harris County, who is on trial in Belton for the felony conversion of $10,000 from an estate.

BELTON, THE county seat of Bell County, is a small Central Texas community of approximately 10,000 residents. The atmosphere is friendly, rural and folksy, and this prevailing attitude extended into the courtroom Monday.

For example, the lead defense counsel, J. Edwin Smith of Houston, introduced himself to the prospective jurors as "Ed Smith."

Smith also introduced the defendant, Clem McClelland, as "Clem" and his wife as "Doris" and their three teen aged children by their first names.

John Moore wrote for The Houston Post, November 13, 1962

He gestured to Briscoe and said, "*You're up first, Mr. District Attorney . . .*"

Frank stood up and walked straight to the jury Box. He said, "*Gentlemen of the jury, I'm going to make a prediction: My esteemed opponents* (he pointed at Ed and Jack) *are going to stand here and talk to you about the Bill of Rights. I, on the other hand,* (He smiled and looked at every juror) *am going to talk to you about the Bill of Wrongs.*"

I saw one juror put his hand over his mouth, and I heard juror no. 4 giggle.

Briscoe walked over to the defense table and continued, "*The Bill of Wrongs that their client,* (He pointed at Clem) *Probate Judge Clem McClelland, has visited upon every family unfortunate enough to visit his courtroom.*"

Clem looked down and wrote on a legal pad as Briscoe walked back toward the jury.

He said, "*Did you hear me use the word 'unfortunate'? It's the right word to describe why we're here today. You see, no one should ever be 'unfortunate' by being at the mercy of ANY Judge, especially when it refers to his ruling on a Last Will and Testament.*"

Briscoe began to pace.

I looked at Doris's face as she looked at Clem's face. She seemed visibly upset so I pulled her toward me and whispered, "*You shouldn't react. The jury's watching us, too.*"

I nodded to her, and she smiled (good girl), and she whispered back, "*You are my smart and handsome son . . .*" I already knew that.

Briscoe stopped pacing and looked calmly at each juror again, "*By definition, a probate judge's job is to carefully process the last will and testament of a deceased person so that all of their property can be retitled or transferred to the designated beneficiaries of the Will.*"

He smiled and shook his head, "*Sounds pretty open and shut, doesn't it? I write a Will so that when I pass on, all of my worldly goods pass to my loved ones or to whomever I choose.*"

He turned to walk toward Clem as Clem kept writing on his legal pad, looking at Frank for a second, and then down again at his pad as Frank said, "*But what if a probate judge decides he's more important than my Will? What if a probate judge decides he can break the rules and use his Public Trust to do as he pleases with my Will?*"

Briscoe turned and began to pace back and forth along the railing in front of the jury Box as he continued, "*What if a probate judge takes it upon himself to divert or manipulate my funds or property so that instead of going to the person I chose, it goes to the probate judge?*"

He stopped pacing and said in a loud voice, "*DAMN! That sounds terrible, doesn't it? It sounds evil, depraved, and even cruel!*"

I was noticing that Frank had a flair for the dramatic. So I guessed I'd have to not only call him the *Devil*, I'd also have to call him the *Drama King*.

I watched him as he histrionically scratched his head and then, to help the jurors have a more interactive trial experience, he pointed his finger at them and asked, "*So . . . then . . . what can any one of us do to stop this bad behavior when we discover it?*" He turned and pointed at the spectators in the courtroom, "*Why, if we're good citizens, we go to our courts . . .*"

Then he turned and pointed at Judge Evetts and he said, "*. . . and we expect our courts to deliver JUSTICE!*"

Clem stopped drawing on his pad and looked at each one of the jurors as they listened and considered what the Drama King was telling them, "*So here we are today. Pursuing JUSTICE! Identifying something that's wrong, and making it right! Because there are a lot of dearly departed who would not like how this judge* (he pointed at Clem) *took it upon himself to mess with their Wills.*"

Frank's voice had risen in volume as he began this phase, "*And what about the beneficiaries of those dearly departed? Who's going to protect their right to have an honest Judge divvy up money and property fairly, the way their deceased parents wanted?*"

Frank, with this performance, became the personification of the word "*Melodramatic.*" Every first year Drama student is taught that any performer who so obviously *overacts* is usually guilty of melodrama. Frank was way over the top. My concern was that this audience wasn't as savvy drama-wise and they probably were giving him high marks for "*feeling so sorry*" for those "*unfortunate*" people Judge Clem McClelland had supposedly ripped-off. Frank, with this performance, had shown that he had no evidence, only speculation about Clem's guilt.

In any other court in the land, this nonsensical performance would have caused laughter. I was amazed as I looked and concluded that all twelve jurors in Belton were in a state of rapture. I studied each juror as they looked at Clem and, to me, they appeared to think what Frank was telling them had to be true. I realized it was the same way Frank handled the Houston Media, but this time it was Belton's jury. This time it was Clem's jury. This was not good.

"Whose job is it to protect a family from a Judge who's going to take the money and property that's supposed to be given to them, and keep it for himself?"

Briscoe thought about the question he'd just asked and he stood at attention at the front center of the Box. He looked hard at each one of the jurors and then melodramatically he pointed to himself, *"I'll tell all of you here today. IT'S MY JOB!"*

Frank stood there for a few moments. He'd told everyone in that courtroom that if something was broken, he was the fixer. Frank ended his speech with, *"In a probate court, the Will of the deceased needs to be judged fairly so the property of the deceased is divided up fairly. The last will and testament IS the last will and testament, and it's a very important document. As you will see, the defendant in this case took it upon himself to think otherwise! . . .* (He bowed slightly to the jurors) *. . . Thank you . . ."*

Frank walked to his table where Pete patted him on his shoulder, and Cap Detrick reached over the railing to shake his hand. Somehow Cap's public display of affection seemed like bad form for an unbiased News reporter, but I guess it was my bias that was evaluating his bias.

I was close enough to Clem's table to hear Ed whisper, *"Do you see their faces, Clem?"*

We all looked at the jury. They all stared at Clem with an exceedingly judgmental point of view.

Clem responded with his own whisper, *"I've been watching them."*

Ed continued, *"They're farmers for Christ's sake. I don't know if I'll be able to get through to them. I don't know . . ."*

Holy moly again. Ed Smith was shillyshallying, and my father was expecting a Percy Foremanesque Opening Statement? Clem struggled to cheerlead his attorney, *"These men are just like me. They'll see Briscoe for the manipulator he is, and they'll decide this case on its merits. Make them think about what's right, Ed."*

Did Clem hire the wrong man?

Judge Evetts was waiting patiently. Then I saw him look up at his wall clock and he decided it was time to nudge the defense, "*Mr. Smith? Please sir, share your Opening.*"

Ed stood and looked at the judge, then at the jury.

"*May it please the court* (He put his hand on Clem's shoulder), *this is Judge Clem McClelland. He used to be the probate judge in Houston, Texas. Used to be. It's a sad state of affairs when a great man is so sorely abused. And all for the sake of a politically motivated district attorney.*"

The Drama King-Devil jumped to his feet, "*Objection, Your Honor!*"

Judge Evetts wagged his finger and shook his head at Ed and said, "*Sustained. No more cheap shots, Mr. Smith, if you please.*"

Ed nodded and said, "*My apologies, Judge. Earlier Mr. Briscoe made some remarks that he wanted put into the record so I felt I should do the same.*"

Judge Evetts nodded and said, "*Proceed.*"

Nice shot, Ed. I looked at Doris and she seemed to relax a bit.

Ed did a swagger-walk toward the jury to establish his desired dominance on this playing field, and he began with, "*I call this case 'The Day They Trampled Clem's Rights'... Clem's rights, based on our founding father's Bill of Rights, have been trampled on by this*"—he pointed at Briscoe—"*district attorney and his office.*"

He made eye contact with every juror, "*Have you ever heard of a Court of Inquiry? I'm going to tell you what it is and let you decide who the guilty party is here today.*"

Ed then spent an hour explaining how Mr. Briscoe had used an ancient 1876 law to force Clem and others to take the Witness Stand to be "*grilled*" by the DA and his Winged Monkeys.

Ed's description was too intellectual. He should've simply shared how unfair Frank had been.

He did describe some of the tricks Frank had used to elicit information, but he should have shared how Frank shaped the unlawfully acquired information into a contrivance that was designed to make Clem look as guilty as hell.

As Ed spoke I watched the jury. About ten minutes into his diatribe I'd figured he'd lost half of them. I saw yawns, I saw some look out the windows, and I saw some check their watches.

I watched the Drama King and his Monkey and they both smiled. They both knew this jury of cow-milking hayseeds would never understand how Clem's Constitutional rights had been trampled, and they both knew the hayseeds wouldn't care. They were farmers and their lives depended on the weather and the fluctuation of corn prices. They couldn't and they wouldn't understand that if Clem's rights could be trampled, so could theirs.

What Ed failed to analyze was that Clem's tragedy would never be the farmers' concern so it was a complete waste of time for Ed to discuss it. Looking at Ed as he tried to effectively perform his opening, I was convinced he'd already lost it. He didn't look confident. He didn't look happy. He looked like he wanted to be anywhere other than Belton, Texas.

Then I looked at Doris as she looked at her Clem. I'd never seen the depth of dismay on her face that I saw that day. She'd been right about Percy Foreman. Even on his worst day Percy would have taught some fancy new milking tricks to that assembly of dairymen.

And finally I looked at Clem. Yes, he was still tall and majestic, but I wasn't sure I liked his hair cut that short. I appreciated he wanted to make the milkers comfortable and assure them that he was a country boy just like them, but I liked him to look more like Burt Lancaster when he played **ELMER GANTRY** not the **BIRDMAN OF ALCATRAZ**. The more I studied Clem the more I saw Robert Stroud similarities. Clem and I had gone to see Lancaster's performance that past summer in **BIRDMAN** and I remember Clem had watched the prison scenes closely.

Meanwhile, Ed Smith continued to show how little he understood his Belton jury as he persistently tried to convince them that Briscoe had wrongly attacked and smeared Clem, and thereby deprived him of his Due Process rights.

Just when I'd had my fill of listening to Ed, Clem held up his legal pad for me and Doris to see and admire. I had expected to gaze upon some amazing and scholarly legal notes, but what we saw instead was a drawing, a caricature of Frank Briscoe with bloody fangs, bloodshot eyes, cloven hooves, a huge pitchfork and a devilish tail. It was hard not to laugh since it was a funny cartoon, but Doris and I controlled ourselves. We showed our admiration with our smiles.

Clem sketched Frank Briscoe

I watched Clem flip his legal (drawing) pad to a blank page and I figured correctly that he was beginning a new sketch of another Belton courtroom scene.

I saw him stare at Judge Evetts for a few moments and then he quickly went to work drawing a caricature of the Belton Judge. I tried to see over Clem's shoulder and when Ed finally sat I confess I was more interested in Clem's new caricature than Ed's success with the Belton jury.

The new drawing showed a happy Judge Evetts sitting on a stool in his black robe milking a cow (with a huge udder) into a milk pail with "*JUSTICE*" written on its side.

Clem sketched Judge Evetts

Judge Evetts called lunch and our group went across the square to ***BESSIE'S DINER*** at the suggestion of Isaac the Bailiff. Isaac and Doris were becoming friends and he mentioned to Doris that, "***BESSIE'S*** *blue plate special may be the finest meatloaf dish to be found anywhere, and you folks might enjoy discoverin' that for yo-selves.*" So I ran ahead and captured a table for the five of us and we gave ***BESSIE'S*** meatloaf our heartfelt attention.

Bessie's meatloaf was the finest anywhere . . .

Over lunch I was lucky to be present so I could hear Clem's overview of what had happened so far. He wasn't thrilled with the jury choices but, as Jack had commented the day before, "*One sharecropper is as good as another. The true test will be if our cluster of cow-milkers believes or disbelieves Frank and his witnesses.*"

Clem also wasn't very happy with Judge Jim Evetts. I could tell by how he said the judge's name that he didn't respect the judge's ability to honestly judge Briscoe's true agenda. Again, Evetts was a former DA and Clem had feared he'd take sides with Briscoe's insanity.

Finally, Clem was not overly pleased with Ed's plan of attack. Clem said, "*Constitutional arguments are useless with this crowd. We won't win if we don't make a change. The jury was half asleep. I want you to go after Briscoe, both his motive and his agenda, and give this jury a chance to get behind us.*"

And with that, lunch was over . . .

Back in the courtroom both Doris and I noticed that the Devil, his Monkey, and their biased News Reporter were still smiling as they huddled around the prosecution's table.

Have I mentioned how irritating they all were to my young self? If I'd been Clem, I would have lost it and poured water over their heads and watched them melt! And regarding our Ed and Jack, I would've kicked their asses and said something like, "*Gentlemen, why don't you start your damn engines!*" So far, I was less than impressed with either side of the aisle.

As we waited for the judge to re-enter the courtroom, I noticed that Ed and Jack were glum due to the confident attitude of the prosecutor's team. I have to mention again the **Be Positive** mantra of my Coach Wilson and the importance of "*Defense positivity*" if these jurors were going to have *any* chance to choose the righteous side. Doris didn't seem too happy either, so I smiled at her in an attempt to jumpstart *her* engine.

With the judge back on his bench and the jury back in their jury box it was time for Frank to call his first witness and prove all the crap he'd stated as "*truth*" in his opening statement.

Speaking of witnesses, Clem would not testify, on advice of his counsel. I'm sure he wanted to, but Ed and Jack didn't want to give Briscoe or his Monkey a second bite of Clem's apple. The Court of Inquiry fiasco had already caused more than enough damage. So if the Devil couldn't get his talons on Clem, he'd have to find someone else to *in-terror-gate* and have them answer his questions to make his case. The difference was that this time it would be according to lawful court protocol. Would Frank be at a disadvantage? I hoped so.

We all waited anxiously to see who Frank would choose for his courtroom assault on Clem. Ed, who was working on his notes at the defense table, looked over at Clem's portrait of Judge Evetts sitting on a stool in his black robe milking a cow, and he raised his eyebrows. Clem just smiled since he thought his portrait of the judge was a good representation, literal and figurative.

Judge Evetts banged his gavel and said, "*Mr. District Attorney, call your first witness.*"

One of the rules of proper and lawful courtroom procedure was for both sides to furnish a Witness List to the court. That way there'd be no surprises and it would give the opposition time to research each person, and then prepare a list of questions designed to weaken or totally negate that witness' testimony.

Frank Briscoe's first witness was a bombshell to me, "*Yes, Your Honor . . . The State of Texas calls Mr. Guy Price!*"

My mouth was wide open with surprise and when I looked at Doris she had a "*What's this?*" look on *her* face. Guy walked into the courtroom from the rear and (like a weasel) he crept in and up to the Witness Box. I wondered how Clem was feeling, but all he did was stare at Guy.

The court Clerk held up a Bible and swore him in, "*Do you solemnly swear to tell the truth, the whole truth, and nothing but the truth, so help you God?*"

Guy nodded and said, "*Yes, I will.*"

The Clerk pointed at the Box and said, "*Be seated.*"

So finally, here it was. We had all suffered at the hands of Frank Briscoe for over two years. He was fully invested and on the record about Clem's guilt. Here was his first attack and he'd decided to call Guy Price?

Briscoe approached Guy with his customarily foul smile covering his surly face. I was fascinated by all that had happened to put us in that place at that time and I watched and listened closely as Frank approached Guy. He began with, "*Good morning, Mr. Price.*" Guy nodded. "*Let's get to it, shall we? You're a lawyer, and you work in the Houston justice system, is that right?*"

Guy meekly said, "*Yes.*"

Frank laughed softly, walked away from Guy and toward the jury, "*Don't be shy, Mr. Price. Speak up. You have things* (He gestured toward the jury) *these twelve gentlemen want to hear . . .*"

Frank's act seemed rehearsed which set the stage for more of his melodrama, *"Now, is it fair to say that the probate arena in Houston, in Harris County, was and is your main area of professional activity?"*

Guy looked over at Clem who was looking down at his funny portrait of Judge Evetts.

Guy said, *"Yes, I guess that's right."*

Frank Briscoe smiled a big smile and took a deep breath as he delivered his knockout blow, *"Then please tell us Mr. Price, did you ever see Judge McClelland misappropriate money from any of his court's cases?"*

The courtroom Observers stirred and murmured as Guy looked at Clem and Clem stared back. Guy blinked rapidly as I'd seen him do before whenever he was nervous. I'm sure he felt like he was on the spot, but from what Judy had told Helen and from what Helen had told me, Guy was the one who had originally contacted Frank Briscoe, not the other way around.

Guy looked at Frank but he didn't answer. Instead I saw him gulp. If it hadn't been a serious moment I would have laughed. Here was a lawyer who Clem had worked with in his court for years, and here was a man who Clem had helped with the adoption of his daughter six years before. How could this man suddenly conspire with the Devil to betray my Clem?

Frank began a deliberate walk toward the jury as he decided to change his choice of words, *"Mr. Price, this time I won't use the legal term so there's no confusion.* (He turned to face Guy) *Did you ever see or help Judge McClelland STEAL money or property from any of the cases that passed through his court?"*

And then I remember seeing something pass between my father and this man who'd been in Clem's inner circle professionally as well as in his inner circle of Arabia Temple Shriners. I was sure I saw Clem faintly nod at Guy Price who turned to Frank Briscoe and declared, *"Steal money? Judge McClelland? Why that's just plain crazy! He's the most honest man I've ever known!"*

I saw Guy gulp again and it was all I could do to keep myself from laughing. The courtroom erupted with sounds from spectators expecting a different outcome to this courtroom spectacle.

From his face I would've said District Attorney Frank Briscoe was in shock. His mouth hung open in disbelief. He walked swiftly toward Guy in what appeared to be an antagonistic and hostile manner but Guy continued, *"Why, the judge and I have gone fishing together many times over the past 10 years. And I have to say he always gave me the best lures to use* (He blinked rapidly) *so I could catch the biggest bass. He's a fair and generous man."*

The courtroom crowd laughed at Guy's fawning speech but they and the rest of us were a bit confused for why the Devil would want to start his prosecution with a fish tale.

Frank Briscoe was in a purple rage as he attacked Guy with, "*Mr. Price! You're not here to share Judge McClelland's fishing etiquette! You have been called today to share with this jury the information you shared with the Grand Jury of Harris County, Texas! May I remind you, sir, that you swore Judge McClelland had on several occasions STOLEN funds from various estates for his personal use?*"

Guy was no longer fawning and he counterattacked Briscoe with, "*He's a fine man! He doesn't deserve all the bad things you've said about him in the Press, and on television! Your office is way out of line! You should all be ashamed of yourselves!*" Holy moly. I was in shock, too. I couldn't wait to tell Helen Smith that Guy was, well, still a good guy.

Meanwhile, Frank Briscoe was apoplectic. He turned and locked eyes with Clem and they fenced silently for a moment.

Then Briscoe turned to the judge and said, "*I have no further questions, Your Honor.*"

He sat down at the prosecutor's table whereupon Ed jumped up and said, "*No questions, Your Honor*" and *he* sat down.

Judge Evetts said to Guy, "*You are excused, Mr. Price.*"

Guy left the Witness Box with the jury watching him. He walked by the defense table and past Clem with neither of them acknowledging the other. Then Cap Detrick waved a friendly hello to Guy who started to wave back but fortunately stopped himself.

I was amazed by what had just happened. Maybe I had underestimated Clem and his Defense team. I didn't know which end was up or down, but it was entertaining to watch Frank Briscoe get blindsided.

Judge Evetts then said, "*Court will recess for half an hour. My apologies but there are papers I need to sign.*" He banged his gavel, left the court, and entered his Chambers with Isaac close behind. The jury stood and went through a different door, escorted by a Belton Deputy Sheriff named W. L. Gunn, to reach the room where ultimately they'd deliberate and determine Clem's fate.

The onlookers stood up and left and I walked over to meet John Moore of The Houston Post. He was tall and thin and he graciously shook my hand as he smiled at me and asked, "*How do you like the circus so far young man?*" I smiled at his use of that word and replied, "*I'd rather be at the beach!*" He laughed and I was glad I'd made friends with him . . .

It was sweltering in the small courtroom over the next hours as we waited for Judge Evetts. I saw Isaac and I asked him if we could open some of the windows on the outer wall of the room.

He said, "*We sho' can, Mister Kirk. Why don't you help me lift 'em up and we'll see 'bout gettin' some fresh air in here?*"

Isaac and I successfully did our bit for the court's comfort and the Third day dragged on.

While we were on hold, Clem spoke with his two attorneys as Doris and I talked about what a surprise Guy's testimony had been for the both of us.

I asked her, *"Did Clem know Guy was their leadoff hitter?"*

Doris replied, *"When Helen spoke to Judy and then spoke to you about Guy meeting with Briscoe, we figured Guy had convinced the bad guys that he would assist them."*

She paused and looked all around the courtroom, *"Thank God he came to his senses and turned on them. I think he would have regretted it if he hadn't. Clem has always been kind to Guy and his wife and daughter."*

Doris bit her lower lip and then nodded to confirm her take on the Guy reversal.

It was close to five o'clock when the judge was able to return to his day job and he explained how sorry he was for the holdup. We all understood how important he was to the community so we forgave him, but that meant that there would be no more trial that day.

The judge hit his gavel to end day 3, and we again watched the jurors exit the court.

I stared at Frank Briscoe and studied his face, enjoying his obvious displeasure with Guy's turn-around-for-Clem testimony. Frank should've considered that a possible traitor to one side should never be trusted by the other . . .

Day 4 started well.

I saw Clem kiss Doris and whisper something in her ear that made her giggle as we ate breakfast at **BESSIE'S**. Isaac was there as were a few of the jurors. Following the rules set down on day 1 by the judge, we avoided talking to the jurors.

Cap Detrick came by our table with his normal phony smirk, and he asked Doris, *"Care to make a statement for the Press, Mrs. McClelland?"*

I saw Clem's face turn purple and I put my hand on his arm to center him as Doris said, *"Good morning, Mr. Detrick. I was wondering when you'd get the nerve to talk to the real victims of all this garbage. Tell your boss,* (She grinned bigtime) *that's Mr. Briscoe isn't it?"* She waited for Cap to acknowledge this truth and when he didn't she continued, saying, *"Anyway, be sure you tell him we enjoyed watching and listening to his first witness!"*

Clem and I both laughed at how cute she was with her big grin and her black Cat Eye glasses. Cap also smiled, and when he received no other response he walked away.

When we returned and sat back down in the courtroom, I tried to do some homework to keep up with the classes I was missing that week, but mostly I wanted to find and use a phone to call Betsy. Her voice would have helped me endure that emotional week.

The prosecuting team came in and sat at their table followed by Ed and Jack who took their places at the defense table. I wanted to ask them and Clem who they thought the Devil's next witness would be but the jury came in and were seated, followed by Judge Evetts.

I saw the Devil whisper something to Pete Moore. Then Briscoe stood to introduce the key witness to the specific indictment. Yesterday Guy Price was supposed to establish that Judge Clem was a villain. In Frank Briscoe's playbook his next witness would "*prove*" the actual case by describing the specific felonious acts actually committed by Clem.

Briscoe was visibly excited as he announced, "*The State of Texas calls Richard Putney!*"

The court spectators muttered to each other about who this man was. Then they studied him as he entered the courtroom and sauntered up to the Witness Box. At first glance he seemed remarkably slimy, and he grinned at Clem the same way that Cap Detrick had grinned at him.

When the jury members got their first look at the thirty-five-year-old man named Richard Putney I could tell some of them hated him immediately. His short brown hair was in need of a comb, but his teeth were bright and white when he smiled a very icky smile. (*Check out his picture.*)

The elderly court clerk made Richard Putney raise his hand, and he asked him, "*Do you solemnly swear to tell the truth, the whole truth, and nothing but the truth, so help you God?*"

Putney sneered at the Clerk and turned to the courtroom of onlookers. He took a coin out of his pocket, flipped it, studied it and then he held it high for all to see. He laughed a deep laugh and loudly proclaimed, "*Well, I guess for today, I do!*"

The Clerk was not impressed and dismissed him saying, "*Be seated.*"

Richard H. Putney
"I Guess I Was Greedy"

The Devil seemed more comfortable with this witness, probably because they were birds of a feather. I found out later that when Putney had seen the widespread smear campaign in the Houston Media about Clem and his court, he'd approached

Briscoe with so-called facts that he knew would someday be useful and valuable to him. That someday had arrived.

Briscoe smiled and asked him, "*Your full name is . . .?*"

Richard had his smile meter set at full tilt and replied, "*Richard Hamilton Putney, at your service.* (He looked at the jury) *And just so you know, the name "Richard" means "brave and powerful!"*

Briscoe smiled and told Mr. Putney, "*We'll refer to you as "Richard" then, if we may.*"

Richard happily nodded as Frank asked, "*Let's begin with your chosen profession.*"

Richard laughed, and told the jury, "*I'm an attorney, and a very good one, too.*"

Briscoe said, "*Now, please share with us, where did you meet Judge McClelland?*"

Richard looked at Clem with a fond smile, "*I met Hiz Honor at a fund-raiser at the River Oaks Country Club in Houston. He was there to fleece the well-to-do swells of their ill-gotten-gains by using con-man words like "donations" and "contributions." I was there to do the same thing. The difference between his scheme and mine, though, was my use of the phrase "investment opportunities." Same drill, different tactics, same results except he dealt with higher stakes and had better results.*"

Richard stopped and really looked hard at Clem, "*He had the benefit of being a high-class Judge.*"

Briscoe nodded and then he moved closer to his witness, "*And?*"

Richard turned to the very interested jury and continued, "*When I overheard his pitch to the same group that I was courting, I realized he might be my ticket to a higher level of suckers.*"

Putney hesitated, searching for the right rhythm to tell his tale.

Briscoe helped again, "*And?*"

Smugly and with a huge grin Richard claimed, "*I introduced myself to him as a player.*"

Briscoe acted like he'd never heard that word used that way before and in full Drama King Mode he asked, "*A player?*"

Richard translated proudly, "*Uh, 'One who knows how to take advantage of the stupid and the wealthy rich who were born into IT but never learned how to make IT on their own.'*"

Briscoe smiled at Richard, "*And?*"

Richard looked up at the high ceiling in the courtroom and folded his hands in prayer, "*It was a marriage made in Heaven . . .*"

Briscoe looked like he was fascinated by Richard's tale and he asked, "*How so?*"

Richard reacted like a **TIMES** magazine correspondent with a great story to tell, "*I knew some tricks, he knew some other tricks. Together, we were unstoppable. He also was acquainted with some of the newly rich people who had made out in his court, thanks to how he had ruled on their cases.*"

Putney complimented himself, "*It was me who taught him how to rid them of their newfound inheritances.*"

Briscoe shook his head, *"That doesn't sound to me like Judge McClelland was doing anything illegal. He might have shown some favoritism in his rulings, but so what?"*

Richard looked like he could strangle Briscoe as he confronted him, *"Favoritism? A funny word for describing criminal activity! As probate judge, he SELECTED which person in each family would get the goods, man!"*

Richard looked at Frank and then shook his head as he realized he had to explain, *"Hiz Honor could be just as creative as he wanted to be and he'd always get the payoff under the table with no one the wiser."* He laughed at Briscoe, *"Favoritism! Ha!"*

Frank shrugged with a smile as he walked away from his annoyed witness, *"Still no proof of any crime here, Mr. Putney..."*

Richard sat up in the Box, and, incited by Briscoe, he looked at Clem, *"Then let's try this one on for size ... There was this one eighty-year-old broad named Clara Currie who up and died one day. When Clara died she willed all, not a little, ALL of her money to a children's daycare center to help it, uh, stay open and to expand its services."*

Putney grinned at the jury and pointed at Clem, *"Well, that's when he contacted me to be the Administrator to the Currie estate. I had handled several cases for Judge McClelland successfully and he liked my style. So when Clara Currie went tits up, Hiz Honor decided..."*

Jack was on his feet in an instant, *"Objection! The witness cannot read our client's mind!"*

Judge Evetts wanted to hear more so he said, *"Overruled! I'm fascinated by a good tale! Proceed Mr. Putney."*

Richard actually winked at the judge (It was a theatrical wink, probably taught to him by Mr. Drama-King himself) and then he pointed at Clem, *"As I was saying, Hiz Honor decided the old broad's money would be happier in his bank account, the Tierra Grande account, and he set wheels into motion so that would happen. And that's where I came in!"*

Putney stretched his arms out, then put them behind his head to flex them. He was the center of attention which must have been entertaining to someone with his triple-sized ego.

He continued, *"I know a thing or three about how to get control of checking accounts and stocks and other accounts. I know how to hide assets. I helped Hiz Honor undo the Clara Currie Trust and her Will and then transfer and hide Clara's money."*

He put his arms down and folded them as he smiled at Clem, *"It was fun and profitable for us both. I enjoyed taking whatever funds I could out of that account. I guess you could say I got a little greedy but all I was doin' was withdrawin' money from this account before the judge had a chance to."*

Frank Briscoe looked like a Cat who'd swallowed an Elephant. He knew how Clem had run his probate court, having visited there many times. He was sure this jury had understood what his witness, Richard, had described to them and that they'd believed everything he'd said.

He was sure that in his Closing Argument, when he presented the additional evidence that established a paper trail from Clara's bank account to Clem's special Tierra Grande bank account (*that Briscoe's Monkeys had found*), that he'd have Clem dead to rights.

So Frank looked up at Judge Evetts and said, "*I need nothing further from this witness.*"

Frank turned to walk back to his table, nodded to Ed, and said, "*Your witness, Mr. Smith.*"

Ed smiled and shook his head as a smiling Jack Rawitscher stood up instead.

Jack approached and then swooped down on Putney to deliver some defensive heat, "*So you think taking money from other people is fun, huh?*"

Richard opened his eyes wide and answered, "*Whatever, man.*"

Jack attacked again, "*And you think you're as slick as eel shit, don't you?*"

Briscoe shouted, "*Objection!*"

Judge Evetts followed his "*Sustained!*" with, "*It's Mr. Rawitscher, is that right?*"

Jack nodded. The judge continued, "*Well, Mr. Rawitscher, in my courtroom I decide what words won't be allowed. Just so you know, I dislike eels, okay?*"

The jurors laughed as Jack smiled and nodded.

The judge said, "*Please continue . . .*"

Jack walked very slowly toward Richard who sat happily in the Box, "*Now, Mr. Putney, you're an admitted thief and an accomplished con artist.*"

Richard yawned and smiled. Jack asked, "*Would it be safe to say you've never completed an honest day's work in your entire life?*" Putney countered with, "*Yeah, just like some slick lawyers I know . . .*"

The gallery of Onlookers laughed. Jack was relentless, "*Did the District Attorney offer to pay you to come here to Belton, Texas in order to testify?*" Richard shifted in his chair and said, "*He sure did! He promised he wouldn't prosecute me, or I assure you I'd never ever visit any place called Belton.*"

A few of the jurors and a lot of the spectators verbally reacted with angry mumbles.

Judge Evetts lightly pounded his gavel and softly said, "*Order, please.*"

Jack said his final words to Richard, "*So you ARE as slick . . .*" He looked at Judge Evetts and then he finished his sentence, "*. . . as slick can be, aren't you?*"

Putney smiled and nodded at Jack as Jack said, "*I ask the members of the jury: Who should you believe?*" Jack pointed at Richard, "*A lowlife thief . . .*" He turned quickly and pointed at Clem: "*. . . or a distinguished Judge?*"

Frank stood up at his table and angrily shouted, "*OBJECTION, YOUR HONOR! The defense can't ask the jury questions!*"

Judge Evetts with a trace of a smile said, "*Sustained!*"

So there it was: Briscoe had linked his extensive Media extravaganza to the testimony of one scoundrel, thinking that an admitted thief could topple a long-standing Judge. It didn't sound like a quality Chess match to me. It sounded like Briscoe was not as shrewd a prosecutor as he wanted everyone to think.

Over the previous days I'd watched all twelve jury men closely to pick up any signs that would indicate their preference for one side or the other. Doris had done the same and so I asked her what her score was and we unfortunately agreed, number-wise, that Clem was in trouble. At the end of day 4 this jury, at least to me and Doris, had no concern for treating our Clem fairly.

Jury Hears Putney on Fee Split

CLAIMS McCLELLAND SAID "PUT MY HALF IN TIERRA GRANDE"

By John Moore
POST STAFF CORRESPONDENT

BELTON
Richard H Putney testified that the suspended probate judge Clem McClelland ordered him to split a $10,000 fee from the Clara L Currie estate in December of 1960.

PUTNEY SAID he took the money without getting a court order from Judge McClelland because he did not want to split any more fees with anyone.

Later under further questioning by District Atty Briscoe Putney was asked "Why didn't You obtain a court order if you thought you were entitled to the money for your work in connection with the estate?"

"I guess I was greedy" Putney replied.

"I thought I was justified in getting a certain amount of money for my work and I took it. I felt I was entitled to a fee and I didn't want to divide it with Judge McClelland."

John Moore wrote for The Houston Post, November 15, 1962

It was November 16, day 5 of Clem's trial, when it happened. Right after a too small breakfast, Clem suffered an insulin shock and simply slid off his chair. Unconscious, he hit the floor in **Bessie's Diner** before I could catch him. Doris went right to work and poured a glass of orange juice down Clem's throat but, as he sometimes did whenever he was unconscious, he spit out most of the orange juice she'd poured into his mouth. Luckily, enough juice got into his system to help him help us help him. I was able to put him into the back seat of the Cadillac and while Doris sat next to him I drove us to a very nice doctor in nearby Temple, Texas.

The doctor was named Dr. Jay Tibbets and I remember him well since he, too, was a long time diabetic. On our return to Belton from Temple, Doris suddenly slipped into a rare and unhappy state of mind and I had to keep my eye on both of my parents as I drove us back to the Belton courthouse.

Once again here's John Moore's account, this time from the Post's November 16 edition:

> THE PROCEEDINGS were delayed for nearly an hour Friday morning when the chief defense attorney, J. Edwin Smith of Houston, announced McClelland was ill and under treatment by a doctor. One of the defense attorneys said McClelland has sufferred from diabetes for many years and was being treated in Temple for an attack.
>
> McClelland, accompanied by his wife, Doris, arrived in the courtroom about 10 AM and the trial proceeded. During the noon recess, McClelland told a Houston Post reporter that he was "feeling all right."
>
> The defense rested a few minutes after the state had concluded its case. No witnesses were called.

So why was Clem's blood sugar so low that day? In my opinion it was a combination of too much stress from the Devil, a less than compassionate jury, a lying thief, and a small town Judge who'd forgotten how important it was for him to stay impartial.

As for the rest of day 5, it would prove to be the hottest and the hardest day for everyone, and John Moore's writings shared how rough it became in that small courtroom:

McClelland Testimony Bogs Down

Opposing Lawyers Reprimanded for Slowing Up Trial

By John Moore
POST STAFF CORRESPONDENT

Most of the argument centered on the complex financial affairs of Tierra Grande, Inc. a corporation on which McClelland was authorized to draw funds.

Once during the day, Judge Evetts said "Gentlemen, both sides are straining at gnats let's get on with this trial."

The 12 men who are serving on the jury were obviously weary and one juror fell asleep in the warm courtroom.

THE CHIEF deputy sheriff of Bell County, W. L. Gunn, raised some windows and some blinds so that fresh air could circulate through the courtroom.

As the fresh air and sunshine flowed through the windows, several of the jurors squirmed around and looked outside.

It is deer-hunting time here in Central Texas and at least half of the members of the jury had planned to be in some deer camp Friday.

Instead, the jurors were learning a great deal about banking

John Moore wrote for The Houston Post, November 16, 1962

Fresh air and sunshine?
Deer-hunting?

Clem and I would have been glad to go with any of the Belton jurors to any of the Bell County Deer Camps. It would've made more sense than anything we'd done there so far . . .

As day 5 progressed it seemed to me that Briscoe was suffering from an overdose of confidence when he decided that his Richard Putney card was sufficient to win the hand at play. But when the Devil said, "*The State rests*" I expected to see and hear witnesses by the score for the defense proclaiming Judge Clem to be a saint of unparalleled proportions. Instead, our well-paid Defense geniuses simply said, "*The State hasn't made a case, Your Honor, and we move for a 'directed verdict.'*"

FYI: A *directed verdict* is a motion made by the defense (before a case is submitted to a jury) that argues no reasonable jury could possibly find for the prosecution since the tendered evidence was legally insufficient to convict. If a directed verdict is granted there is no longer any need for the jury to decide the case. If granted, the verdict is automatically *not guilty*. Few judges will ever grant a directed verdict since it presupposes or presumes the prosecution team is composed of idiots who should go back to law school to learn how to present a case.

Judge Evetts would never sanction a directed verdict so he simply said, "*Motion denied.*"

Ed, Jack and Clem put their heads together and then Ed said, "*The defense rests.*"

Just like that it was over. Clem's geniuses were certain there was no need to call witnesses to testify about how many cases Judge Clem had ruled on, or how many years he'd sat on the bench for Harris County, or his record as a Shriner, or what a great father/husband he was to his family.

Ed and Jack were so confident that Briscoe's star witness was such a scumbag that no good Christian farmer would ever invite him over for dinner much less believe his testimony. To them the jury was a lock, with no need to prolong their time away from their farms.

When I heard Ed say the "*no need to prolong their time away*" line I wondered why we should care for even a second about the farmers being *put out*. I wanted to tell him, "*Let's not forget we're in this courtroom to keep Clem out of prison.*" Period.

McClelland Trial Ends; No Defense Testimony

The Houston Post Headline, November 16, 1962

McCLELLAND, RIGHT, WITH COUNSEL
Principal Defense Attorney is J. Edwin Smith, Left

The McClelland Game Plan: *Call No Witnesses*

The rest of day 5 was spent with Frank and Ed sharing their *closing arguments.*

The problem for the defense: Ed was still trying to convince a jury who'd already made up their minds five minutes after seeing Clem in his $1,000 suit. Ed continued to beat his drum on the loss of Clem's Constitutional rights, and the jury continued to yawn, look outside, and check their watches. I continued to think there was no hope.

Frank used his normal innuendo approach which was all speculation with no basis in fact.

At one point John Moore and the Post quoted Frank's lame attack word for word, "*The man on trial here was a Judge until a short while ago. He used his office for material gain and I think there is nothing worse than a public official who uses his office to line his own pockets. We have a saying that one of the worst things you can do is to steal the pennies off a dead man's eyes. I submit to you that there is a whole lot more than pennies involved here . . .*"

Ed tried again to preach a sermon on Constitutional Law and how protecting an individual's rights was "*vital to everyone.*" I wanted to shake him and yell, "*C'mon, man, these farmers don't care one bit about the Bill of Rights unless it deals with religion or gun control!*"

Also, in the here and now, Defense attorneys use high-tech projection equipment to "*project*" positive supporting images, so they can influence jurors to declare their clients *not guilty.*

Since this was the '60s, Edwin Smith took an 8x11 inch jailhouse photo of Richard H. Putney and scotch-taped it to the chair in the Witness Box. Then, whenever he referred to the "*ridiculous testimony from this ridiculous witness,*" he pointed at Richard's picture.

Hmm . . . High-tech?

I remember sitting in that courtroom and looking at Clem. My father. My hunting partner.

I sat there and tried to imagine the turmoil he was suffering due to the Devil's political agenda.

I also thought back to whatever prompted Clem to hire Edwin Smith instead of Percy Foreman. I knew it was bad luck that had brought us to Belton, and that Richard Putney was a perversity in a Universe filled with perversities, but Percy would've saved the day if he'd been there.

I was only 14 years old and yet I knew every aspect of Clem's case. I understood the smear campaign that Briscoe had organized and executed. And I knew that this trial had finally turned into an all-consuming monster.

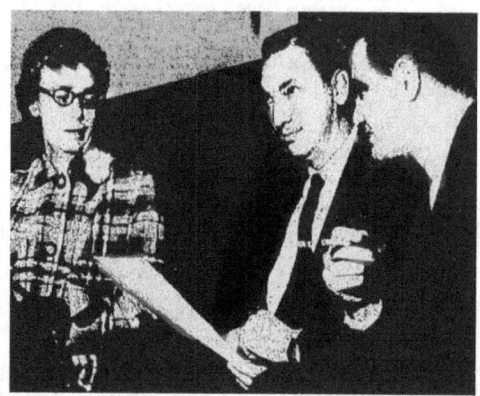

Doris, Clem and Jack discussed the jury
The Brownsville Herald, November 17, 1962

Judge Evetts gave his final instructions to the jury before they began their deliberations. The judge spoke to his jury of farmers as if teaching them about proper courtroom procedure was vital to the future well-being of Belton, Texas, "*Gentlemen of the jury, be aware of your responsibility to both the prosecution and to the defendant. You hold the future of the defendant in your hands and I want you to realize the importance of that fact. I need you to review all the facts presented in the Clara Currie's estate case, not the whims or weaknesses of the participants.*"

He leaned forward toward the twelve men and he seemed sincere when he told them, "*Consider both sides of every argument you heard and then decide for yourself what convinced you to choose guilty or innocent as your verdict. Be careful NOT to draw any negative conclusions from the defendant's choice not to testify. That's his right and you are not to think of it as an admission of guilt. Quite the contrary, Judge McClelland came to our town due to a preponderance of publicity in the Houston newspapers.*"

He continued to educate his farmers by saying, "*Mr. McClelland decided that it was the prosecutors' job to prove his guilt. That means that if any of you have a reasonable doubt as to whether or not he is guilty, you must find him not guilty. If, however, you are completely convinced that he converted funds from Clara Currie's estate, then you must find him guilty."*

The judge also discussed their electing a foreman to be sure that all the jury discussions ran smoothly (in addition to defusing arguments), and to ensure each jury member had their fair say. After a half-hour of instructions, the jury left the courtroom and walked into their deliberation room where they'd remain until they agreed on a verdict. I wasn't confident these twelve men could agree on the time of day, but as long as they kept breathing and deliberating, there was hope.

While we waited, Doris borrowed Isaac's office in the courthouse and phoned home to Micki and Anne. She told them to be there in Belton no later than 8 a.m. the next day. When they asked her how things were going, she lied and said, *"Everything's fine. Your father looks great and IS great. Kirk's not too bad in the looks department either."* A mother's love.

I asked Isaac if I could use his phone *"to call Betsy, my girlfriend"* and he shook his head, *"I could lose my job if you was caught sending sweet nothin's over my line. Sorry."* Ah, well.

I sat there in the courtroom all afternoon. It was quiet and it gave me time to consider and analyze what I thought Clem's case signified. If a hint would help, here's a Clem platitude: *Nice Guys Finish Last*.

Around 6:00 p.m. Deputy Sheriff Gunn came out to tell the prosecutors and the defense team that the jury was close to making a decision, but that Judge Evetts was going to let them go home for the night. The Deputy told both sides that Judge Evetts would see everybody back there at 9 a.m. the next morning.

At 8 a.m. on day 6 the McClellands all met for breakfast at **BESSIE'S DINER**.

Micki and Anne had an early but uneventful 180 mile drive from Houston to Belton and the five of us were discussing the trial highlights so the daughters would be in the loop.

I was the contrary voice and I said, *"I have a bad feeling that this might not be much fun."*

Micki was eager to jump in with a Miss-Know-It-All attitude and she proclaimed, *"Of course it will! Doris has been calling us all week to say everything's going great."*

Then she leaned forward over the table and whispered, *"These country hick's could never look at our Clem and think guilty."*

To which Anne said at strength 10, *"NOT GUILTY!"*

Doris, who'd been mostly restrained at breakfast, bravely nodded, and said, *"From your mouth to God's ears."*

Anne nodded and said, *"Exactly!"*

Clem nodded, and I saw him softly laugh too.

Clem had been watching some of the locals dining at the packed Diner. It seemed that a *Verdict Day* had significant entertainment value for the agro-crowd.

My guess was an event like Clem's trial and subsequent verdict was equivalent to a hanging in the old days.

Clem directed his gaze back to his family and he took charge, "*Now, I want you to listen closely to me. I need you to remember this is not a Football game.* (He looked at Anne) *No yelling or screaming . . . No emotion no matter what happens. Just behave like this is your father's court. We've been in the public eye for too damn long, and it's time we moved forward.*"

After breakfast we walked to the courthouse and into a Meeting Room that Isaac had set up for us. We had just settled in when Ed and Jack came in and said, "*It's time. The jury's back.*"

Clem looked at each of us and then he stood up and embraced Doris and gave her a kiss similar to the kiss he'd given her at our new house celebration party years before. I watched them, especially Doris as she looked up at Clem and ran her hand through his hair.

He spoke softly to her and said, "*I feel like a turkey at Thanksgiving . . .*"

She laughed and patted his strong and handsome face.

She later told me how brave she thought he was. Even though our Clem faced a firing squad he was still making jokes . . .

The McClelland family, in step with each other, walked proudly into the Belton courtroom which was filled to the rafters with Beltonites straining to see Clem.

Doris and I showed Micki and Anne where to sit and Clem sat between his two attorneys at the defense table. The Devil and his Monkey and their bootlicking Newsman were already in place as the judge motioned to Isaac, "*Bailiff, bring in the jury!*"

I noticed that the KTRK-TV Cameraman, Jeff Wilson, had set up his Camera facing the judge since the judge would soon be reading the Verdict. I watched Jeff attach a 400 foot magazine to his 16 mm Arriflex Film Camera and run the new mag of film through the Camera's gate. I noticed that Jeff had run a Cable from the Camera to a Microphone that sat in front of the judge.

Once the jury was seated the judge waved to Jeff who began to roll film. Jeff waited a few seconds then he waved back at the judge: Action!

I recall that from my point of view *the whole thing* stopped at that moment.

I saw the entire courtroom in a series of freeze frames: Clem sitting between Ed and Jack. The judge and Isaac, waiting. The twelve men in the jury. The room full of curious Beltonites. Doris sitting between Micki and Anne. My hands folded in front of me, shaking. I flashbacked two years to Clem sitting in our Living Room telling us, "*Everything will be all right. Nothing's gonna change.*"

And then I heard Judge Evetts say, "*Will the defendant please rise?*"

Clem and Ed and Jack stood up.

Judge Evetts turned slightly and asked the jury, "*Has the jury reached a verdict?*"

The jury Foreman stood up and answered, "*Yes, we have, Your Honor.*"

The Foreman was probably chosen since he was the tallest juror and, with no sign of emotion, he handed a piece of paper to Isaac who crossed to the judge and handed it to him.

The judge adjusted the location of the Microphone in front of him, he looked at the verdict, he looked at Clem, and then he began to read, "*In the case of The State of Texas versus Clement Bramlette McClelland, we the jury of Belton, Texas do hereby find that the defendant, Clement Bramlette McClelland* (he looked at Clem again) . . . *is guilty.*"

Anne screamed, "*NOOOOO!*"

The Gallery of Onlookers looked on for more outbursts from the McClelland family but they got none. Doris hugged Micki and Anne on either side of her and I just stood there lost, as I looked at the jury, as I looked at Clem, and as I looked at Frank and Pete and Cap as Pete and Cap slapped Frank on his back.

I felt dizzy but I knew it was time to suck it up, not to show the loss that I knew each member of my family felt, not to think about how this verdict would change everything I ever did or thought for the rest of my life, and not to think about how life was just plain unfair. It was time for me to be tough, to help my sisters, mother and father leave that place and get home safely.

As I tried to move I found that my legs wouldn't hold me up. I sat down and the room began to spin to a point where I had to close my eyes. But closing my eyes made me dizzier so I had to open them. That was harder since I then had to watch Clem as he listened to Ed and Jack, "*Don't worry about this, Judge McClelland. We'll appeal this verdict. There are so many holes in Briscoe's case, it's a joke!*"

I watched Jeff Wilson as he shot backup shots to use in editing this climactic scene for a News story Houstonians would enjoy watching tonight with dinner and tomorrow with breakfast.

Then Judge Evetts banged his gavel and called his court to order, "*Quiet in my court, if you please!*"

Everyone obeyed and stopped talking. Isaac motioned with his hands that everyone should sit back down and take their seats since the judge still had important business to conduct.

Judge Evetts was sensitive again concerning the location of Jeff's Microphone, and when he had positioned both it and himself for what he'd hoped were optimal audio and visual recording, he continued, "*I see no reason not to move forward on this case and to pass sentence.*"

I heard Doris inhale. She had not expected Justice to move this swiftly.

The judge continued, "*So here she goes. In accordance with the Statutes laid down by the great State of Texas, I hereby sentence Clement Bramlette McClelland to 10 years confinement, to be served at the State Penitentiary in Huntsville, Texas.*"

The Gallery of Onlookers and Spectators gasped. The judge looked at his court and spoke, "*I remind all present that the defendant has the right to appeal the verdict and I order that he remain free on his bond until which time that his appeal is granted or denied."*

He smiled at his courtroom full of people and said, *"My court is adjourned."*

He banged his gavel as Isaac opened the door to his Chambers. They both entered, and then quickly closed the door behind them.

I watched the Gallery talking to each other, I watched Briscoe and Moore and Detrick talk to each other, and then I watched Jeff point his Camera at some of the jurors. When Jeff turned his Camera and pointed it at my tattered and torn family, I heard Clem tell Jack Rawitscher to help him herd the McClellands back to the Meeting Room.

McClelland Is Found Guilty, Gets 10 Years

Jury Out for Only Hour, Sets Maximum Sentence

By John Moore, POST STAFF CORRESPONDENT

BELTON — Clem McClelland was convicted of felony conversion and given the maximum sentence of 10 years in the penitentiary by a Bell County jury which deliberated a little more than an hour Saturday.

WHILE THE 45-year-old McClelland was seated before the judge's bench waiting for the new bond to be posted, his wife Doris came and stood behind him. Later, one of his teen age daughters ran up and kissed him while dabbing at her eyes with a tissue.

McClelland was released and left the Bell County Courthouse without saying a word.

He was just as silent when an assistant prosecutor told the jury that "McClelland has picked the pockets of the dead," and when his own attorney branded the state's star witness as "a cheat, a thief and a liar."

SMITH, THE chief defense attorney, said he would continue to fight for McClelland's freedom in the appeal courts if necessary.

"Frankly, I'm sort of numb," Smith said.

The all-male jury refused to go to lunch and started its deliberations during the noon hour.

Roger Cone, a telephone company employees of Temple, was foreman. The jurors sent out for dozens of the documents used as evidence and apparently examined them again inside the jury room.

DISTRICT ATTY Frank Briscoe of Harris County said:

"It was an appropriate verdict, consistent with the evidence.

"This verdict may have some effect on some of the related cases, including McClelland and others who have been indicted."

McClelland still faces trial on 8 felony indictments. Briscoe said the other cases would be set for trial as soon as possible.

I forced my legs to walk in step with everyone else but it took my full concentration to make them move. I had mentally prepared myself for the worst possible scenario but when I heard Judge Evetts' sentence of 10 years for Clem, something inside of me died. Please understand it's a memory that's hard for me to share.

In the Meeting Room I saw Clem work to appear strong for his family. He was a strong man, but I knew him. I knew he was mad as hell with no outlet for his anger.

In our hunting days he and I had discussed what to do when the world seemed to spin out of control, and I hoped that *he* was doing what he'd told *me* to do. I started to count my blessings: Good health, Betsy, Doris, Clem, Oscar, Gigi, Micki, Anne, Josephine, Woodrow, Steve, Chris and Betsy . . . did I count her already?

Then I saw Clem pull Ed aside and hand his Cadillac car keys to him, "*Here you go, Ed.*"

Ed looked at the keys and protested, "*I can't take these, Judge.*"

Clem said, "*A deal's a deal. I'm going to have to make a lot of adjustments. Might as well get started.*"

I walked over to a window with a view of the back parking lot behind the courthouse, and I saw Clem's black Cadillac Deville parked nearby. A lot of good times were about to drive away.

We piled our suitcases and ourselves into the Station Wagon that Micki and Anne had driven to Belton, and after saying farewell to countless joyful memories, we left Belton behind . . .

Clem was in the driver's seat and Doris was in the back with Micki and Anne. I sat in the front passenger seat. There was no way I was going to sit next to my sisters because I was tired of listening to their moans and groans. They made me claustrophobic. To this day they still do.

Micki was concerned about her loss of popularity saying, "*All of our friends have been tiptoeing around us, afraid they'll hurt our feelings. Now they'll just run away from us!*"

I muttered, "*Great friends . . .*"

Anne was concerned about her life in general saying, "*I don't know what to do! How can we go back to school NOW?*"

Doris took both of their hands and held them as she said, "*NOW is the time you should worry about your father instead of yourselves. Turn those frowns upside-down!*"

Micki wouldn't listen to her and said, "*None of my friends will want to talk to me anymore!*"

This time Clem smiled as he made a joke, "*That could be a benefit.*"

Anne was crying and she howled with, "*How are we supposed to act? Our father's been found guilty and he's going to jail!*"

Clem with a very calm voice said, "*Just keep your chin up. You've done nothing to be ashamed of . . .*"

Doris had listened enough to their wailing and pointed up ahead on the side of the road, "*Clem, why don't you pull into that Roadside Café up ahead so we can fill these wailing mouths with some food?*"

Clem said, "*Good idea. I could eat the south bound ass off a north bound cow!*"

Incredible. Clem had been found guilty, and here he was making jokes and acting like his family was on a jolly road trip.

He saw the Roadside Café, pulled in, and parked. Doris walked toward the Cafe with my sisters but when I exited the Wagon I noticed that Jeff Wilson's Channel 13 KTRK-TV Van was parked several cars away in the same lot. I held back to talk to Clem, "*Look. We haven't talked for a while but I just wanted to tell you that I love you.*"

Clem gave me his brightest biggest smile and said, "*Thanks, boy. I love your support, Kirk. I'm a very lucky man.*"

He and I hugged and then I patted his shoulder and said, "*Give me a minute by myself. I'll catch up with you inside.*"

Clem looked at me with concern, "*Are you okay?*"

I answered, "*Yeah. I just want to say a prayer.*"

Clem nodded and turned to walk toward the Café entrance. I waited a beat and then I walked quickly to the rear of the Channel 13 Van. I tested the back loading doors and they opened right up. Suddenly I was looking down at two cans with a 400 foot magazine in each. "*McClelland Trial #1*" was written on one and "*McClelland Trial #2*" was on the other.

I had to think fast and move faster. For some reason I chose "*McClelland Trial #2*" and with no hesitation I opened up this large can and there was 400 feet of exposed 16 mm film. I held it up and pointed it toward the sun.

I said, "*Burn, baby, burn!*" and then I counted, "*One, two, three, four, and five!*"

I didn't have time to think about what I was doing.

I closed the Film magazine labeled #2 and then looked hard at the mag can labeled #1. I was about to pick it up when I heard a car pull into the parking area very close to where I stood. I quietly closed the Van back doors and, without looking behind me, I slowly walked to the Café's front door and entered . . .

I've thought a lot about what I'd done in that parking lot. I've tried to excuse myself: I was young; I was trying to protect my family the same way I'd done for months whenever I destroyed hate signs or fended off crazy phone callers.

But this was different. I had destroyed Jeff Wilson's film. No excuse. Holy moly . . .

When we returned home safely to Houston I remember thinking that our neighborhood looked and felt like a ghost town. I wasn't over-reacting. I remember there was no sign of neighbors or dogs or cats or children on bikes. There was nothing but low, dark clouds rolling in from the west-northwest, about where the town of Belton, Texas was located. It was eerie.

In the Den/Television Room I turned on the TV, and tuned it to KTRK Channel 13 so we'd be able to hear their *excuse* for failing to capture the verdict. I looked forward to seeing my family smile with *good news* for a change. There were predictable complaints from my sisters:

Micki, "*This is the worst day of my life. Why should any of us watch this again?*"

Anne, "*Do you think that Camera recorded my scream?*"

Clem put our watching his verdict on TV into perspective for us, "*I need to watch and study this. My focus now is on how and if I can appeal this verdict. But if you can't handle watching this again, you can go to your rooms.*"

I was glad that neither of my sisters bailed. I wanted them to feel relief when the Channel 13 news anchor had to explain their station's loss of the Belton courtroom film images.

I turned up the Volume as the KTRK-TV News Hour logo appeared, complete with their nightly news music theme. The TV Anchor was Dave Webb again and he said, "*Good Evening. Tonight's top story is Judge Clem McClelland's trial for converting estate funds for his own private use. Our Cameras have followed this trial all week and tonight we have a verdict . . .*"

I watched Anne turn her head away from the TV Screen to hide her eyes in Doris's blouse. Micki stared at the television as we all saw a wide establishing shot of the Belton courthouse. I couldn't believe what I was seeing, and then I couldn't believe what I was hearing.

Judge Evetts began his verdict speech, "*In the case of The State of Texas versus Clement Bramlette McClelland, we the jury of Belton, Texas do hereby find that the defendant, Clement Bramlette McClelland* (he looked at Clem again) *. . . is guilty.*"

I was in shock, and not nearly as smart as I thought. With Jeff's Camera still on Judge Evetts' face we heard Anne's scream Off-Camera, "*NOOOOO!*" and heard various vocal reactions from the locals. Then we saw/heard Judge Evetts shout, "*Quiet in my court, if you please!*"

Needless to say I was upset again, that second time because I'd expected a ruined film and instead saw a black and white perfectly exposed film of my family's most depressing moment.

I had expected a reprieve, a break, an opportunity for relief. There was none. As part of my brain continued to listen to the judge's monotonic monologue about Clem's 10 year sentence, the rest of me felt sorry for Clem and Doris. They had truly received the short end of the stick.

Then I also felt sorry for me. I was too young and too inexperienced and at that point in time I was totally unable to contemplate how overwhelming this verdict would be for us all.

I walked out of the Den without saying anything to my devastated family. I went through The Billiard Room out the back door, past Gigi and Oscar who wanted petting, and out to my garage. I opened the door and then I loudly slammed it closed.

I saw lightning followed immediately by thunder. Several times the lightning hit close to our home and the thunder was deafening. That natural assault on our environment came at a perfect time. I didn't turn on my lights.

I sat down on my bed and I began to cry. I yelled out, "*God Damn It!*"

I shook my head. "*Why'd you do this to us? Why didn't you give him a break?*"

I walked around my new stronghold that Clem had graciously given to me. There was a new bed, a chest of drawers, a TV, a nice writing table and a portable record player with an album collection that I really loved. There was an entire collection of Kingston Trio LPs and there were Movie Soundtracks from films that were important to me. Over my early years these Films and their Music had impacted my beliefs, and they helped define me.

I picked up a brand new hammer from Clem's tool wall and I began to pound the workbench.

Bam! Bam! Bam! And then I lost it. I pounded and cried, pounded and cried, and with the hammer in my hand I started swinging and hitting everything within range. The more I hit, the louder I cried. Album after album was pulverized:

I yelled out, "**BEN HUR!**" and pounded that album to bits.

I screamed, "**KING OF KINGS!**" and pulverized it.

I cried out "**LAWRENCE OF ARABIA!**" and my hammer showed it no mercy.

I was out of my mind as I shrieked, "**EXODUS!**" and destroyed that vinyl disc forever.

I hit "**WEST SIDE STORY**" over and over until it no longer existed.

I couldn't do anything to help my dad. Ours was a family without hope.

The thunder continued to roll.

The rain fell in sheets outside the McClelland home and on the roof of my garage.

Dismay changed to despair. I felt helpless.

I would have done anything to erase that verdict . . .

CHAPTER SIX

IT DID HAPPEN HERE, 1963–1965

Clem had been found guilty on charges that he had enriched himself with funds from estates he had probated. He was convicted of the offense of *Conversion from an Estate*, and his penalty was assessed at *10 years confinement* in the State Penitentiary. As Judge Evetts had informed us, Clem was allowed by law to appeal his conviction and with Ed and Jack's help, he did.

One night at midnight our phone rang and I picked up my bedside receiver in the garage.

I said, "*Congratulations! You've won a free Jamaican cruise for you and the man or woman of your dreams. The small print on your ticket stipulates the Cruise Liner departs from Galveston Island in 15 minutes, but if you drive real fast . . .*" The Underwriter began to laugh with his deep voice that sounded like a growl, "*Hello, Kirk. You're still a funny boy. Listen, we haven't talked since your dad's conviction. I wanted to call to see how you're doing.*"

I gulped and quickly switched gears, "*Hello, uh . . . Mr. . . . What'd you say your name was?*"

He smiled over the phone and said, "*I didn't, but nice try. I called to check on you and to share with you that your father has no chance with his appeal.*"

I didn't like the sound of that so I asked, "*How do you know that?*"

He answered, "*I know all the appellate judges. Some are okay but some are not okay. The point is they're not elected officials. They're appointed.*"

I asked, "*What does that mean?*"

Mr. Writer said, "*It means your dad's up the creek if he thinks he's got any chance at reversing that decision. Especially with the two lawyers he's retained.*"

Feeling again that this guy was too smart to mess with, I asked, "*So you're a lawyer?*"

He laughed again, "*You're quick, Kirk. Do your old man a favor and remind him that appointees come a dime a dozen and that Briscoe preaches from their guidebook. Clem's going to the Big House and he's wasting his time if he thinks otherwise.*"

I didn't know what else to say so I said, "*Thanks for your moral support, I guess, and if you know a good line to put into an appeal, give me a call.*"

He laughed again and said, "*Sweet dreams!*" as he hung up.

I lay there and thought about Ed Smith and Jack Rawitscher. The Belton jury had taken a total of one hour and 42 minutes to reach a verdict and to set the sentence. The sentence of ten years for Clem to serve was the *maximum* sentence allowed by law.

Nice going, Ed. You really connected with that jury! And good call on your *not* calling any pro-Clem witnesses because you believed the State hadn't proven any crime! Ed and Jack.

My god. Could Clem count on them? Was the Underwriter . . . uh . . . right?

The Underwriter

Clem spent a year writing appeals and traveling to Austin with Ed and Jack to argue before the Criminal Court of Appeals. He and I discussed the demerits of Briscoe's case and the merits of his own case but the year brought only frustration and anxiety to the McClelland household.

On my personal front, Betsy's father had caught Betsy and me trying to go out on a date during Basketball season. She'd told her parents that she and her best friend were going to one of my games but, after the game, when I walked out of the Locker Room expecting to see my sweet baby, I saw my sweet baby's daddy. He held her arm tightly, and he told me that I'd "*fouled out!*" and was "*no longer eligible to play.*" Suddenly I was unhappier than I'd ever been.

Not to be too selfish and not to sound too much like my sisters, I was in a difficult bind because of all the bad publicity surrounding Clem. With Betsy no longer available, my finding a new soulmate would be *très difficile* since almost all of "*the good ones,*" as Steve and Chris liked to call them, would be hard to catch. Then Steve said, "*C'mon, Mac, just go shake your tail feather. You need to get back out there and show them you've still got your best dance moves.*"

Steve's favorite song at the time was ***I CAN'T HELP MYSELF*** by the ***FOUR TOPS***, and as I tried calling several young ladies to fill a painful void in my life, I found myself humming, "*Sugar pie, honey bunch, you know I love you! I can't help myself. I love you and nobody else.*" over and over again. I remember whenever I hummed that song, it hurt my heart.

On the first school morning after Clem's conviction, after the 16 mm film shot by Jeff Wilson had played on all the Houston TV Stations over the week-end, I was eating breakfast with Doris as I made ready for school. My sisters had both refused to go to their Lamar High School, named after the great Mirabeau B. Lamar (a Colonel under Sam Houston and the Father of Texas Education according to my good friend Mildred Henderson). To my sisters it would be, " *. . . impossible to walk down those hallways and have our classmates point at us and whisper . . .*"

So they both decided to stay home and drive Doris and Clem crazy. Micki and Anne were too concerned about being a topic of discussion when, by not going, that's exactly what they were.

On my end, back at T. H. Rogers Junior High, I worked hard to survive that terrible morning.

I was just barely able to force myself to smile at anyone I saw pointing at me or whispering behind their books. It was painful. I would have loved jumping on my speedy Moped and riding to Galveston Island so I could walk alone on Galveston Beach.

At lunch I sat in the lunchroom planning to do just that when suddenly Mona appeared.

Mona was a nice looking girl, very popular, and she had a lot of sympathy for Clem, having followed his story in the Newspapers. On one of the worst days of my life she surprised me by walking up to my table, using her hands to tilt up my face, and then giving me a kiss on my lips. I almost cried out "*Holy Moly,*" but the brainy side of my brain kicked in to save me. I remember reacting with a smile and then watching/listening to her as she said, "*You are way too cute to not have me as your new girlfriend. What do you think?*"

I was instantly infatuated but all I could say was, "*I've always wanted to ask you out but . . . I was afraid you'd say no because of my father.*" She took my face in her hands and said, "*Don't be silly Kirk. I think you're great!*"

Unexpectedly, in a year full of losses, here was a tangible win.

I looked at Mona and then I looked across the lunchroom to see Betsy hold up her right hand. She used her two fingers to make a V for victory sign. She nodded, hoping for the best.

Steve and Chris walked over and sat down with us and both had big smiles thanks to the company I was suddenly keeping. Neither was rude or presumptuous about Mona's insertion into our ranks and Steve moved right to the crux of the matter saying, "*So Mac, his trial was a bust, huh?*"

I was still high with my Mona victory and she sat so close.

I made an effort to answer him:

"*Yeah. They say most Juries make up their minds in the first hour or so. I think the Belton jury made theirs up in the first 5 minutes.*"

Mona moved closer to me, then Chris asked, "*So how are you doin', Mac?*"

I looked at my two old friends and my newest friend and I told them all the truth, "*I'm trying hard not to feel sorry for myself. Clem's the one I need to worry about.*"

Mona moved closer and whispered, "*I'll worry about you.*" Damn. I tried to stay focused on what I wanted to share with Steve and Chris but she was making it hard.

I said, "*When they found him guilty, I didn't know what I'd do.*"

Steve patted my shoulder, "*I've got nothing but faith in the system, Mac.*"

That made me laugh and I said, "*You sound like the man who was just found guilty. He believes in the system, too.*"

We sat quietly for a few seconds as we all considered that, and then Chris and Steve looked at me and Mona and nodded to each other as they stood up, with Chris saying, "*Steve and I will see you guys later.*"

I waved goodbye to them, and nodded my thanks for their positive support.

As they walked away I heard Mona sigh and say, "*They are good friends.*" I smiled at her and looked around the lunchroom. Then I turned Mona toward me, and I kissed her fully on *her* lips. She play-acted like she was swooning, and we both laughed.

Was she real, or too good to be true? . . .

Then November 1962 passed into December. Then Christmas passed, and here came 1963.

My Basketball season shifted to my Track season.

On Clem's warfront, things grew darker as Frank Briscoe and his Monkeys decided to again prosecute Clem, this time on charges of Bribery.

The Devil had narrowed Clem's favorite lawyers down to 5 men. Briscoe said he would prove those 5 men had curried favor with Clem (bribed him) so he'd assign them the best parts of his probate caseload. On the face of it I could understand how it could've been possible, but Clem wasn't stupid. Why would he conduct his court in such a brash and careless manner?

I believed Briscoe was guilty of *payback prosecution* to punish Clem for appealing his Belton conviction. How dare this convicted Judge appeal the distinguished Devil's verdict?

As per usual, Briscoe told the local Media that Clem took bribes, which was dirty pool. I viewed it as a typical act by a jealous Drama King-Devil who lied through his teeth . . .

My Track season changed to my Baseball season so I'd stay in shape for my Football season.

I tried to stay busy and stay out of trouble. I tried to excel at my sports so if I caught a touchdown pass or scored a buzzer basket in Basketball or won a race in Track, I could maybe get the McClelland name headlined *Newspaper-wise* in a more favorable light.

Unfortunately, that fall while playing Football, I suffered a separated right shoulder which benched me for the whole season. It also hurt when it came time to put on a shirt or take a shower. Fortunately, I had my own shower in my stronghold so when I screamed in pain no one could hear me.

Football segued to Basketball, and my shoulder slowly repaired itself thanks to stretching and strengthening exercises that Clem helped me carry out nightly. I don't know what I would have done without his help. Doris would've tried, but she couldn't handle my screaming in pain.

Coach Wilson, Tim #61, Steve #50, Me #81, Chris #13

I posed...   ...and then I actually competed

After a painful Basketball season, suddenly it was spring of 1964 and I was on the run again. It was a Track season that I remember fondly because Clem went with me to all of my meets.

I remember him shooting his 8 mm Kodak Camera as I crossed the finish line at large Track meets held at Del Mar Stadium and Memorial Stadium. I normally ran the 440 yard dash, the 440 yard relay, and the Mile Relay. And then came the Memorial meet...

I was stretching on the Memorial track infield with Clem standing by my side when Coach Wilson, wearing a T.H. Rogers baseball hat and a Rogers sweatshirt, came up to offer me a ridiculous challenge, "*Okay, Mr. Mac. I've got a favor to ask. Chris got some kind of food poisoning last night and he can't run the 880 yard dash today. Wanna fill in?*"

I laughed at him, "*You want me to run the 440 AND the 880?*"

Coach Wilson reminded me of an actor named Richard Egan. They could've been twin brothers but Coach Wilson's charisma couldn't sidetrack me from his ridiculous request. He smiled as he asked me to run the extra race, fully aware I'd never turn him down whether it was a Football or a Basketball or a Track request. And I knew his request was all about points.

He confirmed that saying, "*If you can win the 440 and the 880 it will give us a point total that'll win the whole meet. And I'll get Tim to take your place on the Mile Relay since that will be an easy win for us anyway. So whadayasay?*"

Clem watched me process what my Coach had just asked me to try. As I looked into the two faces I respected and wanted to impress the most, I felt my head going up and down as I said, "*At the end of the 880, have someone there to catch me when I lose consciousness and fall across the finish line.*"

Coach Wilson happily slapped me on my back and said, "*Attaboy, Kirk. We'll win this one!* (back in Coach mode) *Now don't shortcut your warm-up. I need you as loose as a goose out there today!*" He moved away quickly so he could make his name change arrangements with the Race Committee.

Clem smiled, and then he laughed as he shook his head at me, "*Can you do this? You've never run the 880 in competition before.*"

I laughed with him, "*Thanks for noticing. Coach is so busy counting points, he forgot that little detail, didn't he? Jesus . . . Uh, excuse me, Clem.*"

Clem nodded to me. "*I get it, you're worried. Understandable in this case.*"

This was the first large meet of the year and there were 6 junior high schools represented. The first race I had to win was the 440-yard dash.

After chugging down a small orange juice, I stood at my starting block in lane 4.

The 8 Lanes were staggered so the 8 runners ran the same distance before ending at the Finish Line. The Track Referee raised his starter pistol and called out, "*Runners to your mark!* (He waited a beat) *Get set!*" and then he fired his pistol.

All 8 runners took off and we remained in our lanes all the way around the track. I ran as fast as any cheetah could. The 440 demanded I use everything so, when I broke the tape at the Finish Line to win, Coach Wilson and Clem saw me stumble off the track, exhausted.

Clem caught me, while my Coach looked at his stopwatch and congratulated me, "*That's the way to do it! 49.9 this early in the season is way ahead of where I thought you'd be, so good job.*" He made an entry on his clipboard and pointed at the infield, "*Now walk it off so you can get ready for your real race . . .*"

He smiled at Clem and then moved across the field to coach the high jump and long jumpers to keep those points coming in. Clem walked with me as I tried to breathe. It was hard work.

Clem said with a big grin, "*That's my boy . . .*" He raised up his JD flask at me, and winked as he drank.

I said, "*I'd laugh but I'm about to throw up . . .*" I stumbled again. I couldn't breathe.

Clem grabbed me and helped me walk a few paces so I could focus on staying alive. I had nothing left. What made me think I could run both of these grueling races?

We walked along the infield past where Coach Wilson was talking to his Assistant Coach Brewster who showed Coach Wilson the numbers on his clipboard: "*Here are the numbers, Coach Wilson. If he wins the 880, and then the Mile Relay wins, we could win the whole shebang!*"

Coach Wilson was a superstitious man and he promptly corrected Coach Brewster, "*The whole enchilada! How many times do I have to tell you? The whole ENCHILADA!*"

Coach Brewster nodded. "*Right, Coach! We could win the whole enchilada!*"

Clem and I watched Coach Wilson look around at all the other schools attending that meet.

Coach Wilson whispered to himself, "*I never thought we could take the whole meet . . . Jesus!*"

Then he looked at me trying to recover, as I struggled to suck in more air. He asked, "*How ya doin' Mac? Feeling any better?*"

I felt terrible. I felt like I was dying. I said, "*Yes, sir.*"

Then I sat down on the infield and, turning my head, I threw up.

Coach Wilson waved to one of our trainers who ran over to me with water and Orange Juice. I grabbed the water and poured it over my head. I dropped the bottle and tried to open the Orange Juice bottle. I couldn't make my hands work so Clem reached down and opened it for me. I quickly drank some, and hoped I could keep it down. I needed to stay hydrated if I was to have any chance at surviving. Coach Wilson, Coach Brewster, and Clem all stared down at me.

Coach Wilson said, "*Whadayasay, Mac? Is this doable or what?*"

I answered, "*Give me a moment to see if I'm gonna throw up again . . .*"

Our trainer began to wipe the sweat off my face and neck, and I shook my head so he'd stop. I swallowed more of the juice and tried to focus as I talked to Coach Wilson, "*I've got two laps to run. If I were to run this to win, how would you suggest I run it?*"

Coach Wilson's face relaxed a bit and suddenly he began to coach, "*The key to your winning this is to stay at the front of the pack. You have the speed to outrun all of the others, just make sure they don't outlast you!*"

I was beginning to process, and to plan, "*What kind of times do I need to hit?*"

Coach, "*If I were you, I'd run the first lap at about 65 to 70 seconds, and I'd run the second lap so my final time would be around 2 minutes 15 seconds. I think that time will win!*"

I was starting to see daylight. I could almost breathe normal, I was keeping the juice down, and all of a sudden I had a plan of action:

I said, "*2:15, huh? I think I could maybe do that.*"

Coach Wilson put his hand on Clem's back, and his other hand on my shoulder, and he said, "*We'll be there with you every step of the way. Let's go, Mac!*"

I stood at the starting line with 17 other runners. There were 6 schools and each school was allowed 3 runners. Never having run this race in competition, I was pretty scared.

I looked at my opponents: They were all thin since no one could carry fat twice around that quarter mile track. They were all fierce-looking since at the end of this race each one of them would wish they were dead due to the incredible oxygen deficiency that went with this race.

I knew I wanted the starting pistol to fire or I'd throw up again. Fortunately Clem yelled out, "*You can do this, Kirk! Go get 'em boy!*" And yes, he raised his JD flask and drank.

I was about to throw up when the Referee held up his pistol, "*Runners to your mark! Get set!*" He fired his pistol and we all started to sprint to the head of the pack to avoid getting stepped on by all the other runners.

I and a speedy runner from Lanier Junior High were suddenly all alone at the front as we pushed out in front of the other 16 runners, and made the first turn on the first lap. Two of the 16 runners, from Spring Forest Junior High, tried to pass me which was a stupid move since we were on the curve and they were having to run farther as they made their attempt. I picked up my pace and that forced them to fall back.

I saw that the sprinter from Lanier was way out front, and I remembered I was surprised he could run so fast. At that moment Coach Wilson came running up on the infield, and he shouted, "*Don't worry about the rabbit! He'll never have enough gas to make it to the end! Your pace is fine, stay with it!*"

Coach Wilson fell back and I quickly looked behind me to see Clem not far from him in the middle of the infield. There were other track and field competitors on the infield and I noticed they'd stopped jumping or shot putting or pole vaulting. Everybody was watching our race.

The runners behind me remained in the same grouping and as I came to the end of the first lap I saw my Coaches and Clem waiting to give me my time. I also noticed that the Lanier sprinter ahead of me was beginning to lag but he was still moving forward.

Coach Wilson and Coach Brewster looked at their stopwatches and they both yelled, "*62!*" Then Coach Wilson yelled, "*That's great Mac . . . 62!*"

I made it to the first turn and my thoughts were, "*You gotta win this. Clem's right there watching. You can't stop. You gotta hang tough. You can't stop . . .*"

I looked ahead and I said to myself, "*You gotta catch Lanier! You can't let him win!*"

I forced my very tired legs and arms to keep me moving. Halfway around, with half still to go, I was about 30 yards behind him.

But I was gaining on him.

I remember Coach Wilson called the sprinter a "*rabbit.*" That's what he was! I needed to catch him so Clem and I could take him back home to Doris! Clem would gut him and clean him and remove all his entrails and then Doris would throw his meat on the grill so that all the hungry McClellands could eat hearty! These thoughts actually went through my mind.

At the final turn I caught and then I passed him . . . Dear God, how am I ever going to keep going? I have no strength in my legs! I have no air, no wind! Who told me I could do this!

I was at the head of the pack and suddenly there was Coach Brewster yelling at me, "*C'mon, Kirk! You're almost home! Go man go!*"

Then Clem was there on the infield running beside me, "*Let's go, son! Yes, yes, YES! You can do it! You can do it!*"

My eyes were losing focus. I guess I was exhausted. I remember my legs wavered and I had to tell myself to remain standing so I could keep running. I wanted to look behind me to see where the other 17 runners were but my instincts told me I'd fall over. So I tried to look straight ahead. How'd I let Coach Wilson talk me into this? Where's Clem? Where's Doris?

I remember I saw the Finish Line tape stretched out across the track. How would I ever keep myself upright? I knew there were runners right behind me! I had to . . .

Coach Wilson was right there, "*You gotta move! Keep moving!*"

Clem was there, too, "*You can do this, son! YOU CAN DO THIS!*"

It was a footrace then, and I fought for every breath. I was blind. I suddenly ran into the tape at the Finish Line and I could hear Clem and my two Coaches all yelling, "*YES, YES, YES!*"

I fell down onto the track. I had tears in my eyes but I had no air in my lungs. I think my teammates picked me up off the track and drug me toward the infield. I couldn't see anything.

I couldn't breathe. There were no thoughts other than "*I need air!*" It was excruciating.

Then Coach Wilson was beside me and he was yelling, "*2 minutes 8 seconds! That's incredible! 2:08! Wow!*"

Clem pushed Coach Wilson aside and I felt him force me to stand, to walk, to breathe. I heard him whisper, "*That's my boy!*" as he and I walked, and then I finally caught my breath.

The next day was Sunday and the Headline in the Sports Junior High section of the Houston Post was: **Rogers Wins Memorial Meet by One Point!**

I knew that Coach Wilson was a happy man. He'd figured out a way for his average Track team to beat 5 better teams. In coach parlance: He'd hit a home run . . .

As Track season came to an end I was getting dressed for school one morning when I heard a knock on my garage door. I opened it and there was Doris with a big grin on her face. She was dressed nicely with her blue Cat Eye glasses and she stepped inside my sacred domain to say, "*Good morning, Kirk! I came out to make a suggestion to you!*"

I said, "*Okay.*"

She was all smiles and happiness, something I was glad to see but . . .

She gushed, "*Why don't you wear that nice new blue dress shirt and those nice new tan pants that we bought at* **FOLEY'S DEPARTMENT STORE?**"

I couldn't remember the last time Doris had tried to influence my choice of attire, so I was amused at her attempt on that day. I asked, "*What's the occasion, Doris? And don't play games! I know you!*"

She shook her head and denied any hidden agendas, "*I don't know what you're talking about! It's such a beautiful day that I thought we all should wear our best and be thankful for the chance to look our best!*"

I smiled and asked her, "*Gee, Doris, can I have chocolate-filled donuts from* **DUNKIN' DONUTS** *for breakfast?*"

What a crock! I gently shoved her out of my door and then proceeded to wear one of my normal, comfortable short-sleeved golf shirts like I always did.

When I arrived at school I had forgotten Doris's little dance since Betsy met me outside where I usually parked my Moped. Her eyes were so bright and happy, I didn't think about Doris.

When Betsy and I arrived at Mrs. Brennan's homeroom, I noticed Velma was also wearing a happy smile and, as I sat down, I mentioned it to her, "*You're looking extremely chipper today, Mrs. Brennan.*"

She smiled and said, "*As usual, you are right as rain, Sir Lancelot!*"

We were reading **THE ONCE AND FUTURE KING** by T.H. White at that time in Velma's English class so I understood her reference, but my radar was totally activated. The important women in my life were sending me messages I couldn't translate. What was going on?

In homeroom we listened to our Principal read the daily school notes and announcements over our Public Address system. He also announced there was a scheduled school assembly that morning in the Auditorium after homeroom, so when the bell rang we followed Mrs. Brennan in a well-behaved line to our assigned seats, and we sat down. The Auditorium was packed.

After a short speech about the credentials of the man we were going to hear, the Principal introduced us to the President of the Texas Humble Oil company. It seemed that when he'd attended Junior High, when he was living in Dallas a long time ago, he'd won an award called **The American Legion Award**.

Humble Oil said, "*Every year Junior High School faculty members are asked to choose, to vote and recognize two students, one boy and one girl, who epitomize the highest quality of Honor, Courage, Scholarship, Leadership, and Service. The attributes I just listed are necessary for the preservation and protection of the fundamental institutions of our Government and the advancement of our Society . . .*"

I was sitting next to Betsy and Chris and I remember I whispered to both of them, "*Somebody wake me up. This is pretty boring . . .*"

Chris laughed and Betsy shushed me, hitting my recently separated shoulder. I remember a flash of pain just as I heard the Humble President say, " . . . *and I'm proud to announce this year's winners are Kirk McClelland and Anne Bible!*"

I heard applause from the assembly audience and laughter from Chris and Betsy.

Velma came up behind me and tapped me on the side of my head, "*Get that winning smile up to the stage, hotshot! And yes, I voted for you!*"

I nodded thanks to her, grinned at Chris and Betsy, and started walking toward the stage.

I was almost there when Clem and Doris stood up next to the aisle and joined me in a hug.

Doris was crying and said, "*The blue shirt would've been nice but I forgive you!*"

Clem shook my hand and said, "*Good job, son! I'm proud of you!*"

After the three-McClelland-hug the rest of the assembly was predictable so I won't dwell on it. My memory of the event was simply that I was lucky my father was there to hear the McClelland name spoken with respect.

I had no idea how lucky I was to win that award.

I had no idea but, in just a few years, my winning this award would be very important for my hunting partner . . .

American Legion Award Winners: Me and Anne Bible

With barely time to catch our breath, our name was about to be seen in a negative light again. I received my award in April of 1964 just as Clem and Ed and Jack were preparing for his Bribery trial. Briscoe and his Monkeys had scheduled June 23 for the trial and Clem had won a change of venue to Marlin, Texas in Falls County to be tried in Judge John C. Patterson's court.

The names of the attorneys who were accused of bribing Clem were Ross Evahn, David Hudson, E.R. Coffey, R.M. Duren, and my friend and Doris's piano player, Bryson Martin.

R. M. DUREN ROSS D. EVAHN DAVID H. HUDSON E. R. COFFEY J. BRYSON MARTIN

THE HOUSTON PRESS *"Bribery Trial"* printed on June 24, 1964

The Devil alleged that bribes were paid to Clem by these five men to the tune of $25,783 to secure their selections as appraisers, administrators, and guardians in probate court activities.

Briscoe had said that each of these five had an agreement with Clem. They had all bribed him for the benefit of themselves with the understanding that Clem's future acts, decisions, judgments, and recommendations would be *influenced*. That was the defining word. It meant that these five men had a cozy agreement in pending and future cases brought before Judge Clem McClelland in his judicial capacity. The evidence of this activity, so sayeth the Devil, was obtained from the public records of the Harris County Probate Court.

To wit: From December 2, 1960, through May, 1962, Judge McClelland had appointed these five attorneys as Appraisers in Estates for a total of 3511 times. In that same period of time, Clem had appointed 257 other persons as Appraisers, and they had acted a total of 2,225 times. If you looked at the math, something looked fishy. But I wasn't present each time Clem made an appointment to one of those 262 (5 plus 257) persons so I withheld passing judgment.

I did remember eight years before when I'd seen Clem give envelopes to Bryson and Guy in Clem's Chamber. What was inside each envelope? If Clem was getting bribes and there was cold hard cash inside those two envelopes, why was he *giving* money instead of *receiving* money? I was confused both at 6 years old and again at 14 years old.

So Clem and Ed and Jack went to Marlin, Texas in Falls County to do further battle with Devil Briscoe and his Monkeys. Marlin was South-Southeast of Waco,

Texas and was best known for its *"Healing Mineral Waters"* which were supposed to cure whatever ailed you. Clem told me when he'd arrived in Marlin he'd tried a glass or two, but all the mineral waters did was intensify his desire for *his* favorite cure, Jack Daniels.

Unfortunately the jury in Falls County was as brittle and gullible as the Belton jury.

The Marlin jury was unimpressed with Clem's denial he'd taken the bribe money and there was no way that the eleven men and one woman could or would do the math. They couldn't see how 5 attorneys could handle 3,511 cases while 257 other attorneys could handle only 2,225 cases.

And anyway, why did this big-shot Judge have to come all the way to Marlin to defend himself for what he'd been caught doing in Houston? They were unmoved when Clem demanded proof be shown that he'd ever taken bribes from these five men. The jurors were equally unimpressed with Clem's attorneys having decided his attorneys were as *Useless* as Judge Clem was *Guilty*.

After an hour of deliberation the jury convicted Clem McClelland, and the judge sentenced him to 5 years confinement in the Huntsville State Penitentiary with a fine of $5,000.

"*Confinement.*" It's a word that isn't used in normal conversation. Confinement to me described an image of Clem being held behind very tall walls and kept in a dark place far removed from the rest of the world. It was hard for me to imagine.

Another word that, until that time, I'd never thought about, "*Concurrent.*" It seemed that instead of the 5 years being added to Clem's previous sentence of 10 years for a total of 15 years, the judge thought it fair to have both sentences be served concurrently.

By definition, *concurrently* means, "*At the same time or simultaneously.*" Back when I was 15 years old and I heard that word for the first time, I wondered about the judge who had decided Clem would serve both of his sentences at the same time. I wondered if the judge thought because of all the humanitarian gifts Clem had given to Houston as a Shriner and as a Deacon, it was time to show Judge Clem a little mercy and just flat out give him a break.

I would have loved to have been a fly on Buzzard-Briscoe's wall when he learned the word *concurrent* was in play. Too bad, Frank. Win some, lose some.

While my sisters used every excuse they could conceive of to not go to school so they could avoid the embarrassment of suffering "*another conviction,*" Doris did her best to keep her McClelland family operating normally. She was brave and courageous. She never showed what I knew she was feeling: Total Dismay.

I tried to entertain Doris with tales of my four best friends (including Betsy because I was still madly in love with her) and she loved hearing about my riding my Moped all over Houston. The construction of the Southwest Freeway was almost complete and it was fun for me to ride my Moped on a brand new roadway where there was no traffic. Occasionally, when Betsy wasn't able to fool her parents, I'd take Mona for a ride over my wide open Freeway lanes, but she didn't like the wind *mussing* her hair. Hmmm.

Betsy and Kirk   **Mona and Kirk**
(*A different kind of Junior High competition*)

One Saturday Doris invited me to join her as she grocery shopped. I noticed how strained her face looked as she drove past the Highland Village shopping center which was closest to home.

I said, "*You know you just passed our supermarket, right?*"

She was distracted and quick to fib, "*Uh, we're going to a different one today. I heard the **Weingarten** produce department is the best, so I thought I'd try it.*" We pulled into the **Weingarten's** market that was right on the edge of River Oaks, the wealthiest community in Houston.

Inside the market Doris and I performed our usual tag team shopping drill where I pushed the cart and she put groceries in it.

As we walked down Aisle 4 she shared the truth, "*I asked you to come with me today so we could have a talk.*"

Uh, oh. I smiled and asked, "*What'd I do wrong?*"

She shook her head, "*Nothing, silly. I'm worried about Clem.*"

She kept placing items in the cart as I kept pushing. She continued, "*All this pressure is causing his Diabetes to get out of control.*"

I didn't know that, so I said, "*I thought he was handling it.*"

She smiled and said, "*I've been watching your father a lot longer than you. Every day he's walking a dangerous tightrope. Too much sugar, he falls off one side. Too much insulin, he falls off the other.*"

She stopped walking and sighed, "*And now he's taking extra shots of insulin to cover the extra Jack Daniels he's drinking. He's getting worse and I'm worried about his health.*"

I nodded and said, "*Oops . . . I did do something wrong!*"

She nodded. "*We're so concerned about him being happy, we're letting him drink too much.*"

I said, "*I'm sorry. I wanted him to be glad about something, anything. A JD shot is easy . . .*"

Doris lifted up her hand as if to wag her finger at me. She stopped herself and we both laughed. It was like I was 5 years old again.

And then she gave it to me straight, "*Alcohol's a Diabetics worst enemy, made even more treacherous because it's sitting right there in his Bar. You and I need to . . .*"

At that moment a Rich Woman with a faux leopard cloche-styled hat (I'll call her *Ms. River Oaks*) pulled her grocery cart in front of Doris, forcing Doris to stop walking.

Ms. River Oaks was very entitled and with a faux smile she said, "*Excuse me, but you're Mrs. McClelland, aren't you?*"

Doris had good instincts and later told me she was on her guard instantly, "*Yes?*"

Ms. River Oaks smiled an even wider faux smile and raised her eyebrows as she said, "*I've seen you and your husband promoting at some Community Fundraiser or other.*"

Doris was really on her guard then, and said, "*Uh-huh.*"

Ms. R. O. persisted, "*So when I saw you, I just had to ask.*"

She gave me a slimy look, then she leaned in toward Doris to smile a heartless smile, "*What's it like to sleep with that obvious crook?*"

I had then, and still have, good reflexes. I saw Doris about to take a swing at this rich pig so I pushed our cart past Doris and into this pretentious bitch's cart, knocking it over to the side.

Ms. River Oaks was appalled by my behavior and cried out, "*How dare you? Do you want me to call for the Manager, young man?*"

I was cool and intense as I replied, "*Be my guest, you hussy . . .*"

The Rich Woman gasped and shouted again, louder, "*HOW DARE YOU!*"

I gave her my best smile, and then I directed our cart and my Doris toward a waiting cashier.

She and I stood there side by side in line, looking sadly at each other.

There was no escape...

 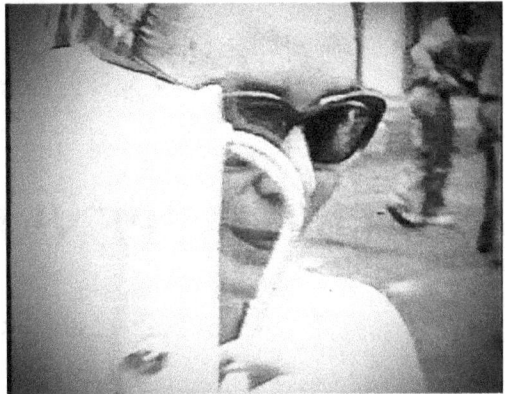

Doris comically hid behind her purse

FOUND GUILTY

Former Harris County probate judge Clem McClelland was found guilty by a Marlin, Tex., jury on a bribery charge and sentenced to five years in prison and fined $5,000.

Clem and Doris endured it all, side by side

CHAPTER SEVEN

WHAT HAPPENED HERE? 1964–1965

Once I realized what The American Legion Award represented, I was glad I'd won. It put the McClelland name back up on the Marquee in a more positive light, and it gave Clem and Doris a reason to be proud of their family. It showed me that I could do good works and maybe have the recognition help our situation. Then, Clem suffered his second conviction.

After Clem's failure to win at his Bribery trial I agreed with The Underwriter about our chasing a dream to have Clem's convictions overturned. The Underwriter warned me that the Appeals process was a waste of time and that the *"appointed"* Appellate judges would soon be overwhelmed with all the different appeals that Ed and Jack were filing. The phrase *"less is more"* from the old 1855 Robert Browning poem never entered their minds.

Why did Ed and Jack think they were smart enough to overwhelm the Appeals system? In my research I found a note in a decision from one of the *"appointed"* Appeals judges, regarding the high volume of McClelland appeals, which said, *"We thank the appellant and his attorneys for keeping us gainfully employed during a lean year."*

That hilarious admission was (and still is) on the public record!

What were Clem's attorneys thinking? Didn't they realize that District Attorney Frank Briscoe would just continue to try Clem on the next indictment? And the next, and the next? Did they forget Briscoe had plenty of time before his 1966 Congressional election, and that Ed and Jack weren't paying for their lawyer time, CLEM WAS?

I realized why Clem wanted to keep appealing. He'd have to leave his family behind and be *"incarcerated"* in the Huntsville State Penitentiary. He'd already lost his judgeship and his license to practice Law. His freedom to live and to love us was all he had left.

BRING CLEM HOME

At the first of June he and I had one of our midnight peanut butter sandwich meetings and he confided in me that he owed Frank Briscoe a debt of gratitude. I shook my head, *"For what? He's taken everything, including my inheritance!"*

I was trying for humor but a dark cloud appeared over Clem's face and his voice faltered, *"I was glad I could be there for your Football and Basketball games as well as for your Track meets. I was there to see you win your American Legion Award. I never could've seen those things if I'd been in my court. Briscoe brought us back our partnership, didn't he?"*

I said, *"Yes, sir, he did but . . ."*

Clem said, *"You're my son. Be aware that when I have to go away, you'll be in charge."*

I didn't know what to say to that, other than to reassure him, *"I'll do whatever you need me to do, Clem. I promise."*

He said, *"I'm counting on it . . ."* and then he reached across the table and shook my hand in a way that I can still feel to this day.

Wow . . . At that moment I realized that Clem had already left the building. His talk with me was his first step toward packing his bags and securing his home before he moved to Huntsville.

It was a sobering moment for me. I was young and clueless about how the real world worked.

Suddenly Clem had made it very real.

Another reality had to be dealt with at the first of June. Clem and I met with a businessman who owned a Construction company amid several other businesses. His name was Charlie Crawford and he smoked a big cigar and drove a very large white *Badillac*. No, that isn't a spelling error. It's just what he called his *"badass Cadillac."*

The reason we met with Charlie was so Clem could negotiate his investing in Charlie's construction company to help the McClelland family with our very real cash flow problem.

With no regular paycheck, Clem and the McClelland family were running on empty in spite of what Mr. Briscoe and his pet Monkeys thought. So Clem reached out to Mr. Crawford to see if he could *invest* in his construction business. Charlie liked Clem a lot so he sold him part of the business and, just like that, I suddenly had a summer job doing construction work.

I was two and a half months away from my two-a-day Football workouts at my new Senior High School so I thought a construction job would be a good way to stay in shape until I began Football again. I was also motivated by the great pay. Charlie looked at me and said, *"Young man, you are fortunate. My workers convinced me last month to give them a raise in their hourly rate, and you're the beneficiary. You get to start at two dollars, sixty-five and a half cents an hour. What do you think about that?"*

What did I know? I'd never had a real job other than the ones that required me to wear a jockey strap and those jobs paid nothing. So $2.65 (and a half cent) sounded pretty good.

The next day was my first work day and I wore thick leather shoes with my normal white socks, blue jeans, and a white T-shirt. I had normal first day jitters and when I saw the crew of workers and the burnt house we were slated to deal with, the sweat began to run off me in waves.

Fortunately Clem had bought me some heavy duty gloves to wear or I'd have been down for the count. My fellow workers had been toiling (they told me) for over a week trying to salvage the walls of a very nice home by removing (wiping) the scorched soot with heavy rags and some special (cheap) chemical compound. I'd had to deal with my ringlets of sweat *and* watery eyes.

After a week of that environment and that labor, I longed for the classroom. I won't share any more details about the next two months other than Clem's investment did create cash flow as he'd hoped it would, and that was good. For me, I was real glad when two-a-days returned. Football and a new coach, Gil Bartosh. A brand new High School, a new beginning, I hoped.

This would be my first of three years at Robert E. Lee Senior High School. All my best Junior High friends were going with me and I even had the luxury of Velma Brennan transferring to Lee where she'd be my full-time Counselor. Velma would also continue to teach me English in her Honors English class. It was one of those special classes where they tried to isolate those that have it, from those who'd disrupt it. I welcomed *it* since I loved Velma's teaching style . . .

Then came the nightmare week when the monster forced Clem away from his home.

I mentioned in the **FOREWORD** of this Book that my happy family would be "*brutally challenged*" and we were. I would have done anything to keep Clem home. Anything.

We all sat at the round table in the Kitchen because the phone sat on the counter next to it. Clem held Doris's hand on one side and Anne's hand with the other. We'd been sitting there waiting for 15 minutes when the phone rang. Doris and Anne and Micki all caught their breaths as Clem released their hands and said, "*Be brave. We knew this day was coming . . .*" He picked up the phone, "*This is Clem McClelland . . .*"

On the other end of the phone line was Warden Carl Jennings who, Clem told us, spoke kindly to him. After they introduced themselves to each other, the Warden explained his call was a courtesy call to inform my father that, since his last appeal had been denied, he expected Clem to report to the Prison at 9 a.m. on Tuesday morning. Clem told Warden Jennings that he understood and that he'd be there "*without fail.*" The Warden told Clem that he looked forward to meeting him and to be sure to drive safely. Clem took a deep breath and said, "*Thanks for your call, Warden.*" And he hung up the phone.

He turned to us and we surrounded him to give him a family hug. Then as a family, we cried. It was a tough day.

Tuesday was a tougher day. Starting early in the morning, the Media encircled the front yard of the McClelland household for the last time. Cameras rolled and Cameras clicked as the Media watched and recorded an event that should've taken place behind closed doors.

Cap Detrick and his photographer waited in front of the house out in the street. He waved at Doris who sat in the Station Wagon in the Carport, waiting for Clem. She didn't wave back.

Micki and Anne stood next to the front passenger side of the Wagon. They both cried.

Josephine and Woodrow both cried as they held the leashes to Oscar and Gigi.

Clem and I stood inside the front door to our home and Clem spoke softly to me so our talk would be private, "*Cliché time, Master Kirk.*" Shades of Josephine. I tried to smile, "*Behind every dark cloud?*"

I watched my father. He was very brave given the circumstance, and he said, "*Not that one, this one . . . You're the Man of the House now. I expect you to act accordingly. I don't want anyone to see you do something and say, 'Oh, he's like that because of his father!'*"

I remember I tried to be witty, to keep him talking so I could keep him there with me forever, "*So you want me to be bad on my own, with no connection to you, right?*"

He smiled his strongest, bravest smile, "*Exactly.*"

Ever since the Warden called, I'd been struggling to ask Clem, "*Serious for a minute?*" He nodded. "*How will we pay the bills while you're gone?*"

I saw him fight himself in order to maintain himself, "*Don't lose sleep over that. I've made arrangements for everything. Just help your mother in any way you can. That's all I want you to worry about. Keep making A's and catch that Football and never come in second when you run the 880!*"

I felt moisture in both of my eyes, "*I can't worry about you, right?*"

Still brave, "*There's no need to worry. I have friends who'll help me while I'm inside.*"

It was getting tougher to stay tearless as he shook my hand and hugged me goodbye, "*You be my good boy, okay? We'll write to each other and before too long you and your mother can come visit me . . .*" He carefully patted my hurt right shoulder as he turned to walk away from me. I was emotionally limp and I used the front door to hold me up. I shouted, "*We'll come visit you soon!*"

He didn't turn but waved to me over his shoulder as he walked to the car. He stopped to say "*Good-bye*" to Josephine and Woodrow, and he knelt down to pat his dogs.

Then he hugged his girls. Both couldn't say anything but they gave brave and strong hugs.

As he turned to enter the car, Cap Detrick yelled to him, "*Hey, Judge!*"

Clem turned and Cap's photographer shot his picture for the evening paper's headline story.

Clem slid into the passenger side of the Station Wagon and closed his door. Doris drove away from the Carport and out onto Ivanhoe Street. Doris honked one time and drove away.

We all stood on the front lawn, watching the car disappear. We all cried.

It was a bad day. The worst day of my life, period.

When Doris returned from her journey to and from Huntsville, she seemed preset to tell us about Clem's positive attitude, about how pretty the Huntsville Prison layout was, and how the guards who walked Clem in through the gate were "*extremely courteous and just plain nice!*"

I didn't expect to see a smile on her face but there it was. And I didn't believe it for a second. I looked at Micki . . . She didn't believe it either. I looked at Anne, and then I understood. Anne was Doris and Clem's main concern and Doris told me later that Anne had been their main topic of discussion during their drive. Clem said to Doris, "*You tell Anne that in your opinion her Daddy will do fine here as long as she doesn't worry. Have her help you around the house.*" The *help around the house* direction was due to Josephine and Woodrow no longer being on the payroll. Clem figured the money he'd paid them would be better used for groceries and so he'd been forced to let them go. This would be hard on Doris.

It also meant that on weekends I'd have to mow and edge the front and back lawns, weed all the flower beds, and replace light bulbs when and where needed. Everything changed at home. Since Micki was now studying at Temple University in Philadelphia, Anne had to help Doris keep the house clean as well as do the laundry, wash the dishes and help Doris do the shopping.

My playing Football shrank my available time for Betsy and Mona. Betsy understood, but Mona was high maintenance and too much trouble, just when I needed *less* trouble.

That first week, after Clem left, I sold my Moped and used $350 from the proceeds to purchase a used Ford Comet. It was my first car and I liked driving it anywhere I could meet Betsy. Since it had no console she could sit in the front seat next to me. It had a gear shift "*3 on the tree*" transmission, and was painted a Peter Pan green color, which brought back memories . . .

That first week I wrote my first letter to Clem hoping it'd be delivered in a timely fashion with none of my thoughts blacked out (censored) by the prison's readers. I wanted to create a "*literary channel*" that he and I could share so he'd be able to look forward to future messages.

My alarm clock showed 2:15 a.m. I lay in bed, thinking about everything. I looked on my bedside table where there was a picture of Clem standing with me. We had our arms opened wide to celebrate my new garage stronghold. We both looked happy. I slid out of bed and picked up a copy of the Houston Post Sports Section where I'd cut out a story for Clem. The headline read: **Tomlin Future QB for Robert E. Lee** and there was a picture of Tom Tomlin with the story.

I picked up my legal pad and I began to write, "*Dear Clem: Let me introduce you to Tom Tomlin, the Quarterback who'll throw me touchdown passes this coming season. In practice this past week he and I really connected. Velma Brennan asked me to say hello to you—she's been a big help. Betsy still loves my singing.*

What else to say? I miss you and I'm counting the days when I'll be able to come see you . . ."

I sat there a few moments trying to decide how I should sign it . . . "*Sincerely*" didn't feel right. "*Yours truly*" was gay before we even knew what *gay* meant. "*Your Duck Blind Partner*" would probably confuse the Huntsville censors. So I ended it with, "*Love from your Best Son, Kirk!*" since that's who I was. For every letter I wrote while he was inside, I'd end it that way.

On the day that I put that letter in our mailbox addressed to Clem McClelland c/o Huntsville State Prison, 815 Twelfth Street, Huntsville, Texas 77348, I received his first letter to me. It read, "*Hey Boy . . . Good morning or Good evening (since you probably just got home from Football practice). I've been learning the rules and regs of the unit I'm in and I think I will be a model prisoner. The only tough part is not being able to see and talk to you every day, so I want us to stay connected through these letters, okay? I want to thank you for all you've had to suffer with my trials and the phone calls and news stories and people trampling all over your freshly cut lawn (don't forget to turn off the gasoline valve when the mower's not in use!).*

You and I have always told each other the truth so I wanted to share with you . . .
The next line was completely blacked out by the censors:

███

Then his letter continued, "*I have in my conscience and in my heart the facts of the cases against me and the facts are that I am not guilty. So here I am now living in Huntsville prison in the "Walls Unit," that's a nickname for the red brick walls that adorn the main buildings here.*"

"*I've made friends with the guards in my cellblock and I'm confident that I'll be safe. I'll share more later. For now, take care of yourself, kiss your girl Betsy, and say hello to Velma B. for me. Your hunting partner, Clem.*"

I sat on my bed, happy to hear from Clem and frustrated by low brow censors acting like they were protecting state secrets by blocking what my father wanted to share with me. Oh, man. This wouldn't be easy for me. I felt brain-cuffed by people I'd never meet, at a time when I needed more than ever to talk to my dad. His stress had become my stress. It was painful.

It was at this time that Cap Detrick decided to publish an interview with Doris that one of his female co-workers had written several months before. He took credit for it, of course.

My favorite line of "theirs" was, "*In the past she had been a warm and forceful woman. Now, for the first time, the force has been converted into anger that burns and flames publicly.*" What'd you expect, Cap? Thank-you notes? Give her a break--Her man's confined in jail!

MRS. CLEM McCLELLAND
What about the children?

Serenity Becomes Strain for McClelland's Wife

by Cap Detrick
Press Staff Writer

The strain is beginning to show on the wife of Probate Judge Clem McClelland.

When the court of inquiry into her husband's financial and judicial affairs began, Mrs. McClelland was a portrait of serenity.

As the hearing in Justice W. C. Ragan's courtroom progressed, her confidence was punctuated with sorrow, bitterness and anger.

Silence, Then . . .

Before court and during recesses, she spoke in "flash-floods" of words. First, she shook her head slowly and said:

"There is nothing I wish to say . . ."

She fell silent a moment. And, then, without preface, she discussed her three teenaged children. Said Mrs. McClelland:

"What can I tell them?"

"My own father died when I was 16.

"I keep telling them they'll get their father back when this is all over. That's all I've been able to say. They have a live father . . .

"Our boy went to play baseball the other night.

"One of the other boys talked to him about the district attorney — about Frank Briscoe.

"The boy told my son, 'My daddy knows Briscoe and he says your daddy doesn't have a chance.'

"My son came home and told me about it. He also said Mother, I hit a three-bagger right after that.'"

The Houston Press story on September 10, 1964

I know that the beginning of September '64 was tough on Doris, but it was hard on me too. I was at a new school, I had a History test to study for, a new scouting report I had to study for our first Football game of the season, I needed to buy a gift for Betsy's birthday, and in spite of what Clem said about his being safe, I was worried about his survival.

Clem was a diabetic. Doris told me he'd have to let the prison doctors inject his insulin for him daily. He'd been injecting himself for over fourteen years and suddenly he was at the mercy of someone else administering to his diabetic needs. I remembered his taking shots whenever he wanted/needed to and suddenly he'd have to ask for or schedule his dosages with someone else?

Another concern for me dealt with his not eating what he wanted to. In my next letter to him I'd ask if I could send him some premade peanut butter sandwiches, but what he really needed was an icebox (refrigerator) inside his cell. I wondered if that was even possible.

Another concern: his insulin shocks. Whenever he had one, he looked drunk or like he was on drugs (more accurate since insulin *is* a drug). His body sometimes shook and he said things.

I worried about the prison population seeing Clem in shock due to low blood sugar, and misinterpreting what he said or did. If Clem wasn't stable and said or did something that sounded or looked hostile, Clem would be in danger. So in that peanut butter letter, I'd be sure to suggest that Clem spread the word about his condition.

The truth: We needed to bring Clem home as soon as we possibly could. We needed to connect with someone who could start doing the necessary legwork to legally get him a parole. I was sure Ed and Jack were working on it but I was unimpressed with their track record.

I remember wishing The Underwriter would call. He'd know who to contact and he'd know what to say. In the meantime I made sure I kept making good grades so my teachers realized I was on a mission to be the best I could be to help my family survive in a difficult time.

Every night when I came home from practice, Doris would have my dinner waiting and she'd put it on a plate, then sit down and quiz me on my day: my two girlfriends, how my car was driving, how Gil Bartosh was coaching, what I was reading in Velma's class, how Steve and Chris were doing, and how I was mentally handling the fact that Clem was behind bars.

She delivered my food to our round Kitchen table where I sat, and she said, *"I've known you your whole life, and I know you're tired and up to your ears with all the things going on. I see that you're suffering. I know you miss him as much as I do, and that's why I'm worried about how this will affect you. Please know that I'm working behind the headlines so we can bring him home as soon as possible."*

I said with my eyebrows raised, "*Well, hello, Doris! When were you planning on sharing this little tidbit? I was just thinking we needed to kick Ed and Jack's ass to get them moving and here you're saying it's already in the works?*"

She reached over and playfully slapped my head, "*Don't say 'ass'!*" I nodded "*Just know that I'm doing lots of research to find the right path to use to get him out of . . .*" She stopped before saying '*that horrible place*' but I knew where she was going. "*I still have contacts downtown and access to the Law Library at the courthouse thanks to Helen Smith. I'm using her card with her blessing. And she said to say Hello to you.*"

So it seemed I had underestimated the women in Clem's life. Doris and Helen were both on the job with one mission in mind: Bring Clem Home! Well, hot damn! The question then on the table was *how?* Doris told me, "*There are several organizations whose sole purpose is to free inmates from jail. For Clem to have their help he has to prove he's worthy of their efforts and if he is . . .* (she cleared her throat) *a good prisoner, he'll benefit from their experience with the Texas prison system.*"

I asked, "*What does that mean?*"

She answered, "*There is paperwork that I have to fill out that's equal to a dissertation for a doctorate degree. It's very complex, about 2 inches thick, and it's meant to scare away most people from dealing with it. Well, I'm not most people and the only thing I'm scared of is not having Clem here with his family.*" She started to mist up but stopped herself and continued, "*We, you and I, will show that devil Briscoe that he chose the wrong man to mess with. Clem is no pushover. We're going to make it look like we're playing by their rules, and then we'll sneak around and use the right language and take the right steps to get where we have to get.*"

By this time my tongue was hanging out. I asked her, "*Which is . . . where?*"

Doris sat up straighter in her chair and answered, "*The Court of Criminal Appeals, where we'll request they grant him an early release . . .*"

I nodded and asked, "*And they'd grant that grant because . . . ?*"

Doris said, "*That's what I'm going to figure out. There are cases on file and that's where the research becomes necessary. It will be a slow process but I know I can do it.*"

My turn to cheerlead, "*And so you shall . . .*" I laid my hand on her arm and saw the fire in her eyes as she calculated the length of time she'd have to spend in the library stacks doing research.

I changed the subject just a bit when I asked, "*Have you decided when I get to visit Clem?*"

Doris answered, "*The timing's not right yet. As soon as I can, I'll make it happen, okay?*"

I said, "*Okay, and thanks for the food.*" Green beans, mash potatoes, and pork chops.

Doris looked like she was glad for the subject change, "*I made your favorite. It's not brain food, but it tastes good.*"

I said, "*I wish I had a better appetite. Sometimes practice takes it away . . .*"

Doris the Coach said, "*Gotta keep in shape if you want to play varsity, Mac!*"
Kirk the Player said, "*I will; I do!*"
I knew what was coming.

Whenever I ate postpractice vittles, Doris would try to surprise me with her famous Fake Vomit Face. Suddenly there it was! We both laughed. I tried to keep eating as I shook my head at her. Doris said, "*You're right! I'm sorry!*" as she Fake Vomited again.

I laughed and yelled at her, "*STOP IT!*"

You guessed it: A nightly event. As she kept doing it, I kept eating and we kept laughing.

I was officially in the tenth grade. I was almost sixteen years old, and I played Football, and I made good grades. When I graduated, I planned to go to The United States Military Academy at West Point. I was prime West Point material. Hmmm, where'd all that come from?

Every Thanksgiving since the beginning of time, Clem and I would go to my Uncle Chalmer's ranch near San Antonio to hunt Deer, shoot Quail, and play Poker. Chalmer was Clem's older brother and he owned a 5,400-acre ranch near George West, Texas that was filled with ugly mesquite, tumbling tumbleweeds, Javelinas, and Coyotes as well as the deer and quail.

While we hunted and slept at Chalmer's ranch, Clem and I met some of his friends. They were important and retired Colonels, Admirals, Majors, and Generals that Chalmer had met at West Point and during World War II when he became a Colonel while fighting in the Pacific.

By day I hunted with Generals and Colonels and they all had fantastic war stories to share. In the evenings as my Uncle's cook prepared what we'd shot that day, I heard about the Point and how military strategy and battlefield tactics were taught there every day to every cadet.

**Clem's older brother
Chalmer Kirk McClelland**

At the Colonel's ranch my fondest memory was simply sitting at the Colonel's table listening to men who'd successfully commanded troops in battle. My young ears rode high with their stories of specialized troops deployed over various campaigns. My young mind conjured questions and I was never held silent by adult or military protocol since all I wanted to hear were answers. And the answers I heard on those Thanksgiving nights still move me to this day.

There were other reasons why a military career appealed to me. I'd lie in bed and try to put faces on the men who had been described to me and ultimately I'd see the face of John Wayne. His war movies like **SANDS OF IWO JIMA** and **THE FLYING TIGERS** and **BACK TO BATAAN** were classic screen epics and they inspired me to study at the Point and learn how to lead men into battle. Another reason: every cadet at West Point was paid a monthly salary while he received a free education. To me that was way better than having to pay for school. Finally, I knew that I'd never be a nine-to-five office worker and after seeing what happened to Clem, there was no way I'd have anything to do with the law.

I also wouldn't pursue some professional calling or uninspired business career. Not when there were troops to be led, battles to be fought, and victories to be won. So the more I talked to Uncle Chalmer and the more I talked to Clem and Doris, the more I thought West Point would be a good fit for me.

For West Point to even consider me I had to have an appointment from a Congressman. Clem had a friend for many years named Robert Casey who said he'd appoint me. 'Bob' Casey held the Twenty-Second Congressional District office in Houston for the House of Representatives from 1959-1976 and in 1964, when I asked him to appoint me, he sent me a letter that said,

"I applaud your ambition, Kirk. Keep making those good grades and if I'm still your Congressman when you graduate, I'll give you the appointment. Please remember that my appointment will only allow you to compete for entry. Nothing is automatic, but having met you and knowing your parents for as long as I have, I'll predict you will certainly become a proud member of the Long Gray Line."

When I shared with my counselor, Velma Brennan, that I was bound for West Point she was positive as usual and advised me,

"I know how you feel about doing everything full speed ahead, Mr. Mac. If having to compete with the best of the best will keep you straight and sober then I agree with Mr. Casey. Keep making your grades and competing in sports to prove you're not afraid of additional activities. Show whoever's looking that you're a doer who thrives on it."

I said, *"Well, I don't really thrive on it, Mrs. Brennan. I just do it."*

She laughed her Velma laugh, *"Do yourself a favor and keep that secret a secret, okay?"*

Our coach for the Robert E. Lee "*Generals*" was Gil Bartosh and he was a great Football player and a great coach. He was known as the "*Granger Ghost*" because of the way he scored touchdowns during fog-shrouded High School games on Friday nights in Granger, Texas.

I learned how to play Football under Coach Bartosh. He was in his midthirties and an inspiration to everyone but Larry Klump who didn't listen to anybody's rules. Someone forgot to define the word "*Coach*" to Klump, so he and Gil Bartosh never dealt from the same deck.

One cold and rainy afternoon Gil decided he was going to *toughen up* his team by running each of us through a *Bull in the Ring* drill. We all hated the Bull drill: One player stood in the middle of six players who surrounded him. Coach Bartosh then blew his whistle and pointed at one of the six players who made up the ring. When a player got the nod, he attacked the player in the middle and then quickly backed out. The Bull in the ring had to stay loose and quickly adjust by turning around to defend himself and stay on his feet.

It was a good drill because it *did* toughen us up and strengthened our reflexes and helped us to learn our center of gravity.

But it was raining, and we were getting frostier the wetter we got. We all wanted to *hit* the showers and drink hot chocolate but Coach Bartosh was smiling at us and saying things like, "*Hit him harder!*" and "*Did he ring your bell, Mac?*" referring to me of course, and, yes Coach, he *did* ring my bell. I lost consciousness once during practicesand it happened during the Bull drill.

On that wet afternoon it was Larry Klump's turn to be the Bull. He was larger than his other teammates who were attacking/hitting him when Gil pointed at them, but he didn't like being on the receiving end of a beatdown. After three or four hits, he was starting to lose it. That's when a player named David Davis got the nod from the coach, and Davis hit Larry hard in his back. Klump hit the ground and yelled loudly as he ripped off his helmet and charged Davis who removed his helmet just in time for a major smashup. All the rest of us in the ring started grabbing both players so there wouldn't be additional bodily harm when Klump shouted, "*You dipshit! You think you can hit me that hard from behind and not pay?*"

Gil "*the Granger Ghost*" Bartosh

Coach Bartosh wasn't a big man. In his day he was a Running Back best known for getting away from large Tackles and Guards, not for going head to head with them. So when he blew his whistle and then grabbed Larry Klump by his shoulder pads and pulled him away from David Davis, I was impressed. Coach spit out his whistle and hissed at Larry, "*I've warned you about your mouth, Mr. Klump.*"

Klump, innocent, protested, "*I called him a dip stick, Coach! That's not a cuss word!*"

Coach Bartosh smiled, "*You're right! I was born yesterday, Larry. Give me 20!*"

Klump looked at Coach with hatred and I saw him as he thought about doing something stupid. But then he hit the ground and started pumping pushups, switching back and forth from watching Coach to watching David Davis the whole time.

After a long hot shower I drove my Comet home in time to see our mailman drop off a letter from Clem into our mailbox. I parked in the driveway and snatched his letter from amongst various junk mail parcels and ran around the Carport to my garage room.

Once inside I sliced open the envelope that held his letter with an opener that Helen Smith had given me with "*Judge Clem McClelland*" inscribed on its handle. The letter read, "*Hi Boy . . . Thanks for sending me a copy of your Scouting Report for your upcoming game with WALTRIP High School. I liked the notes on the best defensive players and offensive players and their team's specific "best plays." It looks to me like your Coach Bartosh is pretty sharp and I hope you learn from his battlefield tactics on the Football field and maybe use his attack plan in future warfare stratagems. Why not, right?*"

"*I think you should consider.*

▬▬▬▬▬▬▬▬▬▬▬▬▬▬▬▬▬▬▬▬▬▬▬▬▬▬▬▬▬▬▬▬▬▬▬▬▬▬

On my end I've had some productive conversations with other prisoners here and I don't know if the censors will allow me sharing what I've learned . . . but here goes:

There are rules for surviving in prison and the most obvious one is Respect Other Inmates. It's not smart to say or do anything that could offend anyone else.

Another one: Follow The Golden Rule. Another one: Don't steal. The word is that stealing can get you killed faster here than any other act.

This next one will make you laugh: Don't Cut in Line! Seriously, the other morning I saw

▬▬▬▬▬▬▬▬▬▬▬▬▬▬▬▬▬▬▬▬▬▬▬▬▬▬▬▬▬▬▬▬▬▬▬▬▬▬

Some good news: I've finally been assigned a job. There are some inmates who prefer to sit around. Not your dad. I want to contribute to whatever society I'm part of. I've been assigned to kitchen duty and it makes sense. I've got orange juice and fruit close by so, if I have insulin problems, I can balance my act."

"*I hope you're helping your mother with her daily life. Be there for me, Kirk. I want you to be extra sensitive on this so I can keep my sanity. It breaks my heart every time I think of her looking around our home for me to talk to or watch a TV show with. I'm counting on you . . .*

Good luck when you play WALTRIP! Your hunting partner, Clem."

Just as I finished reading Clem's letter the phone rang. I was hoping it'd be Betsy but instead it was the deep growling voice of The Underwriter saying, "*Hello, Kirk.*"

I responded tentatively like I always did, "*Hello . . . again. What's happening?*"

His low voice said, "*I'm calling to see how you're doing. Is everything working out?*"

I answered truthfully, "*I don't know what you expect to hear. I don't know who you are. I don't know what to call you. Why don't you tell me your name?*"

He growled and chuckled, "*I can't. I'm concerned about you. This is how I stay in touch.*"

Why was he concerned about me? Why was I still talking to this spook? I asked him, "*Why do you care about me?*"

As usual he chuckled, but then he said, "*I know what's happening with you . . . I know how frustrated you are, how angry you are. I know because the same thing happened to me.*"

That was new. I started to ask, "*Your father . . .*" and he interrupted me, "*My father was found guilty and sentenced to twenty-five years for a crime . . .* (He hesitated) *He was killed in a cellblock fight during his second year. Prison is a dangerous environment. You need to tell Clem to stay safe.*"

He was scaring me with his story but I had to ask, "*What did your father do?*"

The Underwriter said, "*I won't call again. Just know there's someone out there who feels like you do, Kirk. Take care to have a productive life.*" and then he hung up.

I was worn out. I'd suffered a cold and wet *Bull in the Ring*, and I'd been blessed by a letter from Clem in jail, and a cryptic call from someone I didn't know who showed more compassion to me than my closest relatives. I hadn't heard boo from any of my Uncles, their wives, or any of my first cousins concerning *my* losing Clem. The Underwriter had talked to me about *my* loss, and that made him okay in my book.

It was Sunday afternoon and we were playing touch Football on our previous Football field at T.H. Rogers. No pads, no helmets, no cheerleaders. This was Football for fun. The object was to play for points and each of us had to block and run as fast as possible to win those points. On the field were Steve Taylor, Chris Hale, David Davis, Wright Moody, Tim Toler, Hunt Reynolds, me, and Tom Tomlin.

Tomlin called a *Stop and Go* play where I had to run 10 yards, stop, and then run as fast as humanly possible for the goal line so Tom could throw the ball over the opposing team's heads into my waiting arms.

He threw it perfectly, I caught it, and I scored.

The player covering me was Tim Toler and, as usual, he whined, "*C'mon, Mac, I touched you long before you scored!*"

I smiled and tossed the ball back to Tomlin, "*Sorry Timothy, with only one hand. It takes two, baby!*"

As usual everyone offered their opinions. It was a normal whinefest ending with all eight of us looking and laughing at each other. C'mon, it was Sunday and a beautiful day.

Out on the street a new yellow Pontiac GTO Convertible rolled up and parked. There were two large passengers and one of them was Larry Klump. As the two of them exited the GTO we could see they were dressed in suits for Church. They walked over the Football field to join us.

Klump had his regular full mouth grin spread across his face as he walked straight up to David Davis and pushed him, hard. Davis wasn't small but he stepped back as Klump cackled, "*Well hello, Mr. David Davis! So glad to see you today!*"

Klump kept pushing him and talking trash, "*I didn't see you in Church today, Davey! You might want to say a quick prayer!*"

Klump was still pushing him as David tried to hold his ground, "*Back off, Larry!*"

Klump with a bigger grin said, "*Time to pay the Klumpster, Davey, boy! You take cheap shots all the time . . .*"

He wagged his finger at David, "*. . . but not with me!*"

Klump then hit David in his face with his fist, as hard as he could, and David went down.

I liked and admired David. He was a good Football player and a good pitcher for Lee's baseball team. So I couldn't just stand by. My instincts shouted at me that this was wrong. I didn't think. I got involved. As I mentioned before I was thin, Larry was big but I moved fast and suddenly I was standing in front of David like a shield against a large, angry monster.

I spoke calmly, and with poise like my Speech and Debate teacher had tried to show me, "*Not today, Klump. Yeah, you're big and tough, but get lost. You're ruining a good game.*"

As I stood there I was reminded of the Bugs Bunny cartoon **Bully for Bugs** where Bugs stood in front of a huge angry bull with big red eyes and smoke coming out of his ears as he prepared to ram Bugsy.

Like a bull seeing red Larry grabbed my sweatshirt and tried to force me to the ground. Thanks to my isometric and isotonic drills (introduced to me by Coach Bartosh) Larry didn't quite have the strength advantage he'd expected. He and I were face to face, both breathing hard as we tried to gain control over the other. Neither of us spoke. This was physical.

While we wrestled that way, Klump's friend had run back to his GTO out of my sightline. Klump pivoted trying to find a better angle so he could take me down. His breathing was labored as he tore my sweatshirt. I smiled at him as I tore his dress shirt and then I pushed him away so I could raise my fists. I still didn't see Klump's friend but Klump did. He grinned and put his hands on his hips as his friend snuck up behind me and jammed a Colt .45 handgun under my chin. He hissed, *"If you wanna fight, what say we use this?"*

At that moment I saw all of my fellow players freeze. I joined them. The gun felt cold on my sweaty neck and it looked like a cannon. Clem had received a .45 just like it when he'd served with the Coast Guard during World War II and I remembered he let me shoot it once.

It had a kick, and it was loud.

I heard Klump laugh and I watched him take the gun from his friend and point it at my face. Klump, still smiling, shoved me roughly to the ground. I was about to stand back up when Klump leaned over me and angrily said, *"If I were you, convict, I'd stay the hell down!"*

He tilted the gun and pointed it down at my crotch. I saw Steve and Chris start to move.

I lifted my hand and unsteadily said, *"Hold still, Steve. You, too, Chris."*

Klump held the .45 pointed there for several long seconds and then he tossed the gun to his friend. They laughed and patted each other on the back as they walked to their yellow GTO.

Steve and Chris extended their arms to me to help me stand up. I was shaking as I looked around at my team mates. Steve and Chris were the only ones who had tried to help me when I had tried to help David. Speaking of David, I stood there waiting for him to say thank you or *"I'm sorry you stuck your neck out for me."* All I saw him do was look down at his shoes.

Having experienced a gun pointed at my manhood for too damn long, I was in a blind rage. I turned away from my *friends* and I ran to my Comet. If the Comet had had any power I would have peeled out to send my friends a message about how freaked out I was. Clem had advised me to always make sure I knew who I could count on in an alley fight. I was outraged by their fear of the idiotic Larry Klump, and how this stupid incident had made me feel lonely.

I pulled up to our Carport at 4514 Ivanhoe and I parked and exited my Comet.

I ran through the Kitchen door and into Clem and Doris's Master Bedroom. Doris wasn't there and that was good since I didn't want to answer any questions about why I was rummaging through Clem's closet and the drawers in his Dressing Room. I found shirts and suits and shoes and pants and classic Playboy magazines. Under a pile of socks I found what I was looking for.

It was Clem's .45 Colt, identical to the one Klump and his friend had pointed at me. I held Clem's gun in my hands and I can't share the anger I still felt. It was beyond size or measure.

I took Clem's gun and I moved quickly through the downstairs of the house. I took up a position at the Living Room window. I was tense as I looked left, then right. I heard Anne coming down the stairs so I hid the gun behind the window curtains.

Anne sarcastically called out to me, "*How's Mister Perfect today?*"

I responded with my regular perfect wit, "*Still squaring my hypotenuse, big sister*" which usually shut her up. She walked away.

I remained at the window, gun in hand, waiting and watching for a yellow GTO.

After a long time I saw Steve drive up to the house and park in the Carport. I moved to the Kitchen door and stepped outside to join him.

I was still in shock from that afternoon but I'd known Steve forever. I asked him, "*What's up Cecil?* (I'd called him that because it was his father's first name and it always made me laugh. Sometimes I shortened it to '*CC*'. . .).

He tried to look me in the eyes but it was hard for him. He said, "*Hey, Mac, listen. I, uh, came by to apologize.*"

I responded quickly, "*Don't sweat it. We're copacetic.*"

He was downcast and his eyes kept moving away from mine, "*It just happened so fast. You jumped right in. I stood there with my dick in my hand.*"

I raised my eyebrows, "*I thought that was a Popsicle stick.*"

Steve was relieved by me making a joke, and he asked, "*So you forgive me?*"

I was relaxing for the first time that day so I tried another joke, "*Just be sure the next time the ugly Klumpster pulls a gun, you step in front of me and give him a better target.*"

We leaned against the Comet. I needed to talk to him more than he needed my forgiveness, "*I'm glad you came by. I wanted to yak about something.*"

Steve was always happiest when he could be helpful, "*Speak to me, Clementine.*"

I shared, "*I had a dream a few nights ago. I was a bank robber and I shot anyone and everyone who got in my way.*"

Steve was swift to say, "*Sounds like a normal teenage wet dream to me, Mac.*"

I took a deep breath and hiked up my shirt so I could show him Clem's .45 Colt.

Steve gasped, "*Whoa! What are you doing with that?*"

I answered, "*This thing with Klump today. I've been standing at the window waiting, hoping he'd show up so I could blow him away.*"

Steve freaked out, "*Whoa again, Mac. You're kidding me, right?*"

I answered, "*I wish I was.*" I pulled out the gun, "*I've been shooting this gun all day in my head.*"

Steve didn't know what to say, so with wide eyes, he said, "*Jeez, Mac!*"

I continued, "*That jerkoff pointed a gun at me, Steve. Exactly like this one.*"

Steve began to see how serious I was and he pleaded, "*Hey, c'mon, Mac! You need to get real here. You're one of the good guys. You're not Klump. You need to put that thing away!*"

I hefted it up and I really looked at it. I was still mad as hell and if Mr. Klump had come looking for me I was pretty sure I'd have shot a hole in him.

But for Cecil's sake, I said, *"Yeah . . . Okay . . . Hey, you know, I've had this in my hand all day and I never checked to see if it was even loaded!"*

A lie. Of course I'd checked it. Clem had taught me proper handgun usage.

I laughed a fake laugh trying to comfort Steve but, from the look on his face, I don't think he knew who I was or where I was coming from. Well, golly, Steve. Me neither.

After we finished our talk Steve went home and I hid the .45 inside a tool box in my garage. Then I combed my hair, brushed my teeth and changed my clothes for a date I'd planned with Betsy. It was Sunday night and I was meeting her at her Church.

She'd told her parents she and her best friend were taking Sunday Night Communion but she was really going to meet me. I pulled the Comet up to the bench where she sat in the Church's parking lot and when she opened the Comet's front door and moved to my mouth with a serious full-on French kiss, I caught my breath and said, *"Thanks, Elizabeth! I needed that!"*

Betsy had suffered a lot over the past year as she and I tried to make our relationship work. She'd put up with me worrying about Clem, and she'd put up with her father watching her every move to be sure she and I never connected. Ha! Her father didn't understand the basics of young love but since I'd fouled out and was ineligible to play, I wasn't going to explain it to him.

The next kiss was totally mine. Her smile and the way she looked at me were heavenly.

I whispered, *"Heavens to Betsy!"* and she laughed an adorable laugh.

I repeated what I'd already asked her, whispering, *"Will you marry me?"*

She laughed like she always did and whispered back, *"Only if your father walks me down the aisle!"*

I smiled and nodded at her as we played with the concept. *"I'll ask the Huntsville Warden to perform our ceremony and to deliver us unto each other, but only if we can use the prison conjugal van afterward!"*

She laughed and punched my hurt right shoulder. Ow! In pain I said, *"I'll sing* **MOONLIGHT BECOMES YOU** *but only if you sing* **HIGH NOON!**"

She continued, *"I want to honeymoon at Alcatraz* (it had closed the year before) *and sleep in the same cell as Al Capone!"*

I said, *"You are a very funny lady, aren't you?"*

I didn't wait to hear her answer as I kissed her with my full-on tongue in her beautiful and delicious mouth. It was like we were praying in her Church. Me marry her? Absolutely!

Football season shifted to Basketball season and just as I was about to compete in my first Track season for Robert E. Lee, I started losing significant weight. Doris didn't notice at first since I was always eating, playing and sweating. But then she and I used her scale. We looked at my weight and I'd lost 25 pounds since the last time I'd checked it.

Doris said, *"I'll make an appointment for you to see Dr. Nicosia."*

Dr. Nicolas Nicosia had been my doctor since the day I was born. He'd delivered me, he'd taken out my tonsils, given me an appendectomy, and he'd also accompanied Clem and me several times when we'd gone duck and goose hunting in Katy, Texas. I remembered one dark and cold morning sitting in our duck blind when Dr. Nicosia commented to Clem, *"Judge, I don't know about you but it's colder than my ex-wife's tit in here. When do we go back to your place and have a hot J D toddy?"*

I remembered his reference to his ex-wife's tit when Doris said his name and I smiled, but it was a pain to have to go to his office on Westheimer Road so he could give me a blood test. In those days checking my blood sugar level was a lot harder. First, there was Nurse Nancy. As I stood on Doctor Nick's professional scale in their hallway, Nancy gave me the story, *"At your last checkup you weighed 150 pounds . . ."*

Her hand knocked the counter weight on the beam from 150 to 125 pounds where it stopped.

". . . so you've lost twenty-five pounds." Well duh, Nancy. I already knew that.

Secondly, Doris and I sat in Doctor Nick's private office as he studied my results, *"I have your blood test results here and I have good and bad news. The good news is Doris knows how to treat diabetics, thanks to Clem."*

I looked at my mother and she sighed when she heard the good news.

Doctor Nick then said, *"The bad news is I don't understand how this could have happened to Kirk."*

He smiled at me and then shook his head, *"Diabetes usually skips a generation. Clem has it, now you have it. Something else must have broken down to bring it on. I don't get it . . ."*

He led us out of his office as he continued talking to Doris, *"I've contacted Memorial Hospital and they're waiting there for you to deliver Kirk. As quickly as possible, Doris, okay?"*

Unhappily, she nodded.

I remember riding shotgun as Doris drove my thin, diabetically unwell body over hill and dale to reach the Hospital as quickly as possible.

Doris was upset, thinking she had somehow let me down and that my damaged physical health was her mistake. She drove fast as she cried, *"It's all my fault! I've been too distracted! Dear God!"*

I didn't know what to say except to acknowledge things were changing again.

I looked out the car window and noticed our speed as we moved past car after car.

Doris sniffed and said, *"Forgive me. You know you're my favorite son. Wait! You're my ONLY son!"*

We both laughed. What else was there to do?

She sighed, "*I'm so sorry, Kirk!*"

I rolled down my window, stuck my head out and started making Siren noises with my mouth. It was fun and the wind felt good against my face.

Doris laughed and yelled, "*Louder!*"

I increased my volume and Doris sped through several traffic lights as cars honked at us . . .

As we were checking in at the Hospital's main lobby I heard the Head Nurse mention Dr. Nicosia's name and I also heard the reason I was being checked in, "*Blood Sugar at 500 mg/dl.*"

I would learn that my sugar level was very high and I'd also learn that normal people's sugar range was around 100 to 125mg/dl. My pancreas had up and died and it would no longer produce any insulin.

That's why I was there. My body didn't have the necessary insulin to process sugar correctly for energy, and instead of the sugar being used to give me my *get up and go* it was building up in my blood and causing my machine to shutdown with *no go* at all.

I gave Doris a hug and said goodbye to her in the main lobby and then I was taken to my room on the first floor of the Hospital. As I walked with the guide to my room I enjoyed looking at the candy stripers (young girls who volunteer and who wear a cute pink and white uniform). When I walked into my room I had the unexpected pleasure of meeting Nurse Libby.

Nurse Libby was in her late 30s, a Southern girl with a big personality. She looked like the redneck version of Angie Dickinson but she sounded like Minnie Pearl.

I slipped out of my street clothes in the bathroom and into a blue hospital gown.

Libby said, "*Do you know what you are sweet cheeks? You are one lucky li'l Di-o-betic!*"

I didn't feel lucky as I came out in my new outfit.

She continued with a big smile, "*You get to inject yourself every day for the rest of your life with a drug that fifty years ago didn't even exist.*"

She made me sit down on my bed as she continued, "*Did you know that? Up until like 1920 if someone was di-ag-nosed like you just were, they'd go into a coma, then they'd wither up and die.*"

Nurse Libby was touchy-feely

Her eyebrows went up, as did her forefinger which she let go limp, and she made a whistling sound as her forefinger seemed to lose any interest in life and fell. It was funny to see and hear.

Her act continued, "*Sometimes, they'd die within a month! So we're gonna teach you how to take advantage of the God-given blessin' known as insulin!*"

Then I watched as she drove a needle and syringe into an orange she was holding. Next she handed me all the props and called them out so I wouldn't get confused, "*Bottle of insulin . . . orange . . . syringe and needle . . .*"

Then Libby grabbed my gown and pulled it up! When she put her hands on me I jumped!

All I had on under that gown was my underwear! I was otherwise naked under that thing! Then Nurse Libby slapped my upper right thigh, very close to home, and exclaimed, "*And that's where she goes!*"

She moved her hand across my flesh to show me how lithe and flexible it was. Holy moly! She was excited as she instructed, "*There's a right and a wrong way for a Di-o-betic to do this business so let's do 'er right!*"

She continued, "*You've got some easy-to-inject flesh right there in your thigh* (she pushed it with her finger), *so that's where I want you to shoot!*"

She was too excited, but I didn't have a Nurse remote control so she persisted, "*Draw back 20 units and get yurself ready!*"

Just as I was letting Libby touch my inner thigh, a lot, Steve-Tim-Chris were walking down the corridor, having just received directions from a cute candy striper as to my room's location.

I'd asked Doris to call Steve and Chris to let them know my situation, and they told me later that they and Tim thought it'd be fun to surprise me.

When they saw my room number, they also saw my door was ajar and heard Nurse Libby's lilting voice. Steve put his finger up to his lips to be sure all was quiet on the Mac front and they leaned against the door to eavesdrop.

Inside my room Libby has just said, " . . . *and get yourself ready!*" Outside, Steve looked at Chris, Chris looked at Tim, and all put their hands over their mouths to keep from laughing.

Inside my room I pressed the needle into the bottle of insulin and withdrew 20 units based on the numbers on the side of the syringe. Nurse Libby again touched my inner thigh and said, "*Put 'er right in there, partner!*"

Out in the corridor, the trio heard the Nurse and their eyes opened wide.

Inside my room I didn't want to appear afraid, so I stuck the needle into my thigh and yelled, "*OUCH!*"

Nurse Libby wagged her finger and scolded me, "*Don't be a baby! Push it in, give me all of it, right where it counts!*"

Out in the corridor, when the trio heard what Libby said, they couldn't help but laugh.

I heard the laughter so I stopped injecting, pulled out the needle and yelled, "*Hello? Who's out there?*"

The three eavesdroppers entered, eyes wide.

They had very funny expressions on their faces and I remember Nurse Libby smiling the second she saw them, "*Well, lookie here! More students for me to teach! Hey, boys!*"

It was obvious that Libby liked young boys so I imitated her twang as I introduced them, "*Nurse Libby, this here's Steven, that cute one's name is Chris, and that there's Timmy.*"

Libby nodded and waved as she said, "*Hiya!*"

Then she turned to me, "*Let's see you finish what you started, partner!*"

I suddenly had an audience so I had to focus. I jabbed that needle straight into my thigh and, yes, it hurt as the insulin went in and, yes, Tim fainted dead away.

Steve and Chris were quick and caught him. I didn't see that one coming so I laughed as Chris and Steve slapped him a few times trying to revive him. Chris and Steve called out his name as if he was in the next county, "*Tim! Tim Toler! Wake up! Wake up!*" They kept slapping him. I kept laughing.

Tim opened his eyes and when he realized he'd fainted, he was groggily embarrassed, "*What . . . what happened?*"

Steve smiled and said, "*No problem, Timothy, you just fell on yer ass!*"

Nurse Libby took charge and guided Tim over to my bed. As he lay down the three of us watched her try to nurse him back to health. She asked him, *"Tim, is that right? Tim, do you faint like this often?"*

Tim wasn't happy as he replied, *"No, ma'am."*

Always the good friend I contributed: *"Shouldn't you put a hospital gown on him just in case, Nurse Libby?"*

Tim promptly jumped up and waved his hand at me:

"I hope you feel better, Mac. Gotta go!" and he quickly left my room. We all laughed.

Nurse Libby smiled at the three remaining boys and said to Chris and Steve, *"It was a pleasure meeting you . . ."* and then she walked out my door as she said to me, *"I'll be back later so you can inject your next shot in time for dinner. And be glad YOU don't faint at the sight of needles!"* and she left.

I did feel a little dizzy, thanks to the new changes, so I sat down on my bed.

I continued to practice injecting the orange with the syringe and needle. Chris and Steve watched, and shook their heads at this new development. Steve smiled and told me, *"Chris and I were going to bring you a gift but everything in the gift shop had sugar in it!"*

We laughed, but I suddenly realized my love for sweets would have to take a back seat to my good health. Damn! I loved my Chocolate Chip cookies, my Oreos, and my Cokes. Damn!

Steve was still smiling as he continued, *"So we've got something else for you."*

He walked over to my window and pushed the curtain aside so we could see the parking lot outside. He pointed across the lot to a chain link fence on the other side of the roadway.

"As we parked in the hospital lot, we saw a hole in the fence that surrounds the **JUST DRIVE-IN** *next door. You love movies, Mac. You could sneak out of here, go through that hole and watch a movie there tonight for free!"*

I laughed at the thought of me wearing my gown and crawling through a hole in the fence to go see a free movie. No thanks. It would have to be a great film for me to go to a drive-in without a car or without my Betsy!

I said thanks to Steve who pointed at my TV hanging from the ceiling and restated his dare, *"Anything would be better than that, Mac. Check out that fence-hole. Our gift to you."*

I said, *"Thanks guys. I'll see what's playing, and if it's a good movie I'll tell you about it."*

I walked them to the door and, after again thanking them for their gift, I hit the hay.

When I awoke from my nap, I lay there in my hospital bed thinking about how this change, this *"diabetes change"* would be a permanent change. I realized that West Point was no longer a choice for me. Diabetics couldn't serve in the military. A commander of troops couldn't burden those troops with insulin shocks. A commander of troops couldn't stop a battle to pull out his syringe to inject insulin, or risk his troops as he calculated whether he'd eaten enough dinner before charging yonder hill. To say I was devastated when I lost the Point comes very close. It hit me hard. I lay there in my hospital bed trying to decide what I'd do with my life instead. There weren't that many attractive options available to me and that was pretty depressing.

I got out of bed and put a white robe over my blue gown. I slipped on my blue slippers and I took a walk, playing with my orange as I strolled down the hallway. I threw the orange up in the air and caught it behind my back. I tried not to think how this damned disease would affect everything for the rest of my life. I threw the orange up and caught it under my leg.

As I walked I spent some quality time checking out the candy stripers in their pink and white jumpers. Most were close to my age and good diversions from obsessing over my new disease. I'd made two trips around the first floor corridors when I heard a groan followed by a giggle in a room across the hall from mine. The door to the room was open several inches and when I walked toward it I heard another groan and giggle. My curiosity drove me forward and I knocked on the door. I heard a whisper, then a laugh as a male voice shouted, "*Well sure, why not? Come on in!*"

I pushed the door open and entered. I saw a smiling man in his 30s under the bed covers with a beautiful brunette candy striper who sat on his bed. The man wore a hospital gown and when he saw me his smile grew bigger.

When I said, "*Hey, sorry, didn't mean to butt in!*" He said, "*Butt in? No way, my friend! Come in, come in!*"

The man pointed to the candy striper and introduced her, "*This is Glorie Day. She's been helping me with my back!*"

He kept waving me in, so I moved closer to them. I noticed that Glorie pulled her jumper down a bit and I saw the man adjust his hospital gown. He thrust out his hand for shaking, "*Come on in! I'm Bob, Bob Gilbert!*"

I shook his hand and then I mimicked my host, "*I'm Kirk, Kirk McClelland!*"

Bob was quick to bond with me. We both had on gowns, and we both admired Glorie as a reason for smiling. Bob continued, "*Pleasure to meet you, Kirk! This hospital has introduced me to some nice people so far, and here you are, another one! Tell me, what are you in for?*"

Bob seemed playful so I played with him,

"*I'm in for as long as it takes to cure my diabetes!*" He laughed at me and said, "*That's cool, man! I'm in for my back, a water-skiing injury!*"

Glorie Day leaned over and whispered into his ear. Then she buttoned a button, smiled at me and left the room.

When the door was closed behind her he whispered, "*She's an important part of my back* (he winked) *and front therapy!*" We both laughed.

I moved around his room to see if this guy had any other hidden surprises.

He asked, "*So you're a diabetic, huh?*"

I answered, "*Yeah.*"

With a big smile Bob said, "*Wait 'til I make you a frozen Daiquiri! Then you'll really know what a sugar high is!*"

Bob looked like a water-skier. He had a closely shaved beard, probably weighed 160 pounds at a height of 5 feet 10 inches.

I continued to analyze this man who was easily twice my age and prone to silly reasons for hospital visits. Then I looked at myself in his mirror. I was too thin, and not well. There was no reason why it wouldn't work, so I said, "*Listen, Bob. We've just met and you don't know me . . . but . . . do you like movies?*"

It was night. Nurse Libby had watched me give myself my shot of insulin before dinner and it had been easy (as of this writing I calculate I've stuck a needle in myself over 37,000 times). After dinner Bob and I dressed in our street clothes and, trying hard not to giggle or make noise, we slipped out the back exit of the hospital. We walked normally since we were simply two guys who had just visited loved ones. When we reached the edge of the parking lot we sprinted across the street to where Steve had said there was a big hole in the drive-in's fence. There was, and it was large enough for us to slip through.

Just like that we were inside the grounds of the **JUST DRIVE-IN** movie. We walked past row after row of parked cars to reach the concession stand where there were outside tables with a perfect view of the huge drive-in screen. On that screen **FROM RUSSIA WITH LOVE** was playing and we could hear the film's sound from the speakers inside various cars parked nearby.

We sat out in the open at a table next to the projection hut since I had always loved the sound of movie projectors. Bob was a gentleman and bought us two slices of a pretty good cheese pizza and he also bought me my first ever diet-coke (as of this writing I've consumed over 37,000 diet-cokes).

As we sat and dined under the stars, we found that we shared a sense of humor.

With the appropriate accent, I said, "*The cuisine here routs our former hospice, eh Miss Moneypenny?*"

Bob laughed and replied, "*Right you are, Mr. Bond!*"

Then we saw my favorite scene from all the James Bond films, between Tatiana and James:

JAMES BOND "*You're one of the most beautiful girls I've ever seen.*"

TATIANA "*Thank you, but I think my mouth is too big.*"

JAMES BOND "*No, it's the right size . . . for me, that is.*"

Bob and I laughed.

After the movie we snuck back out our hole and crossed the street so we could return to the hospital exit. We had just turned the corner of the corridor when we saw Nurse Libby pacing in front of the Nurse's station. She was pissed and speaking loudly to a candy striper, "*Where's my li'l di-o-betic patient, Rachel? I know you know where he is!*"

Bob and I looked at each other. If we were going to survive the night we had to sneak back to our rooms unseen by Libby. I motioned for Bob to go to his room first and he almost made it. Libby kept yelling at Rachel who, crying, ran away from Libby.

She ran around our corner and when Rachel saw me she screamed and pointed, "*Here he is, Nurse Libby! Here he is!*" The little narc. Bob and I froze in the hallway as narc-Rachel ran away, still crying.

Nurse Libby took her time as she walked down the corridor toward us. She ignored me and focused on Bob, "*Mis-ter Gil-bert! You are officially on my beat-up list, do you hear me? Your li'l Donkey Island jaunt was so stupid I can't think of anything stupider!*" She pointed at me, "*You cudda killed this young boy!*"

Then she turned to me, "*And you! You still don't get it!*" She pulled at my arm, "*Wake yerself up, young man! This is what YOU'LL be doin' for the rest of yer life!*"

She jabbed me in my arm with a needle and syringe causing me to howl in pain. OUCH! She happily injected the insulin into my arm and then removed the syringe.

Damn! It burned! It stung! I rubbed the new puncture. OW!

Then Nurse Libby pivoted and shoved Bob against the hallway wall. He smiled because, as he told me later, he enjoyed getting physical with any woman.

Libby growled, "*As fer you . . .*" She looked at Bob's smile and shrugged, "*. . . you are the dumbest ass-dult I never hope to see again!*"

Bob was still smiling as she stormed off. He waved to me and whispered, "*See you tomorrow!*" as he entered his room and closed his door.

That was the start of what would turn into a risky relationship for me and, by association, for Clem. I stood alone in the hospital corridor rubbing my abused arm. Damn, it still hurt! I entered my room and closed the door. I would stay for a week and then they sent me home…

I was slow to re-gain my weight since I had to learn how much food to eat and how much insulin to take, to be sure the food would be able to benefit my body. As I juggled that, I also had to juggle my classes so I could keep my grades up.

Mona was giving me grief about taking her to some River Oaks gala event. Betsy's father was threatening to transfer to California so she wouldn't be tempted to have me in her life anymore. My new Track coach wanted to know how long before I'd be able to hit the track. And I was behind on my writing letters to Clem.

Too many distractions! To tell the truth, Clem and Betsy were the only ones I worried about.

Timing was everything. Three days before the weekend when Doris and I were slated to go visit Clem at Huntsville Prison, I received a call from Betsy. She was crying and said, "*The bastard's done it! We're moving to Los Angeles! I'm so sorry, Kirk!*"

I didn't know what to say. This was the first girl I'd ever proposed to. I'd already lost Clem and West Point that year, so losing Betsy would make it my trifecta of bad news. She cried, "*We tried to make it work, but I guess we weren't meant to be . . .*"

I agreed, "*Star-crossed lovers, huh?*"

She tried to make a joke, "*Eyes-crossed in your case, blinky . . .*"

I said, "*Hey, California's not that far from Houston. I'll climb aboard the 20 Mule Team Borax Wagon and see you in a couple of months. Hyah, Mule!*"

Betsy had heard me lead the mules before, so she laughed, "*You're really funny, Kirk. How can I not miss you?*"

She started crying again so I quoted her the Borax motto, "*Don't forget, Bet, 'Good things stand the test of time!'*" But that made her cry more.

One of my bright lights during that dark time was Velma Brennan. I discussed with her what she called "*useless stuff that every High School student suffers,*" and she kept me real whenever I started to slip into self-pity. Did she study psychology in College? I didn't care as long as she listened to my aches and pains and gave me good advice for my treatment.

On the day after I had spoken to Betsy (as she'd packed for California) I sat in Velma's Counseling Room located next to her Honors English classroom. The Counseling Room had a sofa, a phone, a clock, bookcases filled with books lining three of her walls, and pictures of a smiling Velma with past favorite students that she'd successfully counseled over the years.

On her desk I also saw a Rolodex that she told me held the names of contacts at Colleges and Universities she was currently generating for her special *graduates to be* like me.

She had my file in front of her and she said, "*It's an ambitious plan, Mr. McClelland. This isn't Junior High. Keeping your grades up and making letters in all three sports is a pretty tall order at the High School level.*"

I smiled at her as she suggested that a *tall order* was out of my reach. This was typical Velma psychology. She'd been responsible for my winning the American Legion Award and she was focused on me and two others as potential (future) Valedictorians of our class. I said, "*I know, Mrs. Brennan. In a couple of years when I graduate as Valedictorian, I want the McClelland name to be celebrated. It would . . . uh . . . It would give Clem something to be proud of.*"

Velma smiled at me, and I saw shades of Doris as she said, "*Don't end a sentence with a preposition . . . Who's your English teacher?*"

She put down my file and then she looked at me, hard.

After suffering a few seconds of her staring, I asked, "*What?*"

She answered, "*I was checking to see if you'd grown an inch or two since our last chat.*"

I answered, "*Just trying to sit up straighter, that's all.*"

She went into her counseling mode, "*Okay . . . Don't forget you're a new diabetic. I know you have to take insulin twice a day, so stay focused.*"

Velma Brennan kept me sharp

I said, "*I thought focusing on my future was your job.*"
Velma said, "*It is but I'm lazy, so you'll have to do it on your own.*"
I said, "*Good. That way it'll be done right, and on time.*"
I stood up to leave and she laughed, "*Take it slow. Don't let anything distract you, and you'll do fine.*"
She stood up as I moved toward her door and she said, "*Just know I'm pulling for you.*" She patted my back like she always did and I left.
Outside her room I saw Grace Stewart, a sixteen-year-old Valedictorian wannabe with an attitude.
Grace was tall and leaned down her head as she moved closer so she could whisper in my ear, "*You'll never be Valedictorian, but I will . . .*"
She stepped back and I watched her as she raised her prissy little eyebrows, "*And get this pretty boy, I'll always make A's cause I want this more than you ever will!*"
She smiled her signature obnoxious smile and, as she started to enter Velma's room, she turned back and hissed sweetly, "*Oh, and I forgot. My father's not a stupid convict, either.*"

She waved her signature *thoughtless wave*, entered Velma's room and half-closed the door. I stared after her. I couldn't believe her flood of Graceless venom.

This was still early days for my using insulin, and sometimes the drug did strange things to my imagination. I suddenly had a bizarre black and white vision of Grace's image being projected inside an old time *Nickelodeon shooting gallery* as I heard Velma greet Grace, "*Good afternoon, Grace. Come in and tell me how things are going!*"

My hallucinatory vision continued and I imagined Grace's image taunting me, repeating "*stupid convict*" over and over as I started pulling the trigger on the *Nickelodeon's shotgun.*

I heard *Gunshot* sound effects and watched Grace as she was shot again and again.

I watched her image blow apart and in my black and white vision her blood was red.

Whew! Insulin was an extraordinary fantasy drug whenever it caused my blood sugar to plummet, and Grace was the perfect phantasm for me to shoot in my insulin-induced dreams . . .

It was Saturday morning, predawn, and I put my pillow in the passenger seat of our Station Wagon. Huntsville Prison was 70-odd miles away and I planned to sleep while Doris drove. Before I closed my eyes I noticed there was a Cakebox sitting in the back seat. I was still sleepy so I held back on asking the obvious question of "*What's in the Box?*" and fell asleep instead.

About an hour later Doris patted my head to wake me up and I looked out the windows to see my first glimpse of the Huntsville Prison buildings and grounds.

Clem's New Address

As Doris had mentioned many times the old buildings were surrounded by trees and flower beds and shrubs. She said, "*Landscaping is job one for a privileged group of inmates. Aren't those Day Lilies and those Hibiscus shrubs beautiful?*"

 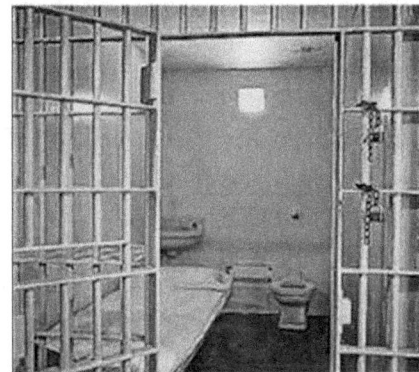

Clem's New Home

I saw one sign that declared 1848 as the birthday of this prison and some of the buildings did look elderly. Doris drove into a parking lot with a sign that read **Visitor's Wing**. After parking she opened the Wagon's back door and removed the Cakebox. I yawned, "*What's in the Box?*"

As we walked toward the Entrance Gate, Doris held the Box by its strings and directed me, "*Stay close to me. The last time I was here, there was trouble.*"

We walked past the Entrance that led to the **Visitor's Wing** of the prison where I saw flowers out front and perfectly mown green grass everywhere. It was all an illusion which began to fade as several large Guards, wearing blue uniforms and holding severe wooden nightsticks, came into view. The garden outside was a big contrast to what we saw inside. There was a long gray-painted corridor with fluorescent lights, and a long line of visitors waiting on the left. The line was composed mostly of women and crying children, 90 percent of which were Black or Hispanic. There was walking room on the right and Doris guided us there, past the people who waited in line on the left.

As we walked I saw a Commissary at the end of the line and three more Guards sprinkled along the line.

Halfway down the long line a Black man and a Hispanic man were arguing loudly about their places in line. Doris was unafraid and kept us far right of their argument as she pulled me toward the Commissary. I noticed that all of the other visitors were hunkering down and looking away from the altercation.

Then I saw the Guards move in on the debate. One very large Guard, who looked like an NFL linebacker, swooped in and banged the two male visitors on their heads. They both fell to the ground and no more words were exchanged. I kept looking back at the two unconscious quarrelers as Doris kept pulling me toward the Commissary.

A large Guard in his 30s, guarding the Commissary window, smiled at us and said, "*Hello, Mrs. Mac, is this the judge's son?*"

Doris smiled, "*Yes, Ronald, meet my favorite son, Kirk.*"

Ronald laughed as he reached out to shake my hand which disappeared inside his large claw, "*We used to play that same joke in our house. Then we had another son, so whadaya do?*"

Ronald led Doris to the front of the Commissary line. A White woman with 2 small kids was about to make a fuss when Ronald held up his palm and shook his head at her. She went mute.

Doris pulled a $20 bill out of her vest pocket and handed it to the smiling inmate who was missing some teeth. He took her money and handed her a tray with 3 soft drinks in plastic cups and two baskets of cookies on it. Ronald then guided us to and through the **Visitors** door.

There he transferred us to a gray-haired Guard in his 60s named Sergeant Dunham who greeted Doris, "*Hello Doris!* (He smiled kindly to me) *Hello, son. Gonna see your dad today?*"

I politely said, "*Yes, sir. It's been a while . . .*"

Sgt. Dunham took us down a long line of Black and Hispanic families who were all sitting and waiting at a long table. As we walked past these people I whispered to Doris, "*Why are we so special?*"

She whispered back, "*Good friends in higher places than Frank Briscoe, thank God!*"

Several Guards roaming the area nodded to Doris as Sgt. Dunham led us down the long table. It was separated by a one foot high glass partition and at the head of the table there were two closed doors, one on each side of the glass, and an elevated platform where two Guards sat. Dunham nodded to Doris as he walked away. The Guards smiled as Doris handed the Cakebox to them. The closest Guard said, "*Thanks*" and put the Cakebox on the platform's floor just as Clem came through the door on our side of the glass. He shook the Guard's hand and then swung around to grab Doris. They hugged and kissed, and I noticed that the two Guards enjoyed watching them.

Clem then grabbed and shook my hand as he gave me a hug. We looked and grinned at each other for several seconds and I watched him go back out the door on our side of the glass to enter the inmate's area through the other door on the other side of the glass. It was a quick dance and it was over before I knew it had even started.

Doris gave Clem his drink and cookies over the glass and he started walking down the length of the table. I followed Doris down our side of the table past the other waiting families. We stopped at the last open seats and sat down. Just as Clem sat down opposite us the floodgates opened, and the other inmates who'd been waiting surged in and took their seats across from their loved ones. It was all fascinating for me to watch.

Over the foot high glass, Clem asked the first question, "*So how's my boy?*"

I lied and said, "*Not bad. The real question is, how are you?*"

He smiled and I felt my heart tug as I remembered the two of us in our duck blind asking each other the same bullshit question. Clem looked at me happily and he answered, *"If you're good, I'm good. Are you doing everything your mother tells you?"*

I nodded. *"Always."*

He asked, *"How about your insulin shots? Are you sterilizing your needles like I described to you in my letters?"*

I answered, *"Yes, sir, just like you told me to."*

Clem nodded and said, *"Good, and thanks for YOUR letters! I enjoy every one you send!"*

It seemed he was enjoying our strange quality time together prison-style.

He asked, *"So how's Betsy?"*

I gave him a Frankie Laine lyric answer, *"She's 'as gone as the wild goose in winter'... Her father moved his family, Betsy and her mom, to California."*

Clem shook his head, *"Well, I didn't expect that one, boy. I'm sorry."*

He looked at Doris and all she could do was shake *her* head. He continued, *"I wish there was something I could say to help you. I know how you feel about her."*

I watched him and saw he was struggling. It'd been a long time since he'd been able to give me fatherly advice.

But he was still Clem, and still very wise. He asked an insightful question, *"So tell me. How are you going to fill the void created by her asshole father?"*

Doris gasped, *"Clem!"* and looked around at the Hispanic families sitting on both sides. She shouldn't have worried. They weren't affected by Clem's word since they didn't speak English and had their own language for describing the *cabrons* and *pendejos* in their society.

When Clem said *"fill the void"* I thought about my meeting Bob Gilbert at the hospital.

I remembered Glorie Day sitting on his lap and how she'd adjusted her candy striper skirt. This guy had invited me into his world but I didn't share Bob Gilbert with Clem because I wasn't sure at that time who *Bob* really was. I also didn't share that this new, possibly deviant character might possibly be in my life, since Doris (my mother) was sitting right there.

Clem had arranged for Sgt. Dunham to give me the grand tour around the Visitor's area so that he could have some alone time with Doris. I joined Dunham and the whole time I was walking around looking at all the unhappy convicts meeting with their unhappy families, I kept peeking over at my parents as they discussed important aspects of our lives.

I held my tongue since I knew I'd charm Doris into sharing their talk on our drive home. On Highway 45 going south back to Houston, here's what she said they discussed...

Clem: *"So how's he really doing?"*

Doris: *"He misses you so much. It's tough not having you around. You made a big impression with that black belt of yours."*

Clem: "*It seems like only yesterday . . . I worry about him going ten years without his father.*"

Doris: "*Or ten years without her husband.*"

Clem: "*Or ten years without his wife. Ten years is too many, Doris. I've tried to talk myself into doing them but I don't think I can . . . I . . . I wish I could just blink and be done with it.*"

Doris: "*I need you to trust me. "Early Release" is still a good chance and I think we can do it. Trust me, Clem. I want you home more than you'll ever know.*"

On the drive home Doris told me that's when Sgt. Dunham and I returned from our *tour*.

I sat down, and Clem waved *Thanks* at Dunham as he walked away.

Clem asked me, "*What did the Sergeant show you?*"

I answered, "*The torture chamber!*"

Doris choked on her drink as I continued, "*It was so cool!*"

Clem raised his plastic cup and Doris raised hers as they both smiled and said, "*That's our boy!*"

The rest of the visit we talked about Clem's job in the kitchen and how fortunate he was to "*have friends*" who'd helped him get it. Every inmate wants to work in the kitchen.

We talked about "*Prisoner's rights*" and how most are taken away so the prison system can maintain order, discipline and security.

We talked about how there were two inmates on Clem's kitchen detail who hated each other and how Clem had mollified them both without disrespecting either of them. He'd borrowed both of their kitchen knives, and returned them safely to the knife drawer. Wow . . .

Huntsville Prison Mess Hall -- Thanksgiving

At that moment an alarm bell sounded. Everyone stopped talking and then everyone began talking very fast. I heard some women start to cry and I heard inmate husbands/boyfriends try to calm them down. Clem simply said, "*Okay, time's up. Any last business before you go?*"

I said, "*Yes, sir, serious now, all right?*"

Clem smiled his wonderful, kind, compassionate smile and said, "*I'll try.*"

I said, "*Velma Brennan and I are trying to map out what I'm going to do with the rest of my life. Any suggestions?*"

Clem smiled sadly and said, "*Anything but the law, boy. Anything but the law.*"

I drove us back to Houston. I liked to drive and look at the road whenever I needed to think about the world, and our visit to Clem had given me a lot to contemplate.

After visiting the Huntsville State Penitentiary, I concluded we needed to bring Clem home as soon as we possibly could.

I asked Doris, "*What's with the Cake?*"

Doris was engaged in surfing the radio, trying to find a station that she could tolerate.

At that moment she found **BOBBY HATFIELD** singing **UNCHAINED MELODY** on a Huntsville radio station and she shared, "*I love this song. It was written for a prisoner to sing in a prison film. Did you know that?*"

I shook my head, "*No.*"

She continued, "*Every time I hear the "long, lonely time" lyric I make a wish that Clem and I could go back . . . 25 years ago . . . Then we'd be able to start all over again.*"

I looked at her as she wiped her eyes and tried to be strong.

I wondered how in the hell she'd ever survive and live without him . . .

CHAPTER EIGHT

WHY DID IT HAVE TO HAPPEN? 1966

I replayed the low points over the previous eight years: The Media smears in the early '60s, the Court of Inquiry, the two trials, Clem's imprisonment in Huntsville, and my becoming a diabetic. On the positive side I looked at my bank account and saw that it had grown to just over $3,500. This was due in part to working for Charlie and Clem's construction company the previous summer, and living/eating at home courtesy of Clem and Doris. It was also due to my receiving serious money in my last Christmas stocking. Some of my relatives had kindly contributed hard cash to my well-being, so I thought it was time for me to take advantage of it.

I'd been reading about a new car offered that year by Chevrolet. It was the Malibu Super Sport and when I read how racy it sounded, I thought of me. I drove my Comet over to **RICHARDSON CHEVROLET** on the corner of Hillcroft and the freshly opened Southwest Freeway. This dealership boasted *"acres and acres of stunning 1966 Chevrolets serviced and ready to go"* and claimed to be *"the largest dealer in the great Southwest!"*

I parked my Comet in front of the dealership, walked into their showroom and instantly fell in love with the brand new off-white off-yellow Malibu SS that sat there. As I looked at the smooth lines of this car I was confronted by an eager-to-sell salesman named Sam Jenkins. Sam was in his late twenties, had light brown hair and a ready smile as he gave me his card and said, *"Hello, you can call me 'Jinx'. Let me tell you a little bit about this car!"*

Jinx pointed inside the car as I walked all around it, *"As you can see, it's got a Muncie 4-on-the-floor, heavy duty suspension, front and rear Antiroll bars, and a fast power-assisted steering package. Let me show . . . uh, it's Kirk, right?"*

I nodded as he opened the hood and continued, *"This car has a special 396 transmission with 375 horsepower which is probably too much horsepower for a car with a small chassis like this one."*

He pulled me under the hood and lowered his voice to *share* some inside dope, *"Listen, Kirk. I really like my job and I like helping people find the car of their dreams.*

But I gotta tell ya, this one is different. I took it out when it first came in yesterday and there was something about it that didn't feel right. It really does have too much power."

He put his hand on the Malibu's carburetor and said, "*My father used to have a garage and body shop so I grew up watching and listening to cars he repaired in his shop, ya know? When I put my pedal on the metal of this Malibu it just took off. Very few cars with an engine this size and with this much power will ever function properly. So it's my . . .*"

I smiled as I stopped him, "*Let me take it out, Mr. Jenkins. I'll know in the first 100 yards if it's too much for me.*"

He paused and smiled back. I don't think he liked me interrupting him, but he nodded. "*Okay, Kirk. Jump in and we'll see if you can handle it.*"

I opened the car door and sat on the driver's seat. I looked at the white and silver four speed shifter and engaged the clutch. The inside had a nice brand new smell. I looked at the speedometer and noticed the car's top speed was 160 mph.

Jinx got in on the passenger side and pointed to the open dealership doors so I could drive through and exit the showroom. I started the engine smoothly, engaged the clutch, shifted to first gear, and slowly *motorvated* out into the dealership's parking lot. I turned onto Hillcroft and in no time I was slipping through the gears on the Southwest Freeway's new lanes. The second I put my foot on the Malibu's pedal I knew this was it. The engine felt and sounded like rolling thunder, with a roar that gave me goose bumps as I drove onto the Freeway. It trembled as I tested the second and third gears. I felt it beg, to show me what it could do. Then I hit fourth gear. Wow!

In measuring-lingo, it was a ten plus. It had the speed and the rush of a race horse and as I separately tested the power of each gear, there was no question this horse would be mine.

It hummed, it roared. It crooned "*drive me and love it,*" and that's what I did. Damn! Suddenly there I was falling in love again! And I didn't care if it bounced all over the roadway because as it bounced it also flew!

The interesting truth of my first Malibu SS experience: It was not overpowered. The tires, the wheels, the brakes were perfectly trimmed and it handled like a dream. It matched my personality and it satisfied my gigantic ego. I'd always wanted to be the fastest, so I wanted a car that could power shift me through its four gears as fast as mechanically possible.

As I drove faster I noticed that my salesman was getting anxious so I shared with him that, with his permission, I had one more test for the Malibu. He said, "*I guess it's okay, just as long as you buy the car!*"

I laughed so he'd feel better. I turned down a feeder street that led to the new Sharpstown subdivision of Houston. There was no traffic visible around us as I sped along, and then I hit the brakes and quickly turned the steering wheel as I executed a 180 degree turn that made him scream at the top of his lungs. The tires squealed and smoke filled the air as we came to a complete stop at the edge of Sharpview Drive. Jinx tried to catch his breath.

I said, "*You're quite a salesman, Jinx*" and stuck out my hand. "*You made the sale!*"

Two hours later after all the paperwork was done and I'd turned over the Comet's ownership slip as part of my transaction, I drove my new car off the lot and into my dreams. I couldn't believe how good the car felt in my hands. It was unreservedly sensual-to-the-max.

I further justified my purchase by telling myself, "*If I can't have my Betsy, I'll have my Malibu!*" And with that, I christened my new car "*Heaven*" (short for "*Heavens to Betsy!*").

I loved how solid *Heaven* felt as I sped along the Southwest Freeway on my way home.

I swerved back and forth as I switched from the inside, the middle, and the outside lanes.

I was on a full tilt rollercoaster ride and I felt happy for the first time in a long time.

One perk that Jinx had added to my Malibu package was an 8 Track Cassette sound system. His boss at **RICHARDSON CHEVROLET** had added the 8-Track system to select sports models as a promotional item and so I was listening to the instrumental version of **APACHE** by **THE SHADOWS** on my new system and it was cool.

I played with my new car using the gears to downshift every time I came up to a red light or stop sign and after a few tries, it became effortless. I hit Westheimer Road and in a matter of seconds I'd run the SS through all 4 gears and reached 100 mph. With **APACHE** still playing I turned off to the right at the **POST OAK APARTMENTS** with a new destination in mind.

I drove around this large complex of apartment buildings until I found the one that included number 227. I parked the Malibu and walked up the outside staircase to the second floor where #227 was located. Here was the Apartment of Bob Gilbert, the water-skier, my companion at the James Bond drive-in movie. On his door there was a cowbell hanging on a hook. I was having second thoughts about ringing that bell when suddenly the door opened and there stood Bob.

He happily shouted, "*Kirk McClelland! There he is! Where have you been? It's been ages since we Just Drove-In!*" Bob laughed and I noticed that he had a tall drink in a Collins glass in his right hand as he directed me to enter his apartment with his left hand, "*Come in, come in! I'm glad you came over! I had some ladies here last night and I was telling them about you, so this is great! Hey, let me make you a frozen Daiquiri! I promised you that you'd love it! Whadayasay?*"

I said, "*Sure, but make it small. Remember--Diabetes!*"

I entered Bob's domain and saw a typical bachelor pad with warm paneling and several soft looking sofas and a dark leather recliner chair positioned on a clean white carpet.

The only abnormality I saw were boxes of books stacked high against one wall. Bob steered me to his bar which was similar to Clem's bar, complete with several stools. I pointed at the boxes against the wall and asked, "*What are those?*"

Bob answered, "*My Law books. I sell them for a living, to support all this.*"

Behind the bar Bob hit a switch on his blender and I heard the loud sound of a frozen Daiquiri being made. As Bob mixed I walked around his Living Room to look at the pictures hanging on his walls. I saw Bob with different girlfriends all of whom looked younger than Bob. I looked and I kept asking myself the question: What are you doing here, Kirk? Who is this guy?

There was a large (*at that time*) 28 inch television on the wall opposite the bar and it was tuned to a Press Conference with none other than Frank Briscoe. I asked Bob, "*Do you mind if I turn the sound on?*" and he said, "*Go ahead.*"

I pushed a control button on the front of the set and heard the Devil say, "*To answer your question, I'll do the same thing in Congress that I did here in Houston as the District Attorney: My job!*"

I softly said, "*Son of a bitch . . .*"

An off-screen news reporter asked Briscoe, "*Do you think you can beat George Bush in this election?*"

The Drama King smiled and said, "*The people in the Seventh District know me. They've been watching how I do business for the past five and a half years. What has Mr. Bush done besides be a Republican? The Seventh District of Houston has always elected Democrats and*"—he smiled big—"*I predict a Democrat will fill this seat once again!*" He waved to the room of reporters.

I was about to say something to the TV when Bob moved in front of me and turned it off.

He handed me a tall Daiquiri. It was green and the glass was cold. I took a drink and said, "*Wow!*" as I caught my breath. It was also sweet and good, as promised. Bob was eager for my review so I told him, "*You should bottle and sell this, man.*"

He laughed and pointed to the darkest of his three sofas, "*Sit and tell me what's going on at Robert E. Lee High School.*"

Bob Gilbert always smiled

We sat down as Bob clinked his glass with mine and we both drank. I kept looking around at this strange pad, trying to decide if Bob's world was close to mine. I was still young and I was still trying to figure out what I wanted in my life of turmoil. Would Bob open new doors or would he open Pandora's Box? I'm proud that I at least considered (*just maybe*) that Apt #227 might not be a good idea for me. Instead of answering Bob's chitchat question I said instead, "*I'd rather talk about Frank Briscoe.*"

Bob responded, "*Whoa! Did I make that Daiquiri too strong?*"

I thought it would be a good test so, to check his pulse, I continued, "*No, I just had a dark thought. I pictured him dead.*"

Bob laughed. I could tell that he thought I was good entertainment.

He said, "*I know you have every reason not to like this man, but do you have a license to kill, Mr. Bond?*"

I spoke honestly, as I continued to analyze my host, "*I've been having a lot of dark thoughts lately.*"

Bob jumped up, retrieved his pitcher, picked up my glass and poured, "*I think you need to drink up, Mr. Bond. Life is goooodddd! Very good!*"

I nodded and said, "*Right. You're right.*" I looked around. "*So do you have parties here?*"

Bob held up his Collins glass and pitched me, "*Yes, I do! And that's why I've been waiting for you to come over. You will love my parties! And my parties will love you!*

You know why? Because you're good-looking, you're quick with a line, and your father's a convict! You'll be the perfect lothario, Kirk, yes you will!"

I knew what a gigolo was, but I had to look up *lothario* to see what this book salesman was saying about me. *Lothario: A man who behaves selfishly and irresponsibly in his sexual relationships with women.* Hmmm. I'd never been told that I was irresponsible before.

Bob clinked my glass again and said, *"Drink up!"* I did, and then I said bye to Bob.

As I drove home, probably due to the Daiquiris I drank, I visualized another bizarre black and white *Nickelodeon shooting gallery* image, this time with Bob saying *"convict"* over and over again. I heard Gunshots (or backfires from *Heaven*) as the shotgun blew holes in Bob, and *his* blood was the green color of his Daiquiris. Whew! I still had a lot to learn about insulin . . .

I drove three blocks to reach my home street of Ivanhoe. Bob's apartment complex was that close. One quick note about the **POST OAK APARTMENTS**: Whenever there was a disturbance of any kind in that location the Police referred to it as *"Sin Alley."* When I was growing up with my roller skates or skateboard, I used to love to go " *. . . skating in sin alley"* even though Doris told me to *". . . stay away from that evil place!"*

So I had a smile on my face as I remembered that and when I parked my new car under the Carport and Doris came out to see it, she misinterpreted my *sin alley smile* as a *here's my new car smile*. She laughed her delightful laugh, *"It's wonderful, Kirk! It looks brand new!"*

She gave me a big hug and then pushed me out of her way so she could sit in the driver's seat.

She looked at the mileage on the odometer and when she saw *0000045* miles she said, *"Wait a minute. It IS brand new!"*

My '65 Chevy Malibu Super Sport (*Heaven*)

She jumped out of the Malibu and gave me another hug and started to cry/giggle, *"I'm so happy for you. You've done so well trying to be good so your father will be proud. You deserve a new car, and now you have it with the money you earned doing that horrible construction work. I guess stepping on that nail was worth it, huh?"*

Doris was reminding me of a rainy day the previous summer when I'd been working on a new home site and I'd stepped on a piece of wood with a thirty penny nail sticking straight up. The nail had passed through my work boot and pierced my right foot with two inches of steel. The puncture had required a painful tetanus shot to help my diabetic foot fight off infection.

Doris surprised me when she jumped back in and started the Malibu's engine, shouting, *"Get In!"* as she revved the engine a few times. I jumped into the passenger seat just as she backed out of the Carport and the driveway, and then she sped down Ivanhoe Street *"like there was no tomorrow."* Thankfully no small children were out riding their bikes that day.

She drove me all around the area that in five years would be the location for The Houston Galleria shopping mall *"with over 375 stores and over 24 million visitors annually!"* Yes, I'm a proud Houstonian.

After Doris's wild ride she brought us, and my new car, home safely. We went into the Kitchen and she made us two iced teas and we sat down to talk.

I remember that day because of the car and because of what Doris then told me. She'd been thinking about my diabetes for a long time (*about how I became a diabetic*) and she shared, *"When Dr. Nicosia told us you were a diabetic, I went crazy . . . I couldn't believe it. I'd been so careful to feed you and your sister's well-balanced meals so that you'd avoid diabetes. Then when it suddenly happened to you, I used my new research skills to try to discover a reason."*

She pulled out an article and laid it down on the table for me to see, *"At the Houston Main Library I found a paper on diabetic causes published by the New England Journal of Medicine. One scientist ran a test group to study excessive stress as the underlying factor in the breakdown of the endocrine system, specifically the pancreas."*

She tapped her finger on the paper and thought about the stress her family had suffered.

She'd lost me about a minute before, when she was sharing with me she'd gone crazy.

I agreed with her that I *had* suffered a great deal of stress during Clem's trials, but I didn't get the connection. As I had watched and listened to Frank and his Monkeys I'd been more worried about my getting *ulcers* since I found myself gritting my teeth and flexing my fists as I envisioned punching Briscoe's smarmy little self-righteous face.

As Doris shared her research (*which she was proud of and which I understood she needed me to acknowledge*) I considered that my first awareness of stress was when I saw Clem watching Briscoe's TV commercial and guzzling his *Nectar of the Gods* Jack Daniels whiskey. Then I took another round of bad stress when I heard Judge Everts say *"Guilty"* as if he was merely discussing the chance of rain tomorrow.

The truth: I think my pancreas died the day that I wrestled Larry Klump and looked down the barrel of that .45 Colt pistol. I take responsibility for my part of it, and I know I over-reacted. It's just that I'd never felt my balls crawl-up-inside-my-scrotum-to-avoid a-bullet before. I had stood like a statue at our Living Room window with my finger wrapped around the trigger of Clem's gun for a long time. The whole episode had drained my spirit and my physical body.

My entire life I'd always done things my way, to hell with the consequences. I remember pulling back the .45's slide over and over again, pulling the trigger on that empty chamber over and over again. I was angry. I was mad as a rabid dog. I was stressed. I was also ready to blow Larry Klump to kingdom come. This was *my* theory for why I would suffer this major disease for the rest of my life.

After discussing the cause of my diabetes, our next talk that day was Doris's other research project: how to bring Clem home. Doris had discovered numerous pleas to Appellate judges from the families of inmates who had shared their need and desire to go home.

The universal need of every inmate was to cover the economic and emotional impact they all suffered, with emphasis on the economic. Doris was learning that most inmates at the Huntsville Penitentiary had told their criminal judges they simply wanted to put bread on their table. These men and women were not the smartest grapes in the bunch. They robbed a liquor store because it was mostly a cash business, and they needed that cash to buy groceries or Christmas presents for their numerous children. They robbed a bank thinking they could grab more money, and then not have to frequently rob as many liquor stores.

Then, when these future inmates were apprehended, they acquired too late the basic knowledge that digging ditches would not only make them a living it would also save them from having to pay lawyers to keep them out of jail.

If I were to create a bumper sticker to help educate future inmates and deter their future crimes, I might have it say, "*If you steal, you'll do time. Count on it!*" or "*If you sell drugs, you'll do time. Count on it!*" According to Doris's research there were a lot of incarcerated people inside Huntsville Prison who hadn't thought about the consequences of being caught. It was sad but predictable. She found out that over 80 percent of the inmates were parents. Damn. How could children of convicts have an equal chance in our society if their role models were only available to them for an hour the fourth Sunday of each month?

So her research had taught her who most of the inmates were and how they'd tried to appeal to the Criminal Court of Appeals in Austin, Texas. The appellate judges had heard it all before. So unless the McClellands delivered an original plea for Clem's release, it wouldn't happen. Not then or ever. Why? **Because District Attorney Frank Briscoe was still on the job.**

There was nothing to prevent the Devil from doing whatever he wanted to drill the screws into Clem's back and keep him pinned to his Huntsville cell wall.

Doris had learned the Devil-Drama King had told Ed Smith and Jack Rawitscher that if they continued to appeal Clem's convictions, Briscoe would put pressure on the appellate courts to not forgive or release Clem so he'd have to stay behind those bars for ten long years.

That's what motivated Doris and that's why she was on a mission. If her pursuit of that mission also delivered grief to Frank Briscoe, so be it. Every day she devoted hours of her life to searching for new information that would provide her with a key to unlock Clem's cell. She was rock-solid and fearless when it came to finding a new method to open the Huntsville gates and set her husband free. I was proud to know her as I sat across the Kitchen table and watched her struggle to discover a new way to plead Clem's case.

She had several files labeled *"Forms to Fill Out," "Similar Cases"* and *"Creative Thoughts."* They were each about an inch thick which testified to how dedicated she was to the job at hand. If Clem had known just how dedicated she was, he probably would have asked her to say *"I do"* all over again.

Clem's wife then changed hats and suddenly became my mother. She had some advice, *"I was reading about a Dallas man who was in prison for embezzlement and he had a plea before the same CCA* (Criminal Court of Appeals) *judges I'm trying to work with. As this Dallas man's plea was being considered his oldest son was arrested for a series of property crimes for auto theft and burglaries. The Dallas man's son looked like a professional to the judges and they couldn't trust that the father wouldn't become involved with his son's criminal enterprise if he were released, so they denied his parole plea."*

I said, *"Whoa! The sins of the son were laid upon the father?"*

Doris nodded. *"Exactly. I need you to keep making your good grades and not do anything that could jeopardize what I'm trying to do for your dad, okay?"*

I thought about that for a moment, and then I said, *"Okay."*

She continued, *"These judges scare the hell outta me because IF we get to meet with them . . .* (That's where we were. It was not a WHEN, it was an IF at this stage) *IF we get to meet with them, we'll have one chance. If we blow it, Clem's out of luck."*

She laid her hand on my arm, *"Clem's being good. You need to keep being good!"*

I sat there for a minute looking at Doris and her files. I had my regular question so I asked it:

"How's our money situation? I just spent a ton on a new car. Should I take it back?"

Doris fiercely said, *"NO! That's the best thing that's happened to you, to us in a long time, Kirk. We all need you to ride high right now. I need it!"*

As I listened to her I flashed on Chris Hale. When I'd told him and Steve that I was considering the purchase of a Super Sport he'd said, *"Get a fast one, Mac. We'll race it and maybe make us some money."* I thought about how *Heaven* felt in my hands and how she responded to my touch. I thought about how Jinx had been afraid of her power and how glad he was when he took my check and turned her keys over to me. Maybe Chris had the right idea . . .

I've tried to share various influences in my life during my first eighteen years, and one experience involved my new Malibu and Chris Hale.

Chris was the wildest friend that I had. From the night he and I had met at the Boy's Club when I'd ducked his roundhouse swing and punched him to the mat, he and I had developed a bond. We confided in each other and, whenever I saw him smile at me and call me *Mac*, it felt right. He and I had played organized Football and Sandlot Football together since elementary school and we were both competitive about doing whatever it took to score enough points to win. Whenever I had a girl problem he was there.

Whenever I needed to talk about the real world I had Chris.

So when Chris suggested I buy a *fast* car, it wasn't a casual suggestion. He was spinning a web that would result in serious nighttime episodes out on the Sharpstown straightaways. As I mentioned, this was the extension of the Southwest Freeway that was both brand new and unopened. Late at night it attracted drivers with fast cars and Chris introduced me to it.

On the day I bought *Heaven* I called Chris to come over, and 15 minutes later he had the Malibu's hood open and, as I revved the engine, he made adjustments to my ignition timing chains as well as to my fuel and boost pressures. It was Greek to me but I watched and learned.

As he made these minor adjustments he said, "*Mac, this is the sweetest lady you've ever known. Man oh man!*"

Then he said, "*I want to strip out all the unnecessary weight.*"

He opened the trunk and took out the spare tire and all the flat-tire tools and I helped him stash these heavy items in my garage. Then he smiled his trademark Chris Hale smile and said:

"*Now let me show you how to drive this beauty!*"

I handed him the keys and I watched Chris drive *Heaven* out onto the Southwest Freeway. I watched him as he made the Malibu purr one second and growl the next. As I would mention to Clem in my next letter, Chris taught me how to brake as well as how to accelerate correctly.

The whole time I watched and learned, I wanted to change seats with him and get behind the wheel to try out each of the rules for high speed driving as he taught them to me. It was exciting stuff and, man oh man, Chris could really drive! I was aching to get back into my saddle!

Finally he pulled over so that I'd stop drooling. He also wanted to watch me employ the driving techniques he'd just shown me. As I pulled back out onto the Freeway, my good reflexes took over Chris' training and I let him watch as I let her fly. I power shifted and it felt great. Then I braked using my downshifting gears and it felt perfect. And then my teacher said, "*Nice going. Let's take her to Sharpstown tonight and see her race against Caleb's GTO!*"

Chris had been talking about *Caleb* the whole time he was tinkering with the Malibu. Chris had seen Caleb's GTO win against some of the fastest cars in Sharpstown and Chris wanted to see Caleb get beat. I knew then why he'd been so quick to set this up.

Chris smiled his standard smile and said, "*He and his best friend, a guy named Sixer, don't have any competition. Until now. You wanna take 'em on, Mac?*"

I laughed, "*How can I say 'no'? It's a classic Chris Hale setup. I'll say 'yes'!*"

A few days later I wrote Clem as I sat at my worktable where I'd also been reading the Alistair Maclean novel **THE GUNS OF NAVARONE** assigned to my English class. Velma loved the book-that-became-the-movie. She'd said, "*Keith Mallory is the finest novelized hero of this generation. I want you to tell me why you agree or disagree in your report. What makes a hero, and why is Mallory, well, the nuts?*"

Clem and I had seen the Carl Foreman movie version of Maclean's book back in 1961, with Gregory Peck playing Mallory. Velma was trying to show my class the complete difference between the book and the movie, breaking down the story so we'd better appreciate the writing.

I was fascinated by both the Keith Mallory *book* character that I had visualized with my imagination, and the *screen* characterization as it was created by Gregory Peck. I totally enjoyed the movie because of Peck, but I liked the book version better since Maclean used his wonderful words to tell his wonderful story. I put the Maclean book aside so I could write to Clem,

"*Dear Clem:*

You know that everything I do is to make you proud to know me, right? Well, to make you proud of me: I bought the Malibu Super Sport that I told you I was checking out. The car is perfect. I want you to know that Doris and Chris Hale love it, too."

"*You would love seeing Doris go through the 4 gears--She's an awesome driver and she makes me laugh whenever she power shifts! Chris and I have been going out the last few nights and he's shown me some tricks for shifting and braking on the unopened feeder streets around Sharpstown. The straightaways are level and long and no one is driving there so I can open her up and fly! Uh, slowly! Don't worry.*

On a lesser note, have you been following Briscoe's bid for Congress? The people of Houston would have to be crazy to vote for him! I'm positive I will not vote for him. Oh, wait, I'm just 17! Like I said, Briscoe won't get my vote! Ha! His opponent is some guy named George Bush. Did you ever meet him? Bush is working hard to win and he even knocked on our door seeking your and Doris's vote. I didn't tell him that Briscoe had stolen your right to vote but I did wish him good luck and told him to be sure to "... beat the pants off that ugly predator!"

Velma asked me to say hi to you. She and Doris, my new Malibu, and you are my anchors in this best of all possible worlds ... Thanks for hanging tight, and know that I pray 4 U every night!

Wouldn't you know it! I sound like a poet!

Love from your Best Son, Kirk."

I probably wasn't being sensitive when I reminded Clem he'd lost his right to vote the second he'd checked into his new Huntsville address, but I wanted to share with him how much I hoped this Republican "*Bush*" fellow would find success in our devoutly Democratic Houston setting.

After a year of writing letters to Clem, I was still refining the skill I needed to describe to him the important aspects of my life, especially my feelings toward him and Doris. In each of my letters to him I tended to use too many adjectives/adverbs when I should have just talked straight. But I *was* writing more efficiently, and Velma told me my book reports were improving, so I concluded that my frequent communications with Clem were helping me be more literary . . .

It was late on a Thursday night as I drove my Malibu with Bob Gilbert sitting next to me, and Chris sitting in the backseat. I remember my 8 Track was playing **WE GOTTA GET OUT OF THIS PLACE** by **THE ANIMALS** and it felt good to hear Eric Burdon sing his song of pain.

Bob had brought along two large flasks that were full of frozen Daiquiris, and he was refilling a Styrofoam cup held by Chris who loved it. Bob smiled *his* standard smile, "*This is so cool, man! I love getting to watch!*"

He turned from me to ask Chris, "*How often do you guys do this?*"

Chris was funny as usual, "*Whenever I can pry Mac away from his homework!*"

I looked in my rearview mirror at Chris and said, "*Whenever I have cash left after bailing Chris out of jail!*"

Chris laughed as did Bob who tried to hand me a cup of Daiquiri juice but couldn't, since my right hand was wrapped around my silver gearshift.

Then Chris threw a pair of lace panties up onto my dashboard and he said, "*Those are from my MaryAnn, Mac.*" Bob laughed as Chris continued, "*She thought you might want to rub them for good luck tonight.*"

I completed this important ritual by grabbing the panties and rubbing them all over my face. I tossed them back over my shoulder to Chris who took them and rubbed them all over his face.

Bob was having fun as he laughed and said, "*What about me?*"

I played with him and said, "*Three on a rub is bad luck, Bob. Maybe next time.*"

As I drove us along I mentally took my pulse and checked my temperature. I looked at myself in the rearview and asked myself an important question: Was I where I wanted to be? You should know me well enough by now to understand why I asked myself that question. I had been *good* my whole life. There had never been a reason for me to be bad. Then I thought about Clem's last letter to me and how the censors had blacked out some of the words he'd written for my eyes only. How dare they? Those words were meant for *me*, not for some lowlife moron who probably got his psychology degree from a bargain-basement mail-order course.

I admit I'd been chewing on the censor's censorship insult since I'd read Clem's last letter, and I realized I was simply tired of watching my P's and Q's.

That's why I was driving toward that night's event. I wanted to stretch beyond my self-imposed limitations. I wanted to test myself and decide if I was a good or a damaged soul. Here's what was bothering me: Was I genetically doomed to be a future inmate at Huntsville prison now that Clem was one? Did I have a criminal gene inside me that would reveal itself at some future time? Would I end up making really bad decisions if it was already genetically programmed that I do so?

I was a diabetic because I carried the diabetic gene. Yes, I agreed with Doris that my stress episodes had crashed into that gene and shut down my pancreas, but was I on a crash course with any other bad genes? Every young man asks *"If I do this or that, am I making the right or the wrong choice?"* But who could I talk to about this? Coach Bartosh? Velma Brennan? Doris?

I glanced at myself in the rearview mirror again and I told myself to talk to myself before making any decisions. Yeah, sure. Huntsville was full of idiots who had taken advice from themselves, so why not me? Would I fail or succeed in my life? It's an everyman question.

I pulled off the Southwest Freeway at the same feeder street Chris and I had driven on two nights before. I drove about a quarter-mile to a spot where there were many other cars parked.

I saw a group of a dozen young men and the same number of young girls, all standing, waiting.

I parked the Malibu and we all exited at the same time. I pointed to Bob and said, *"Bob, just stand and watch with those people over there, okay?"*

Bob nodded and asked, *"Okay. But what if I want to bet on you or something?"*

I looked at Chris, *"Give your money to Chris and he'll handle it."*

Chris and I turned and walked toward two men who were already walking toward us. Caleb was in his 30s, and he was tall with a slick buzz cut. His smile showed a lot of teeth. Sixer, also in his 30s, was short with long black hair, but he was cuter when he smiled.

I greeted them, *"Caleb! Sixer! Good evening, gentlemen!"*

Caleb had his game on and he greeted me, *"It's the Macman! How's tricks, my friend?"*

I answered with a silly sixties alliteration, *"Rip, roarin', and ready to go!"*

Sixer chimed in, *"You young boys are always in a big hurry. Slow down and enjoy life! Watch the sunsets!"*

I responded in a way to make them think I was impatient, *"I don't have the time! So who's gonna pony up tonight? Or do you want to race for fun?"*

Everyone laughed and I quickly continued, *"I didn't think so!* (I pointed at Chris) *Talk to Chris and I'll go grab my Super Duper Super Sport. See you at the Starting Line, or in your case, the End of the Road!"*

I laughed and waved over my shoulder as I walked back to the Malibu. Bob was standing there and he tried to engage me in conversation but I held up my hand at him as I entered my car, "*I'll catch you later, Bob.*"

My hands were shaking due to prerace jitters. I looked in the rearview and tried to psyche myself into having the strength and the courage I'd need to win this race. I started my engine.

I revved the engine several times, then I turned off my interior lights and wiped off my shifter.

I put on my driving gloves and I looked over at Chris to see him hand our bet to Sixer to hold. I saw Chris talking to Caleb who sat behind the wheel of his purple Pontiac GTO. I knew he was telling Chris I'd never beat him again, and that my win on Tuesday night was due to dumb luck.

Then I saw Chris nod to me as he pulled out another roll of bills which he held high for me to see. I saw him hand that roll to Sixer as well. I knew that Caleb had pitched Chris with, "*This is the Gran Turismo Omologato, man! A GTO! Your Super Sport won't come close!*"

Chris had answered his challenge with the money we'd won from them two nights before.

Due to the increased bet my hands began to shake a bit more as I slowly rolled the Malibu toward them. As on Tuesday, four cars had moved in with their headlights *on* to set up the starting/finish line with two cars *shining* from each side where we'd drive through at the end.

Chris raised his hands up and Caleb lined up on his left, as I lined up on his right. Caleb revved his GTO and I revved my Malibu as Chris shouted to us both, "*Same rules as last time!*"

I heard Caleb laugh and yell, "*Except this time I win!*"

Chris reached inside his pocket and pulled out MaryAnn's panties and he rubbed his face one more time with them. I honked my horn in approval and, following my cue, the four Finish Line cars started honking as well. This was a prestart ritual, and it helped me to relax and focus.

Bob stood at the Finish Line with his eyes smiling at our **REBEL WITHOUT A CAUSE** moment. Just then the four drivers in the Finish Line cars began blinking their headlights from low to high beams and back again as they continued to honk their horns.

That's when Chris happily put on and pulled MaryAnn's panties down over his head.

As the horns honking increased in speed, Chris raised his arms back up high, and yelled, "*ON YOUR MARK!*"

Caleb looked over at me and revved. I looked and revved as Chris yelled, "*GET SET!*"

Chris dropped his arms fast, and yelled, "*GO!*"

Caleb and I hit our accelerators at the same time. Chris crouched down as our tires squealed and caught the concrete pavement. We danced right past him. The GTO moved out steady and strong but my Malibu wobbled a bit as it struggled to get proper traction.

I power shifted early so I could achieve second gear, since I'd learned it was my strongest gear, and I held it for as long as I could before I power shifted to third gear. I heard both cars whining as we both reached 60 mph at the same time (probably six seconds).

I looked over at Caleb and he looked back at me. We were both smiling and loving what we were doing. We were grinding, we were flying.

I looked up ahead at the critical turn-around and I waited an extra second, then I downshifted in time so my Malibu could slide into a neat, controlled 180 degree turn.

Caleb tried to do the same but he was a bit late and suffered a split second adjustment. When he finally completed his turn I was already heading back toward the Finish Line two car lengths ahead of his GTO.

The Malibu was still wobbling a little bit due to too much engine and an inexperienced driver but then I power shifted into fourth gear and, holding the wheel steady, I quickly took off, gaining speed on my way home. I leaned forward as I tried to give my car maximum power.

The GTO growled as it came up behind me, catching up with me incredibly fast. I heard Caleb honk his horn which played the opening notes to **BEETHOVEN'S FIFTH**. Holy moly!

The GTO was the faster car and Caleb was catching me, moving up past my tail end. He had passed my passenger side when I drove through the Finish Line a half-car length ahead of him!

I remember struggling to slow down but it took me at least a quarter mile before I could finally brake and turn around. When I rolled up to the Finish Line the four headlight cars were blinking their lights and honking their horns. Caleb had already parked his GTO and he hit *his* horn again. I laughed at his Beethoven excerpt. It was the first eight *"Victory"* notes from the Fifth symphony and it was meant to celebrate Caleb. On that night it was *my* Victory music.

I reached out to shake Caleb's hand, but before he shook mine he held back and asked, *"Best two out of three, my friend?"*

I laughed and answered, *"I couldn't run again, even if I wanted to. I was skidding the whole way. With your permission, I'll use your money to buy me some better tires!"*

Caleb nodded his regret, and we shook hands, both of us understanding that the GTO was the faster car and that the *turn* had decided the race.

Sixer handed Chris our victory money and Chris patted Sixer on his back. He reached inside his pocket and took out MaryAnn's panties. He smiled his wonderful

Chris smile, "*Hey Sixer, here's your consolation prize. Her name is MaryAnn and she loves me a lot!*"

Chris handed the panties to Sixer who looked pleased with the exchange. He was so pleased that he mimicked Chris and put the panties on his head the same way Chris had worn them. Sixer began to dance around and we all had a good laugh. As Sixer played the fool, Chris pulled the money we'd won out of his pocket. We looked at each other and laughed for a better reason.

Bob joined us, "*In-cred-i-ble, Mac! Or should I call you Mario Andretti? That was so cool!*"

Chris handed Bob his bet with his winnings, and Bob beamed as he said, "*Whoa! Money is way cooler! Definitely* **REBEL WITHOUT A CAUSE**, *man!*"

On the next Sunday Doris went to visit Clem. I couldn't go with her since there'd been some kind of riot and "*children*" were not allowed to visit that weekend. I helped her load her files into the Wagon because she planned to discuss Clem's early release with him. I saw her also put another Cakebox in the backseat and just as I was about to ask her, she said, "*Yes, Mr. Nosy. It's another Cake for the Guards. This makes them happy to see me.*"

I said, "*Okay. What flavor Cake is it?*"

She stayed calm and didn't get angry that I had asked. I figured she knew that I would.

She answered, "*It's not a Cake. It's a Texas Pecan Pie, Mr. Smarty Pants!*"

I smiled at her. She'd forgotten it was my favorite. I could smell one of those a mile away.

So since I couldn't open the Box without offending her I had to guess it was green money. Cold hard cash to keep Clem safe. Cold cash to let him continue to work in the kitchen. In his last letter to Doris he'd told her he finally had his own television set that he watched in his cell at night and during the day when he didn't work. This was all thanks to the cash in the Cakebox.

I smiled as I watched Doris drive away toward Huntsville. Clem was hanging in there.

When Doris returned I discovered my cheerful Pollyanna point of view was off the mark. When she drove under the Carport and I went outside to greet her, I expected to see the Positive-Confident Doris. Instead I greeted the Crying-Miserable Doris. Her unhappy face hit me hard.

At that point in Clem's jail-time I remember she was experiencing more frequent negative episodes concerning Clem. Most of the bad news coming her way had to do with her efforts to just get the *chance* to plea for his early release. The Appeals judges could only hear about four appeals a day and there were thousands of inmates who wanted their chance to plea. Doris was frustrated because she was running out of ideas to use to impress the judges. As of that day and that time, the Court of Appeals schedulers had turned Doris down twice.

She hadn't told me this because Doris had a *parent façade* that shielded her children from the harsh realities of life. If she could protect us by *not* sharing bad information, she'd suck it up and smile happily at us. She'd done it successfully for a long time. She was a good liar.

I sat with her in the Wagon under the Carport on the day she came home after seeing Clem. I held her hand while she cried, and I watched her *façade* crumble. She and I had finally reached the point where she had to share the truth with me, so she did: Clem's lawyers weren't helping Doris like they should have (probably due to a lack of lawyer funds) and the Criminal Court of Appeals had notified Clem they wouldn't schedule a hearing for us (his family) to make a presentation to them. I suspected there were Frank Briscoe riptide currents pulling at our feet.

Clem's request to them had been denied. When he told this to Doris in the **Visitor's Wing** that Sunday, she'd lost it and she couldn't stop crying. She was devastated and frustrated beyond any hope and Clem wasn't allowed to reach over the foot high glass to help console her. Clem was distressed but he used *his parent façade* skill on Doris and said, *"I've prayed for a blessing. I'm confident you'll receive the chance to present my case. Just keep the faith and God will answer my prayer . . ."*

Fortunately Sgt. Dunham was there that day and he'd helped to calm Doris down and escort her back to the Wagon. The problem came when she had to drive all the way home with no one to talk to, and no one to ease her unbelievable hurt.

I finally helped Doris to calm down and steered her to the Master Bedroom where I put her to bed with a sleeping pill and a cool glass of orange juice. She thanked me and I closed her door so she could hopefully get some rest. To say I was a wee bit distressed would've been accurate. I walked around the house quietly so I wouldn't disturb Doris and I made myself a peanut butter and jelly sandwich. Then I went out to my garage to watch a Sunday sport highlights show.

After ten minutes of uninspiring sports commentary I made a decision. I called Bob. I was depressed, very concerned about Clem and Doris, and I needed someone to say something positive to me. I hoped Bob would suit my needs. He answered on the first ring, *"This is Bobby-baby. Who might this be?"*

I said, *"This is Kirk, Bob."* He laughed and he made me feel good when he said, *"It's Mario Andretti, my favorite race car driver! Man, thank you again for the other night! That was so much fun, it almost made me feel young again!"*

I, of course, said, *"I bet you say that to all your new girlfriends, Bob."*

He countered with, *"Only the ones with big mouths!"*

We both laughed. Then Bob asked, *"How ya doing? Is everything okay on the home front?"*

I said, *"Things could be a lot better. Anyway, I thought I'd see if you were busy tonight and if you're up for some company. I'm gonna call friends Chris and Steve and we're gonna cruise."*

I envisioned Bob nodding. "*Why don't you come over here? I'm working on a new Daiquiri flavor and would love to test it on you.*"

I nodded. "*Sounds good. Let me call Chris and see if he's available and then we'll come over.*"

Bob said "*Okay*" and we hung up.

I went into my bathroom and looked in my mirror for a quick face to face: Was I making a mistake? There was nothing "*good*" about going over to a thirty-five-year-old bachelor's apartment, especially a bachelor with Bob's value set. I admitted that my priorities were a bit skewed.

In my defense I was sixteen going on seventeen years old and a hormonal male who loved playing on any playing field with any one. I knew I wanted to go to the head of my class, and I knew I wanted to impress Velma and Gil as I made Doris and Clem proud. How could I accomplish these goals with *Bob's* value set? I turned away from my mirror. On that Sunday night I wanted to feel the same way I'd felt the previous Thursday night when I'd driven *Heaven* to victory . . .

I called Chris to come over and when he'd parked in my driveway we jumped into my Malibu and drove to Bob's apartment. Bob happily invited us in, Chris looked around and said, "*Whoa . . . This place looks . . . uh . . . just like my place . . . except your plants look watered!*"

The apartment's lights were set at half brightness and his rock music was set at a perfect volume to fit Bob's bachelor theme. I plopped down on his blue sofa since it looked comfy. Bob returned to his bar to finish making his new concoction while Chris cruised the pictures on Bob's walls. Bob's blender was loud when Chris pointed to one picture and yelled to Bob, "*Wow! Who's this one?*"

Bob saw who Chris was pointing to and he turned off his blender so he could be heard, "*That's Darla, Chris, but you can't steal her panties. She doesn't wear any!*"

I saw Chris gulp as he continued to look at Darla's picture. Her picture hypnotized him.

He touched the picture frame and, I swear, it looked like he caressed it. He said, "*I'd like to meet her*"—he glanced at Bob—"*if that's all right.*"

Bob looked at me, I guessed for approval, and I nodded. Bob picked up his phone from off the bar counter and dialed. A few seconds later he spoke, "*Say hey, Darla . . . Yes. I know it is! Listen, what are you and Jill doing tonight? . . . Well, that's why I'm calling . . . Yes, get on over here! I've got someone I want you to meet!*"

Bob hung up, smiling, and said, "*Ask and ye shall receive-her! They're on their way!*"

When Darla walked through Bob's door it was fun to watch Chris as his eyes bugged out. Jill was nice looking, too, but Darla was a knockout.

Bob handed each of his guests a glass of his new flavor (Chris and I were on our third drink which wasn't good for my diabetic self) and we all commented on its intriguing purple color.

Bob asked us for our opinion of his purple Daiquiri, but I was more interested in watching Chris watch Darla. She clearly enjoyed his attention and after downing a full glass she asked, "*So when is Bobby-Baby going to get this party started?*"

She was very sexy. If Chris hadn't already expressed his overwhelming interest, I'd have moved closer to her. We all looked at Bob who grinned and moved quickly to fetch a bottle from the bar. He then pushed aside the living room chairs and said in a funny and lustful Master of Ceremonies voice, "*As your Ringmaster, I command you to make a ring!*"

He pointed to the floor and both girls knew what to do. We boys were clueless but happy when the girls grabbed us and Darla said, "*Come sit down here next to me, Chris. Kirk, you sit there next to Jill.*"

With everyone sitting on the floor Bob placed the bottle in the middle of us and said, "*The name of the game is "Spins and Kisses!" If the bottle stops and points at you, the spinner has to kiss you anywhere he or she wants to!*"

I smiled and looked at Chris who looked back at me. The girls said "*Yeah!*" and "*Bring it!*" so they were comfortable with the rules even though we weren't. We wouldn't get the chance to ask questions since we were in unfamiliar territory.

Okay. But being me, I still had to ask, "*Anywhere?*" which produced a laugh from everyone, even Chris.

Bob handed the bottle to Darla and said, "*Here we go! You're first, Darla!*"

Darla was very passionate as she grabbed and then spun the bottle. My heart was beating as fast as it usually did when I competed at Track meets(or car races). On Yer Mark, Get Seeeetttt—

The bottle stopped spinning, pointed at Jill. Darla, like a tiger, slowly crawled across the carpet to Jill and then she grabbed Jill's face and kissed her fully on her lips. Everyone, including me, clapped and screamed and laughed. Bob picked up the bottle and handed it to Jill.

He said, "*Okay, Jill. Now it's your turn!*"

Jill spun the bottle, hard. Finally it stopped spinning, and we saw it was pointed at Darla. Jill jumped to her feet and slowly moved around our ring as if she were stalking Darla. Then she swooped in and put both of her arms around Darla who played like she was prey to Jill's predator. Jill then kissed Darla fully on *her* lips, this time holding the kiss a lot longer.

Chris and Bob and I clapped and screamed and raised our eyebrows!

Bob cried out, "*This is good! I'm learning some new techniques here tonight!*" He looked at me and Chris, and all we could do was look back. This was all way outside our experience-zone, Bobby-Baby! He snatched the bottle again and handed it to Darla and said, "*Whew, Darla. It's yours again!*"

Darla crouched low, close to the carpet, and then she spun the bottle again, looking at Jill with a tantalizing and sexy grin. The bottle stopped spinning, and again it was pointed right at Jill. Chris and I held our breath and waited to see what would happen next.

Darla repeated her tiger technique but this time she stood up to stalk Jill. I was surprised when Darla turned, swooped in on me, and kissed ME! I watched Darla's eyes during the kiss.

They were gentle as she gently kissed me again. Just as I started to get into it, I closed my eyes and she pushed me away to grab Chris! I watched her fiercely kiss him and saw that both of his eyes were wide open and amazed! And then I saw lust and what looked like love as she began to passionately kiss Chris.

Much to his disappointment I watched Chris as she pushed him away and moved toward Bob who laughed and tried to back away from her. When Bob was pushed up against his bar, Darla took his drink from his hands and drank it to the bottom of his glass and pitched his glass across the room where it smashed against a wall. She acted like she was going to kiss Bob who looked ready for it but then, with a grin, she turned to Jill who'd been waiting patiently.

I watched, fascinated, as Darla pounced on Jill and grabbed her upper body with both hands. Then I saw her *fondle* and then I saw her *grope* Jill. This continued for several seconds and then both of them began to rip each other's shirts and pants off. Wow!

There was a concerto of verbal audience support from the male onlookers. The two ladies engaged in a heated kissing and stroking contest, and it looked to us like both gals were winning. Chris and I were popeyed. We couldn't believe what we beheld. In a matter of seconds Darla and Jill seemed to have forgotten the rest of the room. Chris whispered to me, "*Mac, how old are these girls?*"

I shrugged and whispered, "*Who cares?*" smiled at Chris, and we continued to watch.

A month passed that included a number of late nights racing and meeting other friends of Bob's who had temperaments similar to Darla's and Jill's. He knew some interesting people and, as always, when I found myself involved with a new experience that was totally involving, it usually had negative consequences. So it was with the time I spent with Bob in "*Sin Alley*." I wish I could have predicted what would soon happen there . . .

It was February 1966 and I had a new Track coach whose name was George *Babe* Craig. Babe was the Head Line Coach during Football season where he was best known for his punishing *get-into-shape* drills to sustain his *work hard to win* attitude. He looked a lot like Coach Bartosh's younger brother but taller with 50 more pounds of muscle on his upper body.

Track season was proving to be a challenge and after a grueling workout thanks to my new Track coach, I walked through our Kitchen door and laid my books down on the Kitchen table.

I was mentally and physically drained and I had a lot on my mind as I pulled out my Report Card and laid that down on the table, too. I imagined Clem sitting there smiling at me to show how happy he was that I still made good grades.

Then Clem faded away and I saw it was actually Doris sitting there looking down at my card.

She said, *"Oh, this is perfect timing! I'm going to see him this Sunday. I'll take this and show it to him. He'll be so proud of how well you're doing!"* Maybe, Doris. Maybe not.

On the Kitchen counter I saw an open/empty Cakebox complete with a string carrying-web.

I asked, *"Are you taking another cake?"*

As usual she didn't answer me and instead looked harder at my Report Card. Her smile changed to a look of concern and she said, *"Kirk, I see some B's here under History and Latin. What's happening with those subjects?"*

I answered unhappily, *"I have a problem. I got a little distracted on my last tests in both of those classes."*

Doris looked at me with real concern. She understood how important earning the title *Valedictorian* was to me and to my future, so she asked, *"What happens if you get another "B" this semester in either of these courses?"*

I answered, again unhappily, *"I won't be able to keep up my perfect grade point."*

Doris quickly over-reacted, *"But I thought Velma was supposed . . ."*

I held up my hand and interrupted her, *"This isn't Velma's fault. This is my fault. I . . . I just got distracted, that's all."*

Doris shook her head, *"I know how important this is to you. What's your plan, man?"*

I answered, *"I'll handle this. I'm gonna talk with Coach Bartosh tomorrow."*

I told Doris I had a plan but it wouldn't be easy for me to accomplish. I got along pretty well with my Latin teacher but my History teacher was another Mildred Henderson. She would not give me any slack as far as her course was concerned. She'd already informed me that whenever she gave me a test if I answered that the **War of 1812** took place in "**1813**" she'd mark it wrong, because "*History is a pure subject with no room in my classroom for false facts!*" In other words, read all the books assigned and learn who, what, when, where, and why something happened or someone did something and then memorize those facts for future tests.

My other problem was the plan Velma and I had put into motion where I joined every club at Robert E. Lee to inflate my resume. It was all about academic excellence so I could *inflate* the *McClelland* name. If I could be elected president or vice-president of a club or even the Student Council, then I had to give them my spare time to accomplish their required directives. Too many balls in the air makes for a poor juggler. That's when I'd called Coach Bartosh.

The next day at the beginning of sixth period (my Gym class), I tapped on the door to the Head Coach's Office. I heard, "*Enter!*" and I did.

Once inside I closed the door behind me and walked over to where Gil sat behind his desk so I could shake his hand. I saw Coach Craig sitting at another desk against the side wall so I walked over to shake his hand. I hadn't expected him to be present at this meeting but that week had been a week of surprises, so why not?

Gil pointed to a chair sitting in front of his desk and invited me, "*Have a seat, Kirk. What's wrong?*"

I sat down. I was in no hurry to have this session so I tried to delay it by asking, "*How'd you know something's wrong?*"

Bartosh smiled his elegant, fatherly smile and said, "*I figured it out when* (he pointed) *Coach Craig said you wanted to see him, too.*"

He crossed his arms over his head and leaned back, "*I can still connect dots, Mac.*"

I squirmed around in my chair and looked down at my hands as Bartosh continued, "*You've been grumbling and stumbling around here all week.*"

He took his arms down and leaned forward as he said, "*Let's have it.*"

I looked up into his patient eyes and I said, "*I can't do Spring Training this year . . .*"

Spring Training was an annual 2 week Football exercise we did every March so the Coaches and players could keep Football as their priority and keep their Football mentalities up-to-date.

Bartosh's face changed. It was less friendly as he asked, "*You can't or you won't?*"

I answered, "*I won't be able to. I know it's gonna sound stupid but I've got a goal, Coach.*"

I hesitated because this explanation was personal and I didn't think it would impress either of these men. I continued, "*I need . . . I want to be the Class of '67's Valedictorian. That means I have to pull off a perfect grade average across the board. There are five others who are studying full time to make it, but I need for it to happen . . . for me.*"

Coach Craig walked over and stood next to Bartosh's desk. He leaned toward me and asked, "*Does that mean you're not gonna be able to finish out Track season this year?*"

George *Babe* Craig ...loved a Good Time

I nodded as I answered, "*That's right . . . and I'm sorry Coach Craig.*"

Coach Craig wasn't finished with my interview and he impatiently asked me, "*Who's gonna anchor my 440 and Mile Relays if you don't?*"

I was very unhappy when I answered, "*I don't know. I'm sorry.*"

Gil jumped back into the discussion with: "*You and Coach Craig are gonna have to come to some kind of understanding, but damn boy, I've never heard of anyone NOT completing Spring Training and then playing Football in the fall.*"

Gil scratched his head as he continued to think about it, and then he shook it as he said, "*This would set a bad precedent for this team if I let you slide by.*"

I nodded and agreed, "*I know. That's why I wanted to talk to you.*"

Coach Bartosh sighed and then asked, "*Is this about your father, son?*"

I answered, "*Everything I do is about my father.*"

Coach Bartosh stood up from his chair and walked around his desk to the door. I stood up and watched him process our meeting. He said, "*You know you can't save your father by making good grades, don't you?*"

I just stood there, clueless about everything, as Gil continued, "*But if you do think this will help him, I recommend you try to figure out a better way.*"

Gil opened the door for me and ended his speech with, "*If you don't participate and do the work in Spring Training, I can't promise your starting spot will be available to you next season.*"

I walked to the door and turned to face both men, "*I understand, Coach.*"

This was hard work.

BRING CLEM HOME

I cleared my throat so I could continue, "*Let me formally say that I won't be able to finish out Track season . . . and I won't be able to participate in Spring Training this year. I'm truly sorry for disappointing you both.*"

Both Coaches shook their heads. My whole body trembled as I walked out the door and Coach Bartosh closed his door behind me.

After my meeting, I drove my Malibu Super Sport extremely fast on the Southwest Freeway. I was listening to **Ray Charles** singing **Unchain My Heart** on my 8 Track, and I was yelling cuss words every time I shifted gears:

First to second: "Goddamn it!"

Second to third: "Son of a bitch!"

Third to fourth: "█████████."

I felt like I'd betrayed the only people, outside my family and Velma, who cared about me. What was I thinking? I've given that question a lot of thought. How could I have been so diligent about being good before I met Bob, and why was I headed toward his apartment on that day? I would be 17 in a couple of weeks and at that age I still wasn't sure if I had bad genes influencing my decisions or if that was just a lame excuse for my being stupider than stupid.

I took the Post Oak off ramp, drove into the Post Oak Apartments and parked at the foot of Bob's apartment. I climbed the stairs to his "*playground,*" or as Chris had *christened* it, "*Bob's layground.*"

At #227 I pulled on his cowbell and Bob happily opened his door, laughing and greeting me, "*If it isn't Mario Andretti himself! Come into my pit stop for a cool one, Mario!*"

Bob handed me a tall glass of his latest frozen Daiquiri mix, and I nodded my thanks as I put the glass to my lips.

It was cold, good and a relief as I tried to thank him, but instead whispered, "*Wow!*"

I entered his apartment and saw Glorie Day (the candy striper from the Hospital). She wasn't wearing her candy striper uniform at that moment, or anything else.

I again whispered, "*Wow!*" as Bob chuckled and closed his door behind me . . .

After that more positive meeting I was again behind the wheel of my Malibu. I was having difficulty staying awake as I struggled on my short drive home from Bob's apartment. My eyes kept closing and I had to shake my head to stay alert. The problem was Bob had given me an early birthday present: **DEAN MARTIN's** 8 Track tape of **YOU'RE NOBODY TIL SOMEBODY LOVES YOU,** and I was trying to load the cartridge into my player using the same hand I used on my shifter.

I kept fumbling the cartridge as I turned the corner onto Ivanhoe. I was driving too fast up to the McClelland home and when I turned into our driveway, my foot accidently hit the accelerator instead of the brake causing me to smash the front of the Malibu into the back of Doris's Station Wagon. Damn! The Malibu was hurt and I remember steam rising up into the air from my busted radiator. I, too, was hurt, I think, but I can't remember because my head slid down sideways on the headrest for a short Daiquiri induced nap.

I don't know how short my nap was but I woke up to Doris and Anne yelling at me, "*Kirk! Kirk! Wake up! Are you all right? Answer me!*"

I heard Doris holler at Anne, "*Call an ambulance, quick!*"

Doris was standing at the window on the driver's side of the Malibu as I mumbled, "*No ambu . . . ambulance. I'm all right! Just help get me into the house . . .*"

I opened the door and tried to get out of the car. Doris nodded to Anne and they helped guide me into the house. I made it to the Kitchen table and I fell on a chair.

With my head slumping forward I said, "*Get my insulin, please. And my syringe.*"

Doris moved quickly to our icebox, opened it, took out my insulin and a syringe and she brought them to where I slumped.

I asked her to, "*Fill it to thirty units, please.*"

Doris pushed the needle of the syringe into the bottle and withdrew thirty units of insulin into the syringe. She held it waiting for her next instructions. I slowly pulled down my blue jeans and took the syringe from her. I stuck the needle in and injected the needed insulin.

As I knew she would, Doris asked, "*How did this happen? Why do you have to take more? Clem only took more after he'd drunk too much Jack Daniels!*"

As I knew she would, Anne added, "*It's Bob. That's his new friend.*"

I, too, was predictable and said to Anne, "*I told you about him in confidence, big sister.*"

I could tell that my sister could've cared less about what I wanted as she replied, "*Doris needs to know, especially now that you've crashed your racer.*"

Doris gave me a Frank Briscoe prosecutorial stare and put *me* on trial, "*Don't get angry at your sister! Right now you need to worry about me! Who is BOB? And why haven't you told me about him?*"

Anne laughed and answered Doris's question, "*He's an older man who makes great Daiquiris! Look at your son--Living proof!*"

Doris looked at my older sister and decided she was having too much fun so Doris motioned for Anne to leave us. Anne smirked at me and left. Doris waited a moment then attacked, "*Okay, mister. Now YOU tell ME!*"

I was thirsty from all the questions, so I tried a delaying tactic, "*Can I have some water?*"

Doris didn't flinch, "*Not until you've earned it. Talk.*"

I answered rat-ta-tat to curry favor with the High Inquisitor, "*Bob Gilbert is his name, and he lives around the corner at the Post Oak Apartments.*"

I continued trying to answer as quickly as possible, "*I met him when I was in the Hospital, we became friends, and there you have it.*"

Doris inquired, "*How old is he?*"

I rat-ta-tatted, "*Thirty-three or thirty-four or maybe thirty-five.*"

I could tell Doris was concerned, but she played a really good game of poker and knew how to play 'em close as she dug for more info, "*So why do you go over to his apartment?*"

I ratted more, "*He's a nice guy and it gives me a place to hang out that isn't school or here.*"

Doris played her hurt feelings card thinking that would leverage more info, "*I'm sorry "here" isn't so glamorous. What can I do to make it so?*"

I was quick but not very clever, "*Learn to make frozen Daiquiris?*"

Doris was still in the game, "*Ha! Funny, very funny. You know you can't drink those, Kirk. You're under age, and the alcohol turns to sugar the second it hits your system. Not smart.*"

I agreed with her, so I didn't rat or tat.

Doris continued, "*Where does "Bob" live?*"

I answered, "*Post Oak Apartments, number 227. Do you want his phone number, too?*"

Doris answered, "*Yes.*"

I grabbed the notepad off the Kitchen counter next to the phone and wrote his number down.

I handed the pad to her.

I was tired and my head hurt from the crash so I asked, "*Are we square?*"

My mother was relentless, "*One other question.*"

I already knew there was one more, "*Ask.*"

And then she nailed me, "*Is this Bob the reason you had to quit Track and miss Spring Training this year?*"

She was pretty sharp. But we were traveling in uncharted waters that required more analysis on my end before I could share, so I played it safe, "*I told you I had trouble with a couple of tests, and I needed more time to make them up. End of story.*"

She countered, "*I need you to talk to me about what you're doing! I'd hate to . . . I won't disappoint your father by not taking care of his favorite son!*"

I tried to reassure her and make her laugh at the same time, "*I know. I'll do better, as long as our talks are short.*"

Doris smiled, "*Ha, ha!*" She put her hand on my head and asked, "*How do you feel? Are you hurting anywhere? Do you need to go to the hospital?*"

I pushed her off that subject and changed gears, *"I'm fine. Can we talk about my speech for the Student Council now?"* She nodded. I asked, *"What do you think of my idea?"*

She sighed and smiled, *"I think it's great. I can't wait to see it!"*

I smiled and nodded at her, *"See? Short talks are good!"*

And then I gave her a big hug . . .

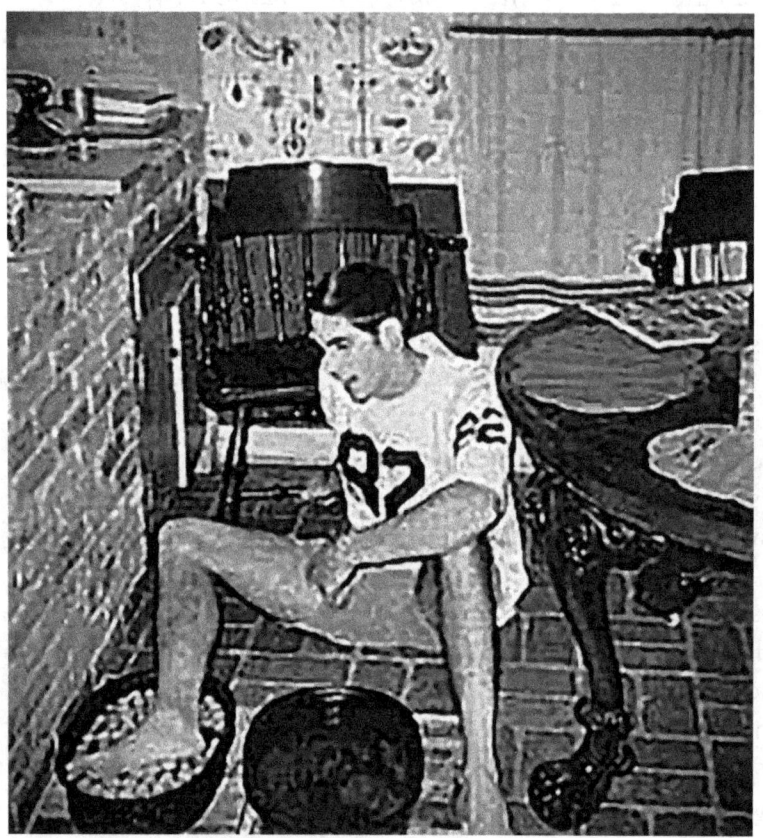

Sometimes I got hurt when I played too rough . . .
(First soak it in ice, then soak it in hot water)

CHAPTER NINE

I WISHED THIS WOULD HAPPEN 1966-1967

The next afternoon something happened that I still can't believe. Fortunately I have tangible proof that it did happen or I wouldn't mention it . . .

Early that morning I took my Malibu over to **RICHARDSON CHEVROLET** and let them deal with replacing my radiator and performing the necessary body work. Fortunately, Chris and I were way ahead with our race bets and I was able to pay for my mistake out of my own pocket. It still hurt to hand over those hundred dollar bills but it taught me a good lesson:

DON'T DRINK AND DRIVE!

I tried to give Doris money to repair her car (her rear end damage was minimal) but she said her insurance would cover it since *"the accident"* had occurred in front of our house and the passing motorist who'd hit her had fled the scene. Amusing and creative role-modeling, Doris.

I was enjoying lunch in the Robert E. Lee lunchroom with Steve, Tim, Chris and his new girlfriend, a pretty brunette named MaryAnn. The lunchroom was packed as usual when Larry Klump strolled up to our table and said to me, *"Well, lookee here. If it isn't our cute little quitter. I hear you chickened out for this year's Spring Training. You finally lost the one ball you had left. Or was it the one on the right?"*

I'd had enough of that pig and I jumped up just as Steve grabbed my arm to hold me back.

Klump moved closer and I shared my angry words with him, *"The truth, lump? When I heard YOU were gonna be there, I told Coach I wouldn't be able to stand the smell . . ."*

Everyone at the table laughed. Fortunately Coach Craig was on lunch duty and was cruising down the aisle in our direction. Klump saw the Coach, sneered at me, and slowly walked away.

I paused and sat down to slow my heart rate, just as MaryAnn sweetly said, "*So are you ready to give your speech tomorrow? Chris told me you've been writing it for about a month. I can't wait to hear it!*"

Steve used his high-pitched clown voice, "**Why, you know what, Mac? I can't wait either!**"

Chris and Tim together said, "*I can't . . .*"

I interrupted them, "*I know. You can't wait either! Okay . . . so you wanna know if I'm gonna be serious with my nomination speech, right?*"

They all nodded, and Chris said, "*Right!*"

I said, "*Wait 'til tomorrow!*" and they all laughed.

I saw Klump look back at us. He probably thought we were laughing at him . . .

After lunch I was walking by Velma's Counseling Room and I looked in to say "*Hi*." Her room was empty and I was about to walk away when I noticed her phone sitting on her desk and I thought I'd call Bob and surprise him. I quickly looked around and started dialing his number. I heard a busy signal so I hung up. I kept a sharp eye out for Velma and then I had an inspiration. I dialed Doris. I smiled as I heard her answer and say, "*This is Doris McClelland . . .*"

I whispered playfully, "*Three guesses who THIS is.*"

I heard her giggle and then she said, "*Hold on. I have an "Unchained Melody" for you . . .*"

I heard her whisper, "*It's Kirk!*"

I heard a rustling sound like she was handing the phone to someone else. Then I heard, "*Hello, boy. Stay cool. If anyone's near you, don't say my name, okay?*"

I was in shock, but somehow I managed to say, "*. . . uh . . . okay.*"

Then I heard him laugh as he said, "*We have to stop meeting like this! So. Let me ask you some questions . . . like I've wanted to . . . (his voice broke) . . . over the past year.*"

I couldn't believe I was talking to Clem. My hunting partner. I'd wanted to talk to him so many times about so many things that he knew, and that he could help me with . . .

Of course he controlled his emotions better than I could, so he asked, "*Uh, how's school?*"

I answered, "*I don't know what to say. How did you . . . Why are you there?*"

He laughed and said, "*I had an attack of prison-itis! Had to see my Doris without looking through the damn looking-glass!*"

I was talking to my father. I was a bit paranoid about Velma showing up. This was her room and her phone and she was strict with her rules.

I asked Clem, "*Okay. How were you able to do this?*"

He answered, "*Can you guess how a "cake" here or there might be healthy for a diabetic?*"

Finally a chance to understand the damn Cakebox!

I asked, "*But what was inside the cake?*"

Clem laughed, "*A thousand special ingredients thanks to your mother.*"

I laughed, too loudly, "*Well, this is fun. How long* (I lowered my voice) *will you be home?*"

He answered, "*The Laundry Truck driver who dropped me will be back in an hour . . . Say, I wanted to wish you good luck tomorrow with your Student Council speech.*"

I said, "*Thanks.*"

He continued, "*Your mother told me about it . . .*"

At that moment Velma walked into her office, saw me on her phone and angrily mouthed, "*Get off my phone!*"

I had to hang up on my Clem. I didn't want to offend Velma so I hung up without a thought.

I smiled and lied to Velma, "*Time and temperature, Mrs. Brennan. Sorry!*"

She said, "*Okay.*" and I excused myself, walking quickly out of her office.

I ran a hundred miles an hour through the halls of Robert E. Lee to the Student Parking lot where my rental car from my Chevy dealer waited. I jumped into the blue '59 Chevy Bel Air and floored it. It, of course, died immediately. I remember wishing I hadn't wrecked my racer the previous night as I tried and tried and finally re-started the rental. I gently coaxed it out of the parking lot and pointed it toward home.

As I suffered the bad luck of a blue Bel Air I imagined Clem and Doris happily seeing each other without being guarded, without the disadvantage of bars on the windows, and without other inmates or their families watching my parents as they kissed each other enthusiastically for the first time in a year. I imagined ice cream and cake and left-over burgers and fries from the **JACK IN THE BOX** on South Post Oak littering our round Kitchen table.

I drove as fast as I could, shifting lanes on the Southwest Freeway, passing cars left and right. I wanted to get home to see Clem. I laughed thinking about his smiling face and knowing that someday we'd remember and laugh at his adventure outside and beyond the Huntsville gates.

Unfortunately his adventure was chock-full of risks and jam-packed with potential disasters. How could he have taken such a chance? What were the odds he'd be successful? What were the benefits compared to the punishments? Holy moly! *How did he do it? Wow!*

A week later Clem and Doris told me some details that I'll share now:

Clem and Doris heard the sound of the Prison Laundry Truck as it drove up the driveway at our home and it parked under the Carport. Doris began to cry. Her quality time with my father was coming to an end and she was lamenting the loneliness she'd feel after he was gone.

Clem kissed her, wiped her eyes and then he started tickling her the way he always did when she needed to laugh. He told me she shrieked "*loudly.*" Then he went to his bar to grab 3 bottles of Jack Daniels, he gave Doris a final kiss/hug, and then he moved quickly to the Kitchen door.

Clem opened the door just as the Laundry Truck driver, Jersey Owens, opened the side panel sliding door so it sat opposite our Kitchen door opening. Clem jumped through it in a flash, turned to wave one last time to Doris, and then closed the Truck's door as Jersey backed up.

Inside the Truck, Jersey asked, *"Any trouble, Judge?"*

Clem shook his head as he stayed down low on the Truck's floor, *"No trouble, Jersey. Thanks."*

As the Truck began to pull away, I drove up in the Bel Air and when I saw the Truck I honked good-bye. Jersey honked back and waved to me but Clem was nowhere to be seen.

I parked the Bel Air under the Carport and walked into the Kitchen in time to see Doris still wiping her eyes as she sat at the round table. I asked her, *"Are you all right?"* She nodded. I asked her, *"What just happened?"*

She pointed at the **JACK IN THE BOX** litter on the table and said, *"Your father came home for a hamburger."*

I laughed and then she laughed. She started to pick up the left-overs and I helped her. As we cleaned up Clem's untidiness, I said, *"Jeez, he took a hell of a chance doing this, don't cha think?"*

Doris nodded as she continued to destroy the evidence of his visit. She answered, *"He did, but your father is your father, Kirk. He's you . . . Isn't he?"*

I didn't answer her. Instead I asked, *"How long have you two been planning this?"* (She smiled) *Okay, let me ask this: Will he be able to get back inside without getting caught?"*

She nodded and said, *"He assured me they've got it all worked out. Please say a big prayer!"*

Doris grabbed me and held me tight as she tried to talk through her tears, *"If he gets caught, it will ruin everything!"*

Jersey Owens was a nervous man. He was a tall Irishman with a sweet smile and a thick nose. He'd been an inmate at Huntsville for over 15 years and he'd checked into the *Walls Unit* when he'd killed his best friend in a drunken bar fight over a luscious redhead. In order to help his *new* best friend, Judge Clem McClelland, he had risked everything.

He'd been a trustee for over 10 years and had the cushiest job on the walk, since he drove to and from Houston three times a week. He'd even developed a relationship with a cute waitress working at a diner close to the **Huntsville Linen Service** just off Woodlands Drive in Houston, and he was the happiest he'd been since he'd become a Huntsville inmate.

Jersey couldn't control Clem, but he loved "*Jack*"

When Jersey was nervous he chewed on his lower lip which is what he was doing as he and the judge left the city of Houston behind them. They were driving north on Interstate Highway 45 headed toward the oak woods of Conroe and Willis on their way back to the piney woods of Huntsville. It was a 69 mile jaunt and it normally took Jersey about an hour and fifteen minutes to make the trip one way.

In the rearview Jersey watched Clem in the back of the truck as the judge carefully arranged all of the Laundry elements that were supposed to be back there. Clem had a clipboard and was checking off detergent, towels, soap bars, bath salts, filters, softeners, and Clorox gallon jugs to make sure everything Jersey was scheduled to pick up was actually and numerically back there.

Jersey saw a smile on Clem's face. Clem was looking down inside a full-sized hamper and then he was looking up at Jersey. He told me Jersey said, "*Judge, you look like the cat that ate the canary. What cha got goin' on back there?*"

Clem looked back down inside the hamper and said, "*The hamper will be easier for me to hide in now that the linen's clean.*"

Jersey said, "*Uh-huh.*"

Then Clem told me he fake-screamed, "*Wait! There's something else in this hamper! Oh my Lord!*"

Jersey went from being nervous to totally freaked out and bug-eyed, "*WHAT IS IT, JUDGE?*"

Clem said he then leaned down into the hamper and pulled out one of his Jack Daniels bottles, and then he held it up so Jersey could see it in his rearview mirror.

Jersey shouted, "*Holy Mother of God! Judge, tell me that's what I think it is!*"

Smiling, Clem walked up to where Jersey was driving and handed him the open J D bottle.

Clem said, "*It's what you think it is. Give it a guzzle, and tell me how it tastes!*"

Jersey took a long swig and he spoke very fast since he was so excited, "*It's everything that's good and true and holy in this otherwise unholy world, Your Honor!*"

Clem told me he saw Jersey's eyes water as he handed the bottle back to Clem. The Truck swerved ever so slightly and hit a bump. Both men laughed.

The Truck settled down, back on course. Clem wasn't concerned but he still had to ask, "*You want me to drive, Jersey?*"

Jersey beamed and sounded like a preacher to Clem's ears, "*Won't be necessary! I have a light inside me now! It will show me the clear path! I see my future ahead of me now!* (He turned back to Clem and the J D bottle) *Another please, kind sir!*"

Clem handed the bottle to Jersey and said, "*Keep it. I'll get another.*"

Clem said Jersey's eyes actually bugged-out, "*ANOTHER?*"

Clem moved back to the hamper and picked another bottle up. He tore the paper and twisted the lid so he could open the bottle and pour a healthy *Nectar of the Gods* swig down his throat.

Jersey watched Clem in his rearview mirror and asked, "*Sweet Jesus, how many bottles do you have back there?*"

Clem told me at that moment the Truck suddenly switched lanes by accident. Fortunately it was an Interstate Highway that had 4 lanes . . .

Forty minutes and two bottles of J D later, Jersey took the Prison exit off of Highway 45 to reach Twelfth Street in Huntsville. This was the location of the Prison and where the Walls Laundry Department was situated for the *Walls Unit* where Clem had his cell.

Jersey was prudent and driving slower so he could stay inside the lane he was supposed to stay in. He was a changed and extremely focused man as he held the steering wheel of his holy Truck with both of his wholly intoxicated hands.

Clem told me Jersey was a little loopy as he said, "*The Texas Department of Criminal Justice promotes positive change in offender behavior.*"

Clem said after Jersey had quoted the Prison *Mission Statement* several times he slapped his own face. Then he started to prep Clem for what they had to do to survive the next ten minutes.

Jersey shook his head and was alert as he said, "*Let's go over it again, sir.*"

Clem sat next to him in the Truck's passenger seat. Clem described that moment to me, as he sipped his J D. His mind was unhappy with having to return to his cell away from Doris and me, so he took that opportunity to watch the rolling Texas countryside as they moved along I-45.

Even though his escape from Prison was outrageously stupid, Clem had to regain some control over his life, if only in his mind. What better way to flush his anxiety and frustration than to break out of Huntsville Prison and go for a drive across the beautiful State of Texas?

Jersey pointed over his shoulder to the back of the truck, "*Get back into the hamper . . .*"

Clem smiled at Jersey, got up sluggishly and moved back to the hamper. He carefully crawled into it but he couldn't control the giggle that slipped out between his wet lips. Then Clem began to sing **THE YELLOW ROSE OF TEXAS**, "*There's a yellow rose in Texas someday I'm gonna see. Nobody else could ▮▮▮▮▮ her nobody else but me. She cried, so when I left her it like to broke her heart. And if I ever see her, we nevermore shall part.*"

Jersey scolded Clem, "*No more singing, Your Judgeship! Do NOT make a sound . . . Do not move around . . .*"

Jersey looked back at the hamper, searching for any visible sign of the former judge, "*Are we clear, Your Honor?*"

Clem giggled again and then shushed himself which made him laugh again. He pulled one of the linen sheets over his head. It covered his face, but the shape of his head puffed upward.

Clem was very loose, but he tried for a deeper, more serious voice, "*Plan sounds good! No Problem!*"

Then he giggled again. Jersey was getting more nervous. He had a lot to lose.

He shook his head, "*Shut up, Judge . . . Please!*"

Jersey drove the Laundry Truck slowly toward the Outer gates of the Prison's front gates.

Clem continued to drink and giggle inside the hamper and under the sheet. Jersey continued to go down his checklist trying to control Clem, "*Now, don't forget. Ronald is the Guard who's on our side. It's the New Guard we have to watch out for. If he sees OR HEARS anything, we're cooked . . .*"

At the Outer gate, Jersey was waved through by the Guards. He honked, they waved, and the Laundry Truck went through.

Huntsville Laundry Truck

Huntsville Guard Tower

Huntsville Prisoners/Guard

At the Inner gate, Jersey saw Ronald who, smiling, motioned for Jersey to drive through.

Jersey honked hello to Ronald and, as he drove through, he looked over at the passenger seat and saw an empty bottle of Jack Daniels. Jersey grabbed it and, scared, he shouted at Clem, "*Got a problem here, Judge! I'm sliding it back to you! I need you to grab it and put it inside the hamper with you!*"

Under the sheet Clem yelled, "*Go for it!*"

Jersey utilized his pitching arm (from his *Huntsville Tigers* baseball team) and slid the bottle back on the Truck's floor toward the hamper.

It was a good pitch, and it hit the front of the hamper.

At that moment, the New Guard (they learned his name was Lester) approached the Truck and he tapped his black nightstick against the front of the Truck. That made Jersey hit the brakes and come to a stop just as the Truck passed the Inner gate.

Through his windshield Jersey watched Ronald and the New Guard, Lester, as they stood next to his Truck and discussed the protocols for guarding Huntsville Prison. Ronald wanted to wave the Truck through and Lester wanted to examine it thoroughly. Simply put, that meant for Clem and Jersey the jig was up, the dance was done, and the party was probably over.

Jersey saw the two Guards continue their debate and, keeping his face pointed forward, he tried to ventriloquize his voice to Clem without moving his lips, "*Clem, the bottle's in front of the hamper!*"

Jersey saw Lester look at him through the glass. He tried again not to move his lips, "*I need you to get it and get it fast, PLEASE!*"

Clem told me he'd been peeking over the edge of the hamper to watch Jersey sweat and he said he found that to be humorous. He reached outside of the hamper and used his long arm to slide down its side.

Jersey coughed and then he ventriloquized again, "*Judge, it's now or never!*"

Clem said his hand felt around the Truck's floor. He told Jersey, "*I can't find the bottle.*"

He kept searching around with his hand and when he finally did find the bottle, he brought it up and over the edge and then down so he could hide it with him under the sheets inside the hamper. Clem was feeling no pain and it took, he said, incredible mind control on his part not to laugh.

Clem told me he was under all the sheets in the hamper so he couldn't see Ronald or Lester but he could still hear them arguing when Lester banged on the sliding side door behind the driver's side. That forced Jersey to open it.

Once he was inside the Truck, Lester extended his hand to Jersey and said, "*Jersey Owens, right? Hi, Jersey. I'm Lester and I'm gonna look to make sure you didn't bring any contraband back with you from Houston, all right?*"

Clem heard Jersey say, "*No sir, no contraband this trip!*"

Clem heard Lester say, "*My chief told me you guys always say that!*"

Jersey later told Clem that he was watching Ronald through the front windshield and he said that Ronald shrugged and mouthed "*I'm sorry*" to Jersey who was totally sober by that time.

Lester walked past Clem's hamper so he could check the back of the Truck. He picked up several inventory items, then he put them back. After a final look, Lester nodded to Jersey, "*No contraband, Mr. Owens! You're good to go!*"

Lester stepped down and slammed the sliding door shut behind him. Lester waved Jersey forward, Jersey put the Truck in gear and slowly accelerated through the Inner gate.

Clem heard Jersey breathing fast as he whispered rat-ta-tat, "*All the saints preserve us! Dear God bless us sinners from on high and may we bathe in the light of Your glory all the days of our lives, thy kingdom come, thy will be done, so help me Jack Daniels! Amen!*"

When Clem heard Jersey's prayer of thanks he told me he laughed and cried real alcohol induced tears. It was the perfect ending to Clem's perfect jailbreak . . .

Huntsville Prison Units   **Huntsville Prison Yard**

After Clem left us, Doris and I spent the rest of the day gathering the items (the props) I would use for my speech the next day. I was running for Vice President of the Student Council and I wanted to make sure I performed well for the people (Velma) who had nominated me. Once Doris and I had the items in hand it was simply a matter of placing the items in their proper location for my very short speech. My game plan was, "*Presentation Is Everything!*"

I did one run-through, with Doris acting as my audience, and then I was good to go . . .

The next day the Robert E. Lee High School Auditorium was packed with students. Each of the nominees for the four Council positions had to stand up on the stage and speak into the microphone and tell the entire student body why each of us would make a good President or Vice President or Treasurer or Secretary. Then each student would return to their homerooms and cast their votes for their choices and thus the Student Council would be democratically chosen and set to run the school over the next year.

I had no desire to run the school. That's why I told Velma to nominate me for the VP slot. The other reason I wanted to run for VP was David Davis was nominated for the President slot.

I didn't want my personal feelings about his inability-to-help-me-when-I'd-tried-to-help-him to get in the way of my having fun with the Student Council election process.

That's right. My plan was to have fun and that's what I did.

After the Principal called the assembly to order he sat down and Velma took over. Sitting behind the podium where Velma stood were eight well-dressed student nominees, two nominees per office, with me sitting in the middle. I was the only male nominee who wore a suit and tie.

I looked out and saw Doris sitting next to sister Anne and Steve (who waved at me and laughed) and Chris and his MaryAnn. Being no stranger to school assemblies Velma got right down to business.

Guess who she called on first: *"Each nominee today will tell you something about themselves to help you decide who you want to represent you in this very important group. Your Student Council shares your ideas and your concerns with teachers and Lee's principals. If there is something you don't like about how Lee operates they will listen to your complaint and if it's a legit gripe they'll represent your point of view. They'll also help raise funds for school social events so* (She turned and pointed to the eight nominees) *these people are your agents to keep you happily involved with your school.*

Keeping that in mind the first nominee who will share with you why he/she should be on next year's Student Council is Kirk McClelland. He will tell you, hopefully, the reasons why you should vote for him. Nominated for Vice President. Clement Kirk McClelland."

Velma looked at me with her normal *"You can do anything if you really want to"* attitude and then she sat down next to the Principal and other high placed members of the Lee staff.

I stood and walked slowly up to the podium. Being first meant I was the ice-breaker, and I wanted to appear nervous so that when I took charge of the room, I would be more powerful. This was a technique my Debate coach had taught me and I saw him smiling at me. I said, *"First of all I want to thank you for nominating me for this job, and second of all I want to thank you for nominating my opponent, since we all know he'll be EASY for me to beat."*

That little joke bought me a lot of votes since the whole auditorium laughed out loud.

I looked over at Bill Wade, my opponent, and I saw he wasn't very happy. So I said, *"Just kidding!"* and waved at him. I turned back to the audience and rolled my eyes.

The students sitting up close laughed when they saw my eye-roll. I continued, *"Just so you know, I am more than qualified for this post because I make it a point to attend Robert E. Lee High every . . . single . . . day!"*

Out in the audience, Doris began to clap as I'd directed her to.

When no one joined her, she stood up as I'd directed her to, and she continued to clap louder. Then everyone got it, and joined her. I pointed at her and said, *"Ladies and Gentlemen, that intelligent woman with the clap is none <u>other</u> than my <u>mother!</u>"*

The students howled at my off-color joke at the expense of my mother who stopped clapping and wagged her finger at me. She then executed her famous Doris shrug, and sat down.

So far, so good. I was on my final turn, *"So let's get down to why you should vote for me. When I started to think about that, I came up with so many reasons for why I'm qualified for this position that, try as I might, I couldn't remember them all. So I had to make a list. I ask in advance for your forgiveness since it's a rather long list and I just couldn't remember all of it . . ."*

I began to pat my suit jacket and first looked in my outside pockets. I said, "Uh . . . I've got that list here, uh, somewhere . . . Where did I put it?"

Then I played like the proverbial light bulb had just turned on over my head and I unbuttoned my jacket to search my inside pockets. I stepped to the left of the podium as I opened my coat. Sewn to the inside of my jacket were Track medals, Basketball and Football ribbons I'd won over my past years in the Boy's Club, Elementary, Junior and Senior High competitions.

There were many, and when the audience saw them they started to laugh, bigtime.

Since I still hadn't found my list, I stepped to the right of the podium and opened up the other side of my jacket which revealed more ribbons and medals and two small trophies. I stood there and held both sides of my jacket open.

The audience stood up, laughing and clapping, to give me a standing ovation. I stood there a moment and then I started to laugh at the wonderful response my peers had given to my silly visual joke. I looked over at my opponent and smiled. Then, since I'd been unsuccessful finding my list, I shrugged, buttoned my coat, and sat down . . .

Footnote: At the beginning of this chapter, I mentioned I had tangible proof that Clem had indeed escaped Huntsville Prison for an afternoon . . . uh, burger.

When Doris returned from watching my Student Council performance at Lee, she picked up her Kitchen notepad so she could make a Shopping list. On the top page of the notepad she saw that Clem had drawn a sketch the day before. The sketch was his vision of me holding up both sides of my coat with all the medals and ribbons hanging down. Underneath his sketch was a message and his signature, "*That's my boy! I know you'll surprise 'em! Your hunting partner, Clem.*"

**Clem sketched his favorite son
(during his jailbreak)**

It was 1966, and over the next few months I corresponded with Clem and went to visit him whenever Doris let me. She was the boss and the mover and shaker for all things Clem. I helped her as much as I could but I didn't get in her way. She and Clem had worked together for a lot of years before I came into the picture and I respected her decision-making authority. What I needed from her was more face time with my dad. I missed him. I missed talking to him.

In 1966 there were approximately 1400 inmates inside the thirteen units of Huntsville Prison. To monitor and maintain the Prison daily, there were approximately 275 Guards plus 100 or so administration personnel for the whole Penitentiary. This was where my Clem was being kept.

I studied the mindset of the 1400 prisoners in that jail. I read article after article about life in the Huntsville Prison system and it was obvious that every inmate had fantasies of innocence as well as righteous anger in their minds about how they got there. They fantasized about how they should simply be allowed to go back home. Each prisoner wanted to be released and returned to his life since his old life held more promise than his present prison life offered. I thought about those obvious facts because during the time Clem was living there, with a prison population that was full of captive and unhappy men, a number of "*incidents*" took place.

There was a riot where hostages were taken and people were killed. It was, and always will be, a dangerous place. The harsh reality inside Huntsville Prison was that Clem had lost control of his life. When he'd first arrived he'd had to stand naked in a room full of other prisoners and correctional officers of both sexes. He'd had to bend over and be deloused as probing fingers searched him for drugs. He'd been called names and treated less than fully human. Over the past year, during a normal day, he'd had to stand next to some of the worst human beings in our society, and he'd had to suffer every indignity, every insult, and every lousy meal that every inmate in The Walls unit was fed. This was what my Clem had suffered.

I've never forgiven Frank Briscoe for his obsession to go after Judge Clem McClelland. At that time, in 1966, he was still unbelievably determined to keep my father locked up inside. Did my father do the things that Frank Briscoe had said he'd done? In reading newspaper articles and stories from that period, I found some of the statements that Briscoe had made to Clem's Juries. Here are two, "*If you do not find this man guilty, you will be abusing your oath as jurors as much as he abused his oath as a public Judge*" AND "*His pocketing of probate funds was the kind of crime for which there is no justification . . . stealing funds from orphans, the dead, and from lunatics.*"

Did Clem abuse his oath? Did Clem pocket probate funds and thereby deprive widows and orphans? Did decent and Christian Clem make bad choices that had come back to haunt him? The question I wanted to ask Briscoe at the time was, "*Do you really think it will benefit you and the citizens of Houston if Clem McClelland continues to stay in that hellhole of a prison?*

Briscoe's run for Congress would occur later that year, in November. After reading the press stories and watching the TV interviews, I was sure he had convinced himself that prosecuting a sitting Judge successfully was THE necessary step toward his achieving a seat in Congress. And while Frank slept at home with his wife Clem slept in a cell within the depths of a dangerous jungle.

It was late at night and I was thinking some dark thoughts about Mr. Briscoe and how he might look after spending the night in The Walls unit with some of the violent criminals he'd locked up. I had a smile on my face when suddenly our phone rang. It was one o'clock in the morning so I answered with, "*Who the hell's calling here at one o'clock in the morning?*"

I heard the familiar voice of The Underwriter saying, "*Hello, Kirk. It's been a long time but I wanted to check up on you.*"

I said, "*Hello, Mr . . . what was your name again?*"

He laughed, "*You've gotten older but you're still singing the same song.*"

I smiled. "*Sorry, I had to try. What's up?*"

He asked, "*How's your luck with the appeal?*"

I answered, "*Not so good. Doris is working hard but she's missing some key element that will open the door for us.*"

I heard him smile as he asked, "*Can I help?*"

I answered, "*Hell, yes! We need an argument that will allow us to get a hearing. You know the process. Without a hearing, Clem has no chance at early release.*"

Then I shared with him what I hadn't shared with anybody else, "*You've got to understand that Doris and I are willing to do anything to get him home. She and I are so frustrated that a day doesn't go by where one or the other of us doesn't cry.*"

I tried not to let my voice break, "*Can you hear my voice breaking? That's my heart!*"

I think he smiled again as he asked, "*Do you have a pen and paper?*"

I took a deep breath and answered, "*Yes, sir.*"

He said, "*Write this down . . .*"

Oh my God. My prayers were being answered. I'd prayed night after night that this man would call and share his knowledge with us. He wasn't toe-brained like some people I knew, nor was he motivated by money. He just wanted to help. Holy Mother of Christ. Thank you, Jesus.

I tried to steady my voice, and then I said, "*Ready.*"

The Underwriter said, "*You need to remind these Appellate judges that prisoners who were not involved in violent crime but who were earners back home will not jeopardize public safety. States like Texas, Georgia, South Carolina and Mississippi have reduced their prison populations by adopting a more systematic approach to sentencing guidelines.*"

I asked, "*Are we talking about parole?*"

He answered, "*Yes. Without parole to give prisoners a HUGE incentive, they'd have to build a lot more cells and build much higher walls! Do you know currently how many prisoners or inmates there are behind bars, inside all the State prisons in the country?*"

I answered, "*No, sir.*"

He said, "*200,000 . . . and I estimate 40 percent of that number could be released today without jeopardizing public safety, because they are NOT violent criminals.*"

As of this writing there are *now* 1.3 million prisoners inside all the State prisons. Of that 1.3 million, 718,000 are violent criminals. Going back to 1966 the Underwriter coached me, "*You need to remind the Criminal Court of Appeals that your father is not a violent criminal.*

He misappropriated funds . . ."

I interrupted him, "*So you suppose!*"

He continued, "*You're a true and faithful son . . . Okay. Try this: He deposited funds that weren't his and then he filled out and signed a deposit slip to deposit those funds in his account. I think he called the account "Tierra Grande," isn't that right?*"

I said, "*You're well-informed . . .*"

He agreed, "*Yes, I am. Now, here's my advice: You need to get in front of those judges and beat your chest and growl at them to wake them up so they'll be fair toward your father for his many years of service as a Judge, and for all the work he did for those Crippled Children.*"

I considered what he'd told me.

I said, "*You've given this a lot of thought. Thanks.*"

He then laughed and said, "*Good luck to you and your mom . . .*" and he hung up . . .

I'm not going to say that what Mr. Writer told me was the key to the door.

I will say that when I shared what he'd told me with Doris, he helped motivate her to explore several new avenues that expanded her research. He'd educated both of us about what the Appeals judges wanted to hear, and what would seriously bend their minds toward letting Clem leave his cell and come home. The Underwriter had helped us try to be smarter . . .

Me and my touch Football buddies were playing again on the T.H. Rogers Football field on a Sunday afternoon. It was August and Tom, Tim, Chris, Steve, Hunt, Wright, and me were playing touch. It was Football as usual until Tom Tomlin, holding the Football, called, "*Time out! Let's take a breather and drink some of that new Gatorade Chris brought!*"

Tim Toler whined as usual and said, "*I don't like it. It tastes . . .*"

Chris interrupted, "*It tastes great when you've played hard, Tim! You never play hard!*"

Everybody laughed. Tomlin picked up a bottle and pulled me aside. I followed him.

I asked him, "*What's up, Mr. Quarterback?*"

He drank the new green Gatorade like it was champagne and then he answered, "*Mac, you know we started our two-a-day workouts this week.*"

I nodded and said, "*I know.*"

He looked at me and grinned, "*Guess what? You weren't there!*"

He tossed the Football up and continued, "*You know I plan to make All-State this year.*"

I nodded, and he continued, "*And you know how many Football teams there are in our very large State of Texas.*"

I nodded again, and he said, "*I can't make All-State unless I have good people to throw to. You're good people. Go make nice with Bartosh so I can get what I want.*"

He patted me on my shoulder and walked away as he called out, "*Okay, ladies! It's only 110 out here! Let's play!*"

To a man we all ran to join him. He was the quarterback . . .

The next day was Monday. I stood in my garage room in the morning and I put on my Robert E. Lee Football jersey and a Lee baseball cap. I looked at myself, and took off the cap.

I combed my hair with my hands. Then I began to rehearse my speech, *"Hi Coach. Say, listen, I'm really sorry about missing Spring Training . . . No."*

I cleared my throat and tried for a deeper register with my voice, *"Hi Coach. I'm sorry I missed Spring Training. I WAS able to get my grades back up to my 4 point 0 status but I know it cost me a terrible price . . . No."*

I wandered around the garage trying to find my center of gravity . . . I whispered, *"Jesus.."*

I walked into the Locker Room and saw various players in various stages of suiting up for the first of two workouts for the day. Everyone who saw me shouted, *"Hello, Mac"* or *"Hey, Kirk."*

I headed for the Head Coach's Office and I saw the door open. Coach Bartosh walked out and when he saw me he said, *"There he is! Hello, Kirk."*

I said, *"Hello Mr. Bartosh"* and I stopped to see what would happen next.

He put his arm around me and he guided me back toward the lockers.

As we walked he said, *"I'm glad to see you, but I have one question for you, son."*

I said, *"Yes, sir?"*

He pointed at my locker and I saw a placard with *McClelland* officially posted on it. I also saw all my pads, my helmet, and my jersey, #82, hanging there and waiting.

Coach laughed and asked, *"What took you so long?"*

I smiled, shrugged, and then as he walked away, I quickly and happily began to suit up . . .

At the beginning of the school year I sat in Velma's Counseling Room watching her thumb through my student file. She said, *"I'm glad you worked things out with Gil Bartosh. At the end of Football and Basketball seasons you'll have two of the Athletic letters you wanted to achieve."*

She turned a page in my file and continued, *"Now, as for Coach Craig I predict he'll run your . . . uh, he'll run you hard before he'll give you your Track letter. So get ready. Your day of reckoning with him is coming."*

She put down my file and looked at me like she always did when she wanted to raise my bar, *"Are you aware of how close you are to accomplishing your goal?"*

I said, *"Yes, ma'am and I'm grateful. You've been a big help."*

She chuckled, *"Help? You didn't have a chance without me!"*

I didn't expect that and then she said, *"Your mother told me to say that one to you!"*

We both laughed and I saw that her eyes were full of pride. I liked that.

I told her, *"Doris is right, though. You've been great and I know how important my senior year will be. I won't let anything else slide."*

She looked serious, *"My fingers are crossed. You almost blew it last year. Just keep your eye on your star. No distractions!"*

We both stood up and she ended our meeting with, "*Come and see me if you need me."*

She walked around her desk and marched me to her door, "*Now go play Football. Catch a pass for your mother . . ."*

She winked and smiled as she commanded, "*And score a touchdown for me!"*

Two months passed. Doris and I were in our Den watching the November voting results on television. George Bush was leading Frank Briscoe for the Seventh Congressional District in Houston. This Bush fellow had run for the Senate in 1964 and he'd lost because he was a *Yankee* Republican in a Democratic District. He was also a *Yalie* (he'd graduated from Yale), and he'd lived with his wife, Barbara, for many years in Midland, Texas (where five of their six kids were born), he'd built a thriving oil business and he'd made a ton of money.

As Doris and I watched, George won 57 percent of the votes and beat the very conservative Democrat, Frank Briscoe, in a District that had seen way too much negative press about Judge Clem McClelland. One of the reporters asked Briscoe why he lost and his unhappy face tried to smile but couldn't. With 20-20 hindsight it's easy for me to say but, in my opinion, Frank had smeared the wrong man when a simple prosecution could have had the same result. Excessive Press coverage where Clem was tried daily in the Media had left a bad taste in the mouths of a lot of Seventh District voters. I think Clem ruined Frank Briscoe's run for Congress.

**A Young George H. W. Bush
Defeats Frank Briscoe**

As Doris and I watched television, I created a poem as I looked at Briscoe's defeated face. Ready? "*Hooray and Hallelujah, your ass got handed to yah."*

I shared that little ditty with Doris but she didn't seem too impressed with the results of the vote or with my splendid rhyme. I stood up to turn down the volume on our TV and then I re-joined Doris on our couch. I said, "*So this is good news!"*

Doris sat quietly and mumbled, "*Uh-huh.*"

I frowned, "*Hmm. What am I missing here? The villain got beat! Why aren't you and I celebrating?*"

Doris shook her head, "*Things aren't always what they seem, Kirk.*"

I waited for it. One beat, two beats. She didn't explain what she meant. I was confused.

I was also impatient so I asked her, "*What THINGS? Is this like you not telling me what's inside a pretty cake for Clem? What's going on, Doris? I expect happy times when the bad guys lose, not silence!*"

I watched her compose herself as she stood up. She talked as she walked to the Kitchen, "*I'm very glad that Mr. Bush won the Congressional seat. It's good the best man prevailed. Now, what would you like for dinner?*"

I was a bit dramatic as I pressed, "*Some answers with my beans and rice would be nice!*"

From the Kitchen she said, "*Give me some time. I'll explain it to you soon, okay?*"

I sat on the couch and shouted to her, "*Thanks, but I'll pass on the beans and rice. After listening to all this, just give me another ba-lo-ney sandwich!*"

I heard Doris laugh as she opened her cupboards and began making dinner.

Then came Christmas. Coach Bartosh gave his Football team a great Football Banquet.

Just like in my T.H. Rogers Junior High years, I won a Robert E. Lee trophy for being the only player who wanted to play Football AND make good grades.

Football Trophies: Me, Wright Moody, David Davis, Hunt Reynolds

I showed my Football Letter to a close friend

BRING CLEM HOME

Christmas was hard on all of my family. We missed our Clem. I invited Steve Taylor to join us for Christmas Dinner so he could fill the empty space at our round table. We'd enjoyed a wonderful Turkey feast where prayers of hope and thanks were said. We'd also thoroughly enjoyed Doris's stuffing mix (from a Cook family recipe) and a tasty Texas Pecan Pie a la mode.

Then Doris spoke the following to our invited guest, "*Steve, I want to thank you for joining us for our Christmas dinner.*"

Steve and I were clearing the dishes and glassware from the table so we both stopped to listen to what sounded to us like a preamble to a traditional Yuletide tale. She continued, "*But I need to discuss something with my children that won't be of any interest to you.*"

Steve stood next to the table with a handful of used dessert dishes.

She continued, "*For that reason would it be impolite of me to ask you to say good night and go home?*"

All of the McClelland children were amazed, as was poor Steve who gracefully said, "*No, ma'am. It was a great meal and, with your permission, I'll say good night and be on my way. See ya, Mac.*"

He reached over and handed me all of the dirty dessert dishes and patted my arm as he turned toward the Kitchen door. I'd been blindsided by Doris but I was not tongue-tied, "*Thanks for understanding, Steven. I'll tell you all about it when I see you tomorrow!*"

I laughed but nobody else did.

Doris walked with him to the door and kissed his cheek as she opened the door and said, "*Thanks for joining us. Good night, Steve.*"

He said, "*Yes, ma'am. Merry Christmas to all of you.*"

Micki and Anne called out, "*Good night, Steve. Merry Christmas!*"

Steve was out the door when all of Doris's children attacked her:

Micki screamed, "*That's the rudest thing I've ever seen!*"

Anne yelled, "*How could you treat that nice boy that way?*"

I objected, "*Steve deserves better than that, Doris!*"

Doris had returned to her seat at the table and smiled at the three of us as she said, "*I want to thank all of you for your unsolicited and uneducated opinions.*"

She pushed the remaining dirty dishes out of her way and plopped a file down onto the table.

She looked at the file and then looked up at us and said, "*Now, I would appreciate it if you would all do me a favor and shut your mouths. There are some things that you need to hear.*"

She opened the file on the Table and said, "*I've spent all of my free time over the last 18 months making sure each one of you had whatEVER you needed. I've also paid bills and kept this house running, but if you want to know what my full-time job really was, I've been working to bring Clem home.*"

My sisters had been out of the loop for so long that they both gasped when she said that.

Doris continued, "*That's right. To free him. Under Texas law, certain inmates' families can directly petition the Board of Appeals when circumstances merit. I've spent the last 18 months filing and re-filing for what is known as an "Early Release Hearing." So far they've turned us down twice.*"

Sister Anne was attending Rice University in Houston. She spoke softly to Doris, "*I was right here. Why didn't you tell me?*"

Doris smiled and patted her arm, "*Because I wanted you to be comfortable and move forward with your life. I saw how distressed you were during Clem's trials and I swore I'd protect you from all the explosive grenades that Briscoe and his men were throwing at our family.*"

Sister Micki had her normal attitude when she said, "*I would have helped you if you had asked. Why have children if you can't count on them when the going becomes tough?*"

I tried to correct her, "*When the going GETS tough*" but her face showed no interest. Micki and I frequently used our eyes to shoot daggers at each other, then Doris interrupted our stares, "*I repeat: They've turned me down twice, but I never quit trying. I promise you the judges in Austin, Texas know me on a first-name basis. In fact I'm sure I've made an enemy or two in the hallowed halls of the Texas Court of Criminal Appeals.* (She sniffed) *Well, I don't care because, come this March 22, we're headed to Austin for our hearing! Merry Christmas!*"

All three of us were delighted that she'd accomplished this impossible feat. Doris smiled as her children verbally expressed their emotions and we all congratulated her on her success.

She cautioned, "*Now don't get too excited. A hearing is no guarantee that an early release will be granted. But it is better than a poke in the eye with a sharp stick!*" and then she started laughing and then we all joined her.

Sister Micki said, "*I can't believe this!*"
Sister Anne said, "*I knew this coming year would be good. My astrologist said so!*"
Son Kirk said, "*So who got the cake?*"
Mother Doris said, "*Such a clever boy. But the truth? There were no cakes baked.*"
Both sisters asked, "*Cakes? What cakes?*"

Doris shushed all of us by saying, "*It's not important because it's not relevant. What IS important is that we will meet and talk to, and try to convince three judges that Clem's coming home is vital to all of us and that this family won't survive unless he's released NOW.*"

She looked at me and said, "*A month ago you asked me why I wasn't thrilled when Briscoe lost his Congressional election. The truth is, now that he lost, Mr. Briscoe has nothing else to keep him busy.*"

She was right. I hadn't figured on the good news of his losing being bad news for Clem.

She continued, "*If he finds out we're campaigning for Clem's early release, knowing him and how hard he fought to smear your father and ruin everything for us, I'm sure he'll fight it.*"

Both sisters gasped again.

Then Doris said, "*I'm hoping our hearing will stay below Mr. Briscoe's line of sight . . .*"

I shook my head, "*Don't count on it!*"

Doris looked deeply into my eyes, "*All I can do is hope, and I'm hoping that horrible man won't contest our attempt to bring your father home.*"

My sisters and I held our breaths, waiting for Doris's next surprise. She whispered, "*So I want us to say a Christmas prayer and I want each of you to close your eyes and I want you to think about what I'm saying . . .*"

She bowed her head. The three of us bowed ours.

She prayed, "*Dear Most Heavenly Father . . . Please bless our family. Please keep our Clem safe and well in that horrible prison for just a little while longer. Please guide us so we can do whatever it takes to bring him back to us.*"

The three of us looked up at her as she finished her prayer, "*In Jesus' name, Amen.*" . . .

The following week I received this letter from Clem, "*Hey, Boy, I haven't written for a while due to some conflicts inside the Walls. We've been* ▬▬▬▬▬▬▬▬▬▬▬▬▬▬▬▬▬▬▬▬▬▬▬▬▬▬▬▬

I know you understand how tough it is for me, too. I have to carefully follow all of their rules . . ."

"*So I need you to be grateful for all your blessings: Your good looks, your inquisitive mind, and your humility. Did I say humility? What was I thinking? I meant to say your "confidence."*

I always made sure you could take on any challenge God gave you, and I'm proud of how you do all that you do. Keep it up and know I'm always there, right beside you! I'm about to go to mess hall for dinner. I hope there are no more ▬▬▬▬▬▬▬▬▬▬▬▬▬▬▬▬ *. . . Your hunting partner, Clem.*"

Once again I was frustrated because I had no clue about what the censors blacked out. But what could I do? Maybe I'd complain to our new Congressman, George Bush, but he'd say it was a State prison and questions concerning censorship should be handled locally and not at the Federal level. I'd probably say "*I was always told to "Let George do it" so, well, do it George!*"

On one of our recent visits to see Clem he'd shared with me that, "*Christmas is a rough time of year when you're inside The Walls. If someone hates their situation in here bad enough and you step on their toes, they will find a way to* ▬▬▬ *you up!*"

On that Christmas there was an incident and it was a big deal. It was so big that all inmates were put on lockdown and were told not to talk or write about it.

Clem, of course, *did* write and when he shared with me what had happened, the censors took out their black Sharpies and redacted over half of his letter. After receiving the seriously censored letter, Doris and I went to visit Clem and I had him fill in what he'd tried to describe.

He spoke quietly to us, "*I'm not supposed to tell either of you what happened. There's been no reporting of this incident because the Warden clamped down on the Press and allowed no journalists to visit here for over a week. It was one of our real bad prisoners, and I mean REALLY BAD. He decided to decimate his competitors for the Bad Guy of the Year award* (I giggled) *by slitting some throats.*" I stopped giggling.

I asked quietly, "*When did this happen?*"

Clem kept speaking sotto voce, "*Two weeks ago. This bad guy forgot that solitary confinement would be his payday if he cut anybody. The reason the Warden quelled the Press is the incident stirred up a lot of other bad men who have been acting out and they, too, found themselves put down in the hole.*"

After we'd said goodbye and left Clem, on our drive home Doris had a severe reaction and she told me rat-a-tat, "*I can't believe Clem's still in that horrible place! It sounds like any prisoner is at risk at any time and it's just plain bad luck if you're at the wrong table in the mess hall or working out in the exercise yard or walking down the wrong corridor at the wrong time or getting ambushed in the infirmary where Clem goes for his insulin shots. He's in way too much danger. I need to get him out of there and bring him back home!*"

I had her pull over to the side of Highway 45 and we switched places so I could drive and she could cry. It was business-as-usual for the McClelland family.

Seeing how upset my mother was and hearing Clem talk about the dangers of Huntsville Prison was a lot for me to process at that time in my life. Damn!

After my talk with The Underwriter there was no question that the Appeals judges were the difference between my parents being happy and unhappy. To a teenager who'd already suffered way too much because of one man's crusade to destroy my family, I was beginning to think it was time for me to balance Briscoe's books.

That night I drove over to Bob's apartment. I was sitting on his blue couch when he brought me a Daiquiri and sat down next to me. As we drank, Bob cast his normal happy-go-lucky spell on me and asked, "*So what's bothering you, Romeo?*"

I tended to talk honestly with Bobby-Baby so I said, "*Frank Briscoe. I'm having dark thoughts about him again . . .*"

Bob laughed like he always did and said, "*You need to drink up, then, and think about something else!*"

I said, "*I wish I could. I have this vision where I'm sticking a sharp object into his gut and then I see myself feeding him his balls . . .*"

Bob reacted with his normal grin, "*Whoa! Before you do this, let me check my Law Books under "Sharp Objects" and "Balls" to see how many years you'll get!*"

He laughed at himself, and then I told him my intense feelings, "*Let me ask a question: Do you think I'm willing to do whatever it takes to bring Clem home? It's sim-*

ple: If I don't stop Briscoe he could continue to destroy my family . . . I need to stop him. It's the only thing that will ease my mind."

Bob cheered me saying, *"Ease your mind, ease your mind! Drink up! Let me call Glorie Day or Darla so you can forget about this loser!"*

(***Clem and I had a Madras Coat Day***)
Clem gave me the Garage..........What could I give him?

I looked at Bob. He was right where I needed him to be. He was smiling and reminding me that I had a lot to *lose*. I responded, *"Glorie Day . . . Darla . . . Uh, what were we talking about?"*

Bob jumped up and ran to his bar counter phone, *"See? I'll give 'em a call!"*

Bob kept his eye on me as he dialed. I sat there sipping and continuing to think.

As Bob called his lady friends I tried to get my mind off the Devil and his never-ending threat to my family. Damn! Who could I call to help me take Frank Briscoe out of the mix?

The Underwriter? Larry Klump? Chris and Steve?

Then Bob hung up his phone and he walked over to stand right in front of me. With his big smile he said, *"GentleMAN . . . Start your engine!"*

On that night, as Bob and I waited for our company to arrive, I sat there listening to him tell me stories about *"When **I** was your age . . ."* and *"I was slow when it came to figuring out what really made me happy . . ."*

I studied his predictable and happy face as he shared tales of his misspent youth and there was no doubt in my mind that Bob, on that occasion, had saved me from myself . . .

8 MM Home Movies
**I wanted to help my mother and father
get back together**

Velma's Valedictorian Bowl Game

CHAPTER TEN

THIS ONLY HAPPENS IN THE MOVIES, 1966

Two months later I'd received my Basketball letter, and Track season workouts had begun. It was freezing cold as my fellow runners and I ran around our quarter mile cinder track. There are no mountains in south Texas so the wind cuts across the Texas plains and cuts like a knife.

Fortunately I escaped bad weather during the classroom hours and on a Monday in February I met with Velma in her Counseling Room. I looked at her phone and remembered the special conversation I'd had on it with Clem.

There were seven of us in her room that day, counting Velma. I was the only male, and one of the six females was Grace Stewart. If you don't remember her, she was the one who'd told me Clem was a "*stupid convict.*"

I stood. The girls sat on folding chairs which surrounded Velma as she sat behind her desk.

Velma had a take-charge attitude as she said, "*Thanks to all of you for coming today. You all have achieved 4 point 0 averages on your grades and I wanted to say "Well done" to each of you. Since it's obvious you will all maintain your perfect grade points up to Graduation, Robert E. Lee has to invoke Chance to decide this year's Valedictorian.*"

I stood watching and listening to the girls as they looked at each other and said, "*I don't like the sound of that!*" and "*I studied so hard to get mine!*" and "*What a gyp!*"

I smiled as I saw Grace Stewart look over at me. She said, "*He shouldn't even be here. He wasn't in the Honors Science class!*"

I smiled, pointing at Grace as I said, "*She shouldn't even be here. She wasn't in Honors Football!*"

All of the girls except Grace laughed, as did Velma who then said, "*I was so sure we'd be able to do this in a civilized manner. Are you two going to behave?*"

I performed a sweeping bow a la Sir Lancelot and said, "*Yes, m'lady!*"

Grace couldn't help but pout, so she pouted out loud, "*This is SO not fair!*"

Velma told me later that she'd predicted some of my *competitors* who'd never *competed* in such close *competition* wouldn't be able to graciously process this unacceptable conclusion to their four years of pressure and hard work. Her way of dealing with the unfairness of it all was to ignore it, which I thought made a lot of sense.

Velma picked up an antique bowl and turned it over emptying out six pieces of paper onto her desk. She unwrapped one and held it up so all of the Valedictorian-wannabes could see it. On the paper was the letter 'N'. She said, "*As you can see, on this piece of paper is the letter "N" for "No." There are five Ns and only one Y for "Yes" in this bowl.*"

She returned the papers to the bowl and then she stood, "*May the best Valedictorian win!*"

She handed the bowl to me and said to me, "*Ladies first, don't you agree?*"

I smiled and took the bowl from her hand. I then held it out in front of me so all five girls could easily reach in and take out one piece of paper from the bowl.

As each girl grabbed their piece and opened it, I heard:

Girl #1, "*Shit!*"

Girl #2, "*(she sighed)*"

Girl #3, "████████"

Girl #4, "*Damn! Damn! Damn!*"

Girl #5, "*For Christ's Sake!*"

Having heard all the words and gestures of frustration, I was confident as I said, "And I get the last one, right?"

I reached into the bowl and took out the last piece of paper. I opened it, and I held it up so that all could see the "*Y*" clearly written on it.

I gloated, "*I like Ladies First! It's always worked out well for me.*"

Velma didn't get my off-color remark but she did give me a harsh frown, "*Don't gloat, Kirk. It's unbecoming of you. But I do guess congratulations are in order, right, ladies?*"

All of the girls but Grace said "*Congratulations*" or "*Congrats Kirk.*" Grace was mute. I smiled at her as she glowered at me . . .

That night Doris and I sat at our Kitchen table as I replayed my championship Bowl Game, "*I wished I'd had the Tape recorder with me so you could hear what each one of the girls said when she saw the "N" on her paper. Such improper language from such proper ladies.*"

Doris laughed as she said, "*Velma called me to say you could've behaved better, but she said she wasn't sure how **she** would have behaved in your place.*"

I nodded, and then I confessed, "*Ah, sweet Velma. Did she also tell you that we rigged the drawing?*"

I wish I'd had a camera so I could share Doris's horrified look of surprise, "*You what?*"

I laughed and pointed at her. "*Ha! Got you! Just kidding, Doris!*"

I picked up my books and headed for my garage room when I stopped and told her, "*Coach Craig decided today that we ARE going to the Laredo Track meet this weekend! Just so you know I'm calling Bobby-Baby to tell him I can't go to his party Saturday night.*"

Doris nodded to me, and I walked out the back door. I wasn't aware of it at the time but a few months later Doris shared how scared she was for me. She didn't have Clem to consult with so when it came to deciding if Bob Gilbert was good or bad, she made her own choice.

She told me she waited for my garage lights to turn on inside my stronghold, and then she counted to 5. One, Two, Three, Four, Five. She picked up her Kitchen phone just as I had finished dialing Bob's number. She snooped as I spoke to Bob:

I said, "*Mr. Gilbert!*"

Bob laughed and said, "*Glorie Day's new love interest! How are you, Romeo?*"

I said, "*I'm fine, but it looks like Saturday's a no show for me. Coach has us going to Laredo this weekend to fine tune our Mile Relay team so I wanted to call and apologize. I know you're disappointed 'cause your parties need all the help they can get!*"

Bob laughed, "*Haha! . . . Seriously though, I'm sad. This one's gonna be great! It's guaranteed to erase all dark thoughts!*"

I laughed, "*I'll catch you next time, okay?*"

Bob said, "*We'll miss you!*" and we both hung up.

Doris told me she waited a beat and then *she* hung up. She told me she sat at the Kitchen table thinking about what she'd just heard. She looked around the Kitchen and at the phone as she replayed what Bob had just said. In her mind she kept hearing Bob say "*We'll miss you!*" That's what stimulated her to pick up the phone (*and since the 9-1-1 system wasn't in place until the following year*) and she dialed "0" for the Operator.

When the Operator answered, Doris said, "*I need to speak to the Police, Operator.*" . . .

It was fun to take Friday off from school so we could drive to the border town of Laredo. The event was the premier Track Meet in South Texas known as the Border Olympics.

Riding inside my Malibu was our Mile Relay team: me, Steve Taylor, Bill Klein and Barry Sinclair. We were a lean team, and that year our time for the Mile Relay was so fast that, as of this writing, no other foursome at Robert E. Lee has ever come close to beating it.

I was driving my Malibu on Highway 35 headed south toward Mexico and I drove behind Coach Craig's blue and white Chevy Impala. So far that year Coach Craig and I had developed a workable peace-treaty based on him telling me to run like hell every race, and me doing whatever it took to make him think I was his Track slave.

In fact this Laredo trip was a test that Babe had presented that week to the Captain of the Track team (me) and he had set it up for me by saying, "*Mac, I need to see if you guys have let yourselves be handicapped by your latest record-breaking time OR if you can truly apply your God-given gifts into breaking your new record down there in Laredo.*"

It was a challenge that I realized I needed at that time, and it gave me a decent focus for my excessive negative energy.

Robert E. Lee's swift mile relay team should be a threat
for a first place birth in District 9-AAAA this year.
Top to bottom, Bill Klein, Steve Taylor, Kirk McClelland, and Barry Sinclair.

Our Mile Relay Team

As we rode along the hot Texas highway I directed a question-and-answer drill to my extremely talented team. I started with, "*Barry . . . How badly do you want to beat our best time?*"

Barry, who was the shortest runner, answered, "*I get cramps just thinking about it, Mac!*"

I coached, "*Drink Gatorade! Bill, why do you want to beat our best time in the Mile Relay?*"

Bill, who was the tallest runner, answered, "*Debbie said that if we did beat it, she'd . . .*"

I interrupted him, "*I don't want to hear any low-class language, Bill!* (Steve and Barry laughed at me) *We have to keep our morals HIGH, our cleats CLEAN, and our noses pointing STRAIGHT DOWN THAT TRACK! . . . So Steve, what will motivate you to rise above your silly self-imposed limitations and keep the Robert E. Lee Mile Relay team in first place?*"

Steve answered, "*SECOND PLACE IS NEVER AN OPTION!*"

I honked my horn three times and we all shouted, "*One, Two, Three . . . ROBERT E. LEE!*"

I honked my horn again and then I looked ahead and saw Coach Craig's arm come out of his Impala's side window. He'd waved at me so I'd stop honking. Jeez! I'm the Captain, Coach! I'm in charge of executing high motivation drills for our Mile Relay team!

As I grinned at myself, I thought about what was being said in the Impala up ahead. Babe had brought along his assistant, Coach Paul Vickers, a nice man in his late twenties whose beer belly was probably the result of his undying love for Mexican food and beer. Ay Caramba!

It was my guess that Asst. Coach Vickers was *muy contento* (very happy) that we were going south to this Track Meet. And since the Laredo meet annually attracted the fastest runners in the State, we were all motivated to head down Mexico way. *Sí estar seguro* "Remember Goliad."

Steve sat in my passenger seat and he chatted with me so I could avoid an unexpected siesta, "*When was the last time you were in Laredo, Mac?*"

I answered, "*Chris and I came down last year after I bailed on Spring Training. I had to escape all the looks I was getting at school and at home.*"

Steve was curious and asked, "*So Chris is a good co-pilot, eh?*"

I answered, "*Not as good as you . . .* (I turned to verify) *. . . uh, Steve!*"

The four members of our mile-racing engine laughed.

I continued, "*He's just Chris. How long have you and I known him?*"

Steve nodded, "*Forever.*"

I nodded too. "*Exactly. I'd trust that guy with anything . . . except MaryAnn's panties!*"

In concert, the mile-machine laughed again . . .

So we were very focused, thanks to my cheerleading skills, and we were fast, thanks to God.

When we rolled past where the meet would take place at the **Laredo Shirley Field**, those *chalupas* and *gorditas* had no clue that the *muy rapido* Robert E. Lee Mile Relay had come to their *bonito pueblo* to win.

We checked into the **Laredo Lantern Motel**, and next door at the **Las Kekas** restaurant I enjoyed a fine meal of tacos, enchiladas, tamales, and my first ever beef chimichanga . . .

The next morning Coach Vickers had the pleasure of helping Barry and Bill deal with their inability to digest border cuisine. It was difficult for them both, but I was impressed with Coach Vickers' knowledge of border remedies for all things Mexican. He must have eaten *mucho Mexican comida* over the years since his formula for upset Texican stomachs worked perfectly.

The Finals for the running events began at 1:00 p.m. on Saturday.

The Prelims had taken place on Friday but Coach Craig had insisted his Mile Relay team draw a *bye*. He said that since his team had run and won at every meet we'd competed in during that season (except for our one loss to Houston Memorial three weeks before) we should get a pass.

I liked his style and he was right: It would have been repetitious for us to dazzle the Track fans both on Friday *and* on Saturday. Coach Craig wanted us to run and win, but he only wanted his runners to run **once**.

His game plan turned out to be real smart since two of his runners wouldn't have had the strength to run on Friday and then overcome the Friday night enchiladas so they could run successfully on Saturday.

Babe was lucky that, by 2 p.m. Saturday, Coach Vickers had all of our systems under control, and our Mile Relay was physically good to go. Our relay team was running warm-up laps around the **Shirley Field's** cinder track. The track felt solid, the weather felt hot, and I was ready to push our team to the limit. I gathered our group into a huddle and I shared my realities with my teammates, "*Listen up, guys. I've got a favor to ask. As you probably know my mother and sisters and I are going to Austin next week to try to spring Clem from the State Pen. What you don't know is how important our performance today will be when these three Appeals judges measure me. I've talked to Coach Craig and he understands how our performance today connects to my pitch next week. So here it is: We gotta win. That means we have to beat Houston Memorial. We cannot let Houston Memorial get the lead, Barry. When you hand off to Steve you've got to be running full speed so Steve can accelerate and get ahead of the pack. Steve when you hand off to Bill you have to be at least two lengths ahead. That way when Bill hands off to me I'll have the cushion of space we all know I'll need if I'm gonna have any chance to beat Memorial's speedy anchorman home. So that's what I need you to do for me and my family . . .*"

Barry waved his hand at me and, completely serious, he said, "*But what if I have to throw up?*"

Steve answered Barry saying, "*Just point your muzzle at the Houston Memorial runner behind you and let her fly!*"

That Saturday at 5 p.m. the Public Announcer at Shirley Field announced, "*All Mile Relay teams should be in place. Coaches have your first runners on the track.*"

We'd drawn Lane 4 and I ran out to cheerlead Barry. I patted him on his back and told him, "*Run this like there's no tomorrow!*"

He nodded to me, and he gave me his biggest smile, "*I'm running for Clem!*"

I nodded back and had to fight myself to not give Barry a hug.

The Starter held his pistol high and yelled:

"*Runners, to yer mark . . .*" The runners of the eight finalist teams knelt down into their blocks.

"*Get seeeeetttttttttt—*" All runners lifted up their legs, making ready to sprint at the gunshot.

The Starter fired his pistol and I swear Barry *flew* out of his blocks with both of his legs moving faster than I'd ever seen Barry run before.

On the infield I moved into position with the other anchormen. As each of my teammates made their baton exchange, I'd move closer to the track.

I watched Barry hit the 220 mark and since the first runner has to run in staggered lanes I had to guess what his position was in the race. My guess: He was moving at an expeditious rate that seemed magical. He was the poster boy Coaches used to visualize the description of *hauling ass*.

Yes, he was definitely first and when he handed the baton to Steve he was running full speed. Steve took off like a rocket and by the time he hit the first turn it was clear he wanted to win.

Next came Bill. Bill jumped off early and had to look back so Steve could catch him. It was obvious Bill was thinking about Debbie's promise and that made him start prematurely. Once Bill took the baton from Steve he was off to see the wizard. There was no one ahead of him and there was no stopping him.

I stood on the track in Lane 1, waiting. I had no excuses for losing this race. My teammates had done what I'd asked and the only one who could lose it was me.

The exact second that Bill hit the pass-off mark that I had carved with my foot into the cinder, I took off hell-bent-for-leather with both feet gripping that track as they flew over it. Coach Craig told me later he'd never seen anyone run the first 100 yards of their leg any faster.

I was on that track to win, to make my Coach/teammates proud, and to celebrate my father.

I was flying. My feet were barely touching the cinder track. Then I glanced behind me and I saw the Memorial anchorman. He, too, was flying but I held the inside lane which meant he'd have to run *around* me to take over first place.

I couldn't let that happen. I needed to win that race more than this sprinter did. It wouldn't have been fair if he were to pass me and take this race from me. But what is FAIR? I think Doris told me when I was four or five that it's a place you go to buy cotton candy.

By having the better position I was able to use a technique I'd learned from watching the real Olympics in Tokyo in 1964. In the finals of the Mile Relay the USA's anchor, Henry Carr, had moved away from the infield and *pushed* the second place team's anchor outward into the second lane, making the other runner run 2 or 3 extra steps. The USA team had won the Gold Medal. With that visual in my mind

I moved away from the infield and into the second lane which made the Houston Memorial anchor to firstly, say a bad word, secondly, to lose his footing, and finally, to propel me across the Finish Line in first place.

Suddenly my teammates and my Coaches were surrounding me and robbing me of the air I desperately needed. Back off! Let me breathe! As always after running a quarter mile at full speed it took all my focus just to inhale. When I was finally able to suck it up, it hurt like hell.

I felt Coach Craig's left hand on my right shoulder and his right hand shaking mine.

He smiled and said, "*I don't know what you did, but Houston Memorial's coach is yelling at their anchorman bigtime. Good work, Mac! I'm proud of ya!*"

Steve and Barry and Bill and I took the top platform to receive the Border Olympics Trophy for the Mile Relay. Each of us also received a Gold Medal, which I'd be sure to include in my medal array, inside my jacket, the next time I ran for office.

As we normally did after a race, we huddled with Coaches Craig and Vickers so we could inspect their 5 stopwatches and review our separate times as well as the team's overall time. Barry ran the first lap in 49 seconds, Steve ran his lap in 49.5 seconds, Bill ran his in 48.5 seconds and I ran mine in 48 seconds for a team total of 3 minutes and 25 seconds . . .

The coaches told us they'd meet us outside our Motel after we'd showered and dressed.

We then had a mild American dinner at McDonald's so Bill and Barry would survive the trip, and then we drove back to our Motel parking lot to discuss what we'd do the rest of the evening. Coach Craig pointed across the street to the Laredo CinemaTech movie theater where we saw *A Fistful Of Dollars* touted up on the Marquee. He told Coach Vickers, "*That's a Clint Eastwood movie. Might be fun, Coach.*"

To us he said, "*Good race today, men. I'm proud to know that YOU KNOW you can always run faster. That's an important lesson and you're lucky to be learning it so early.*"

As the Captain of the Track Team I changed the focus to more imperative issues. I said, "*Since I've already seen that film, would it be all right if we go over the border to Nuevo Laredo for an hour or so?*" Both Coaches laughed, and then Babe said, "*Let me get this straight! You want me to let all of you leave the country, go over to a border town that's filled with . . .*"

I interrupted, "*. . . great shops with low prices. I promised Doris I'd try to get her some blown glass for her collection, Coach.*"

Coach Craig smiled and nodded. "*Uh-huh.*"

I kept pitching, "*I've crossed over more than a few times. I know my way around, Coach.*"

Then he surprised me. He looked at his watch and pointed again at the movie theater, *"That movie starts in ten minutes. It's ninety-nine minutes long. When Coach Vickers and I walk out you four will be here, waiting, or I'll blow"*—he pointed at me—*"YOUR glass! Comprendo?"*

I did indeed. I happily replied, *"No problemo, Coach. We'll be right here, waiting for you!"*

We all waved at the Coaches and then turned to run to the Malibu. We jumped in and, slowly, drove toward the Border. The Coaches watched us drive away and then I saw them slap each other on the back as they walked toward a night of entertainment minus the babysitting.

I drove to the Border crossing and stopped at the checkpoint. I held up my Texas driver's license to the Border Guard who didn't look at it. He yawned and waved me on through.

The Malibu and I had been there before so we knew how and where to cross the Laredo Bridge over the Rio Grande and, presto, the Robert E. Lee Mile Relay track team was in Mexico. *Ay caramba!* Or *Hot diggity dog!* if you speak English.

I drove around the Nuevo Laredo streets. Each was filled with tourists and many Mexicans who were walking, standing, and carefully eyeing each potential mark that walked or drove past. Mexican music was heard on every street. It might have seemed like I was lost but I wasn't. Chris and I had made many late night trips since we'd been racing the Malibu. I hadn't shared that with Steve because he was an important part of my normal life . . . until that Saturday night.

Nuevo Laredo was the center of my teen rebellion. Chris and I had worked off the same playbook when it came to matters of car racing or south of the border sex.

Ciudad con Valor—A Valuable City

I'd wanted to share that with Steve, and with Barry and Bill, too. My three teammates hadn't been initiated until I'd driven all of them up to the walled compound known as **La Alta Barrera** or *The High Barrier*.

And then, suddenly, there it was. The wall was green and it surrounded the compound. It was too high to climb over and that was the point. It forced all the young bad boys from Texas to enter that setting through the front passageway.

I parked the Malibu as close as possible to the Entrance of the passageway and announced:

"*Here we are. Donkey Is . . . uh . . . Boystown!*" My teammates exited the Malibu and looked at the Christmas lights that adorned the Entrance and then they looked at the scary Mexican men who stood under those lights, looking at us. With a shake in his voice, Steve asked, "*Mac, this is where you and Chris came the last time you were here?*"

I answered, "*Yeah, c'mon . . . And don't forget: Remember Goliad!*"

I led them into and through the Entrance. Once we were inside the green walls, the compound looked just like the dirty low rent neighborhood of Bars and Saloons that it was.

On both ends and in the middle there were three-story buildings that looked a lot like hotels.

We were in Boystown.

In Mexico everything was exactly the way it seemed. There was no studio landscaping, only ugly dead shrubs. There were no offset lighting designs. A building or a fountain or an outside chair or a swing was either bathed in light or it was just plain dark. The paint changed color from building to building and the freshest coat was probably ten years old.

To repeat, we were inside the bottom most sliver of Mexico, and there was no magic to be found anywhere. Why did young boys go there? Because we'd been warned that it *era muy mal*, or was very bad, and that we should stay away. That's why.

All around the compound were green lights hanging from gutters and dead tree limbs. It had the effect of making that creepy place look like an alien planet. We entered one Saloon. Its name was **PAPAGAYO** and I didn't remember it, so I wanted to look inside to see what it had.

It took a moment for my eyes to adjust and, when my eyes started working, all I saw was sleaze. Yes, we were in Boystown, Mexico, but there's down and dirty and in **PAPAGAYO**'s case, down and dead. I imitated Clem's cow, "*Moooo!*" and we quickly moooved out of there.

The Bar I was searching for was several Bars down and it had a sign out front with a nice mural of a **BLUE DRAGON**. I had history with this location, and I led my team inside so they could look. The establishment was full of people, some working some touring. The actual bar was easy on the eyes and was well-crafted with solid oak wood and a granite top. My teammates were wide-eyed and impressed that such a nice place could exist in such a low-class place.

We entered and immediately sat down at the bar. I said to the Bartender, "*Cuarto Cerveza Coronas, por favor.*"

We looked around. Girls were everywhere standing along the walls, on the staircase, and upstairs, looking down. There were *mucho* bouncers/bodyguards all over, too.

The Bartender set our beers down and waited for me to pay. I gave him a twenty, his eyes lit up and I said, "*Gracias. Keep-o the change-o!*" He smiled and walked away, pocketing the $20.

Steve in his usual master-of-ceremonies mode said, "*Well, here we are in the tourist capital of the world. My grandkids will be so proud.*"

I laughed at him, "*Who's gonna marry* you?"

Steve looked at a young, curvy Latina at the bottom of the stairs and said, "*I bet SHE would . . .*"

Then I saw a familiar face at the top of the stairs. Her name was Concepción.

I nodded to her, finished my Corona, and I quizzed my three teammates, "*So who's for going Up the Stairs with me? Steven?*"

He smiled and said, "*No way, Mac. I'll keep my snake in its cage.*" He pointed. "*Too many diseases lurking up there.*"

I knew Steve had a phobia when it came to germs, so I nodded to Bill, who said to me, "*Thanks, Mac. I'm gonna pass, cause my Debbie would know.*"

I knew Bill's girlfriend and I also knew Bill's inability to lie successfully.

I gazed at Barry who told me, "*You know why I can't, Mac. I wouldn't know what to do!*"

I grabbed Barry's arm and he and I started walking toward Concepción. I encouraged him to drink his Corona which he did, but then Barry protested, "*C'mon, Kirk. I really don't want to . . .*" I countered with, "*Get ready. Tonight's the night!*"

I almost had to carry Barry. So I put my hand under his armpit and tickled him. He was ticklish and his ticklishness helped me transport him to the top of the stairs.

I greeted the lovely Latina, "*Buenos Noches, Concepción.*"

She smiled and kinda recognized me, "*It's Mr. Houston! It is been so long!*"

I replied, "*That's what she said!*" and Barry laughed.

I winked at Concepción, handed her two twenties as I said, "*I expect good things from you tonight*" and I pushed Barry into her capable arms. She linked her arm with his and escorted him to the door to her room. She opened it, pushed him inside, waved *bye* to me, and closed it.

I thought, "*Tonight's the night, Señor Barry. Safe travels!*"

I went back downstairs and had another Corona while waiting for Barry to complete his Boystown initiation. 15 minutes passed, then a half-hour. I looked at Steve and Bill.

Steve said, "*I sure hope this is worth it to you, Mac. Babe's gonna be pissed at you.*"

Bill just smiled and shook his head at me.

I quickly re-climbed the stairs and knocked on Concepción's door as I loudly asked, "*Barry, are you all right in there?*"

He answered, "*I got a bit of a cramp, but Concepción put some kinda lotion on her hands and she's giving me some P.T.* (physical therapy) *for it.*"

I processed that but said, "*Okay, but we gotta go if we want Coach to be happy.*"

I heard Barry tell Concepción, "*Go a little faster. Coach is waiting . . .*" I heard her giggle and I went back down the stairs to wait with Bill and Steve.

Fifteen minutes later Barry and Concepción appeared and she led him down the stairs. I gave her a hug and said, "*Gracias, Concepción!*" and then I threw another twenty at the Bartender as our Track team moved quickly toward the exit.

While we were playing Upstairs, Downstairs in Boystown, there was another drama taking place back at Bob's apartment in Houston. When I spoke to Chris the next day he filled me in:

Chris loved Bob's parties. Chris loved Darla and all the other rebellious Belles he'd met through Bob. Chris loved Bob's frozen Daiquiris.

On that Saturday night Chris was right where he wanted to be. Chris had also brought Tim Toler with him. Tim had been complaining *forever* about being left out of "*all the good stuff*" so, to shut him up, Chris brought Tim along with him.

Chris and Tim exited Chris' car, a blue 1964 Oldsmobile 442 with a 4 speed V8 that Chris was simply crazy about. Chris and Tim laughed at a lame joke that Tim had just shared about "*an alligator wearing a vest being called an INVESTIGATOR,*" and they ran up the stairs to Bob's apartment. Chris rang the cowbell as he opened the door and walked in.

Bob was behind his bar making his signature drink and he called out, "*Chris! And a new friend! What took you so long? Darla, look who's here!*"

Bob's apartment door closed behind them. Chris was feeling giddy about seeing Darla so he told me he never noticed the three unmarked Police cars parked down in the parking lot. He was inside Bob's apartment so he didn't see the six men, who'd been ducking down, as they sat up inside their cars. This was the Houston Vice Squad and three of the six vice cops were dressed in plain clothes while the other three were wearing their Police blues.

As these six officers quietly moved up the stairs, Chris and Tim were enjoying Darla's and Glorie Day's new suntans. They'd acquired them the day before when they went water-skiing with Bob on the Houston Ship Channel between Houston and Galveston. At that moment both girls only wore the bottom parts of their bikinis and, from Chris' point-of-view, they both had the best *baby-doll* look (it was a '60s thing) anyone anywhere had ever had the good fortune to see.

One of the cops stumbled on the stairway but the sound was covered by Bob's loud blender blending inside. The six officers stood outside Bob's apartment where they all silently laughed at the cowbell. One of the officers *rang* it and Bob shouted, "*Someone get the door!*"

Just then the six cops broke down the front door and rushed in. According to Chris there was a lot of screaming as the cops grabbed Bob and threw his pitcher against his bar's back wall, wasting many delicious Daiquiris. Two other scantily clad ladies started swinging at two of the cops and one of these ladies made a solid connection with one cop's jaw, breaking it.

Chris said it was chaos for about two minutes as the Police snatched and cuffed everyone in the apartment, including several who were scrambling to get their clothes on, but couldn't. Bob tried to smile his way through the pandemonium as three cops finally cornered him and made him stand still.

He was trembling and shouting at them, "*There's no crime here! These girls are all lovely! Take these cuffs off, and I'll introduce you to them!*"

One of the cops said to Bob, "*You might wanna hold your water there, Mr. Gilbert! Everything you say, can and will be used against you!*"

Chris described the scene to me: The Police had the boys in various stages of undress on one wall, and the girls in various stages of undress on the other. Then the Police started ripping Bob's boxes of Law Books apart. When the cops realized what the books were, they laughed.

Bob settled down finally and, smiling, he asked the top cop, "*How did you know where to find me?*"

The top cop said, "*Some of your neighbors called us, Mr. Gilbert, but that's not important. What's important is how old each of these young ladies and these young boys are. I assure you, when we call their parents, we're gonna look hard at their birth certificates!*"

Chris told me they then took Bob out his smashed front door and down the front stairs where Bob was put into the same paddy wagon as the boys and girls. Then the Police hit their sirens and took off for central booking downtown where all were processed for future arraignments.

While Chris and Tim and Bob were struggling in Houston, the Lee track team was about to exit from the **BLUE DRAGON**.

I asked Steve, "*What time is it?*"

He said, "*Coach is pacing as we speak, Mac. We might wanna go top speed and an-da-le outta here.*"

As we ran for the front door the Blue Dragon Bouncers moved into our path to block us. I'd forgotten that the locals didn't like any boys to run. It's a disorderly visual for their orderly states of mind. Our Bartender came to our rescue by waving at them and crying out, "*No hay problema!*" and the Bouncers moved aside so the Houston Robert E. Lee runners were able to run around/by/through them.

I took the lead as we ran through that part of the Boystown Pleasure Arena and I aimed our Mile Relay toward the front Entrance. As we ran, our speed drew more attention than I wanted, so I picked up the pace which inspired my teammates.

There were a horde of Mexicans on our tail by that time, but the Lee boys were *mucho rápidamente*. When we reached the Malibu and jumped in, I peeled out from a large circle of dust and pulled away from the pursuing Mexicans.

Fortunately I heard no gunshots in the romantic Mexican night air.

I raced like a cannonball through the back alleys and dirty streets of Nuevo Laredo. I had a collision with an errant trash can as it rolled across one of the darker streets but the Malibu flattened it with a bump and we kept moving.

I sped to the Border crossing. I pulled up to the checkpoint and held up my driver's license. It was a different Border Guard who looked us over and, when he smiled, I saw two of his teeth were on permanent vacation. He indicated he wanted me to pull over into a search area. Uh oh.

The Border Guard reminded me of the bandito in **THE WILD BUNCH** who had called William Holden's character (Pike Bishop) a "*smart, damn gringo.*" This Guard had the same killer smile, and with his gaping holes I didn't look forward to his talking to us. Fortunately the Guard didn't speak. He lifted his finger and pointed at a dim figure exiting his Guardhouse. I saw the figure was Coach Craig and as he walked closer I could see that he wasn't pleased with his relay team's qualifying time for this event. I was cooked. He looked more than angry.

His fists were clenched, and he nodded to the Guard, who turned away so Babe could lean in past my window guard. He asked me, "*I got a question for you, Mr. Mac. Who do you think had the most fun tonight?*"

I said nothing. I knew I'd been careless and it was time for me to hurry-up and shut-up.

Babe cocked his head to get a better look at my face, and then he continued, "*I got to sit next to Coach Vickers and watch Italians playing Mexicans (he shook his head). You, on the other hand, got to go and do what little boys do in a border town full of Mexicans who probably wish they were Italians. So tell me, which of us had the most fun?*"

This was no fun. No matter how I answered, I'd be wrong. I didn't like trick questions, but it was too late to negotiate, so I answered, "*You did . . . ?*"

Coach Craig delivered his only smile of the evening and said, "*We're driving straight to the Motel, we're gonna pack up and drive straight through to Houston. You keep your racer on my tail. Do not pull over for any reason unless I do. Then, tomorrow morning, Sunday morning, at eleven o'clock, I'll see you in the Coach's office. That's when and where I'll have the most fun. Think about that on the drive home.*"

I watched Coach Craig, still shaking his head, as he joined Coach Vickers in Babe's Impala. They waved their thanks to the Border Guard and drove away. The Mile Relay team followed close behind.

What waited for me back in Houston was not new to me. I'd experienced physical punishment several times growing up. Clem, of course, was first. Then came Coach Wilson who'd felt obliged to brand me when I'd sat down on the Football field once to catch my breath. The occasion, of course, was during an August two-a-day practice.

Coach Wilson was such a believer in the paddle as an effective device for altering bad behavior that he'd used it on me again when I'd interrupted him during a halftime pep talk in the Del Mar locker room. Jeez. He'd made a mistake when he'd said, "*After you beat Lanier tonight, you'll remember it was . . .*" I raised my hand and corrected him since we were playing *Pershing* Junior High that Friday night, not Lanier. Did he thank me? No. He smiled his Richard Egan smile and told me to meet him in the Assistant Principal's office Monday morning where he'd proceeded to swat me, hard.

So there I was, a Swatted Man Walking, this time for helping Barry jump *a major hurdle* (it's a track reference) in his young life. I thought that what I did exemplified the kind of help that illustrates "*Teamwork*"! C'mon, Coach, team sports help develop real men!

Sunday morning I'd had a nice breakfast with Doris and I'd shown her my new Gold Medal that I'd won in Laredo. She'd seemed impressed but I could tell something else was on her mind. I'd assumed she was thinking about our trip to Austin that week and I hoped she was focusing on what she'd say to the appeals court judges.

To explain my excursion to Lee that morning I'd told her I was helping Coach Craig with "*some equipment issues*" and that I'd only be gone for about an hour.

She'd waved a preoccupied hand at me and said, "*Drive carefully.*"

I'd replied with my usual, "*I'll drive so fast, they won't be able to see me, much less hit me!*"

It was straight up 11 o'clock when I waltzed into the Robert E. Lee locker room and aimed my soon-to-be-abused body toward the Coach's Office.

I knocked on the Head Coach's Office door, heard, "*Enter*" and I did.

Coach Craig sat at his side desk reading the Sunday edition of The Houston Post. On his desk I also saw the infamous Coach's paddle which he picked up the second I walked through the door. He greeted me with, "*I hope you've considered what you did down at the border, and how much pain and worry you caused me.*"

I said, "*Yes, sir.*"

He looked hard at me, "*Yes, you've considered what you did, or yes, you're aware of the pain you caused me?*"

I answered, "*Uh, yes to both, sir.*"

He nodded as he stood up with the paddle in his hand, and he pointed at his desk, "*You know how this works. Assume the position.*"

I had no clever remarks that morning.

I should've said, "*This sucks*" but I'm not real sure that phrase was in my vernacular in 1967. I leaned over his desk with my back to Coach Craig.

He said, "*I hope you had a good time, Mac, but with pleasure sometimes comes pain . . .*"

I felt myself shaking. I tried to brace myself for the torment that was headed my way.

And then Babe asked me, *"Are you ready?"*

I nodded, and he hit me.

It was a loud swat. As I tried to process the agony I felt in my lower body, I heard Babe take a deep breath and I think I tried again to brace myself. Remembering the complete heat he'd created on my backside, I don't think I could've done anything to prepare for what came next. He hit me a second time and he hit me so hard that I swear the second swat froze my brain.

I felt tears coming. I made no sound since part of the drill was to be able to take it that way. But as I maintained my *position*, my arms trembled.

As I tried to handle my pain a thought crossed my mind: I remembered Clem had disapproved of my behavior over something I'd said once, and back then he'd hit me just as hard as Babe had. What did these adult men hope to teach me? Discipline? Making sure the trains ran on time? To always say *"Please"* and *"Thank you"*?

I braced myself for a third swat because I knew I had really disappointed Babe. I knew if our situations had been reversed I'd have regretted letting the Mile Relay team explore Boystown unescorted, and when the team didn't show up as planned, my imagination would've run wild.

I was relieved when, out of the corner of my wet eyes, I saw the paddle being returned to Coach Craig's desk. Then I saw Babe grab his morning newspaper and I watched as he slid the paper under my outstretched arms. I saw its headline:

Police Raid Post Oak Sex Party and I saw a picture of a smiling Bob Gilbert beneath it.

The picture showed Bob holding one of the Law books that he sold, and the caption read, *"Bob Gilbert looks up his possible sentence!"*

I still made no sound but my mind was racing. How'd the Police become aware of Bob? What did his arrest mean to me and Chris? Did Chris get arrested? Was I in trouble? Would this cause trouble for Clem's early release? Holy Jesus!

Coach Craig said, *"Thought I'd show you this in case you missed it at home."*

He pointed at Bob's picture and continued, *"Word has it you might know this guy."*

He picked up the paper and shared, *"It says here this Bob-guy could get up to ten years and pay a $10,000 fine for sex crimes with underaged girls. Chinga su madre!"*

Babe put the paper down and I picked it up to read it. I was stunned.

Babe said, *"You wanna know what I think? Just like Clint Eastwood in* **A FISTFUL OF DOLLARS***, I think you dodged a bullet!"*

I watched Coach Craig pantomime drawing two guns and shooting them. As Babe mimicked the sounds of gunshots, I imagined the gunshots and bullets flying into the far wall of the office. Babe held up his imaginary guns and blew the smoke out of each barrel. Then he twirled both imaginary guns with another sound effect and he holstered them both into imaginary holsters. He stood there smiling at me and he watched me as I suffered what I'll call a double-shock.

I put down his newspaper and said, "*I'm real sorry about being late in Laredo, Coach. I'm glad we were able to cross the border, but I wish you hadn't been forced to worry about us.*"

I turned and tried to make a clean departure. The pain on my backside was immeasurable, so I gritted my teeth and did the best I could to exit that office without moaning.

I drove my Malibu out of the Lee parking lot and away from the school. I shifted in my seat and tried to find a sitting position that wouldn't touch my intensely injured ass.

Then I stretched to turn on my radio and I heard **BOBBY HATFIELD** singing his **UNCHAINED MELODY.** I sighed as I thought about Doris's favorite song and what the lyrics meant to her and Clem.

As I rolled smoothly toward home down the Southwest Freeway, I listened to the lyrics and thought about how Clem used to sit his bench in his probate court. I remembered him playing his clarinet as Doris clapped and laughed. I laughed as I replayed his running across the **TRUTH OR CONSEQUENCES** stage with a spoon in his mouth, holding an egg.

I remembered Clem playing with his dogs, I thought of Clem hugging and kissing my two sisters on that nightmare day when Doris drove him to Huntsville, and I remembered him hugging and kissing Doris on Visitor's Day at Huntsville Prison. "*Time can do so much, are you still mine? Godspeed your love, I'll be coming home, wait for me . . .*"

When I pulled into the Carport at our home I had two things on my mind: Firstly, putting some liniment cream on my unfortunate extremity and secondly, talking to Doris about Bob.

The news story had mentioned that an anonymous neighbor had notified the Police that the *sex party* would take place at Bob Gilbert's apartment on Saturday night. Did Doris tell them? If she did tell them, then why? She had to know that ratting out Bob would have serious consequences for him. Hadn't she and I learned that putting people at the mercy of the justice system was sometimes the worse option?

I walked around the house and unlocked my garage door. Inside I found the cream that I'd used several years before when Coach Wilson had tanned my hide. There were still plenty of uses left in that tube, so I used one of them. It was wonderful, and I smile when I think of the difference in how I viewed the world *before* and *after* I'd applied that cream.

I went into the house through The Billiard Room door and found Doris and her Appeals files spread out over the Kitchen table. She asked, "*Did you and Coach Craig finish your task?*"

I said, "*Yeah, we did. Can I sit down with you for a minute? I need to talk about something that's bothering me.*"

She pointed at my regular chair and I sat down as she asked me, "*What's up?*"

I answered, "*I need to know if you called the cops on Bob Gilbert . . .*"

I didn't know if Doris was expecting that, but I heard her catch her breath before she said, "*I did, and if you'll listen to me, I think you'll agree it was a smart move.*"

I had just turned 18. I didn't have enough experience to judge anybody, especially my mother, so even though it was hard for me, I again shut-up and listened.

She started by asking me, "*Did you by any chance see the morning Post?*" I nodded.

She asked, "*Did the story make you angry or did you realize how lucky you were not to be here last night?*"

I said, "*I guess I was damn lucky the Laredo meet took place on the same date.*"

She said, "*Uh-huh. Now, do you remember when I was researching the kind of cases that the Appeals judges had historically voted against, and how the son of a convict who wanted early release was living like a criminal?*"

I said, "*I remember the son was a burglar and a car thief.*"

Doris continued, "*And the judges were afraid that once the parole-wannabe was out, he'd be tempted to start helping his son with his son's criminal enterprise. The judges feared that together they'd harm more people because that's what criminals do . . . Am I making some sense?*"

I nodded again. Doris pointed to her research papers and files and she said, "*If you get into trouble NOW, what will these judges think? That the McClellands can't control their Valedictorian son because he thinks he's above the law? Oh my God, Kirk! This is the worst time for you to be testing the limits. Your father needs to have the chance to come home and not rot for the next 8 years in that horrible place!*" I nodded as she continued, "*I'm also worried about your being associated with a sex fiend! I'm worried that your friend, Bob the sex fiend, would cause the three Appellate judges to judge Clem harshly. I'm worried they wouldn't grant him early release because he's connected to a man who disregards laws that protect Houston's underaged girls!*"

I was about to contribute to the conversation but my hope for a dialog had turned into a Doris monolog. She wasn't finished. "*JESUS! Just think of the amount of press that would have been generated if Clem was linked to Bob through you. Think! Clem would lose his chance for parole, and Frank Briscoe would happily win the final round. That's why I called the Police. To protect Clem . . .*"

I asked, "*Can I speak?*" She nodded. "*I feel sorry for Bob, but you gotta know I agree with what you did. And I understand your not sharing your plan with me since I had a race to run. You did good, Doris. You were right on the money with this one. I'm sorry I almost blew it.*"

I stood and hugged her. I told her, "*You're a good mother and a great wife. Clem's lucky to have you. Now, do you mind if I call Chris to make sure he's all right?*"

BRING CLEM HOME

Doris said, "*Of course. And I'm sorry he was the accidental victim. Maybe this experience will make him a better person, I don't know. I can only worry about my men, okay?*"

I nodded to her and walked out to my garage room. I called Chris and, from his description of what happened at Bob's, it seemed he was clueless about Doris's involvement in his arrest. Then he told me about Tim Toler being arrested, too, and I felt more guilt pangs.

The timing was bad for both Chris and Tim, and I made a promise to myself that somehow someday I'd even the score with both of them. But at that time, for Clem's sake, Doris and I agreed that we'd keep our connection to Bob's Saturday night event to ourselves.

I told Chris I'd see him the next day and that I'd be happy to drive him to his arraignment on that Tuesday if he wanted me to. He said it wouldn't be necessary and we both hung up.

Next on my list was Bob Gilbert. I hadn't told Doris I was going to call him but I had to live with myself for a few more years and this man had extended his hand in friendship to me.

Yes, he'd probably been happy to have a male of my age to counter-balance his dirty old man image, but it had always been a two way street between us, and that connection was about to end.

The main reason that bond had to end was there couldn't be anything that would interfere with Clem's early release. In my juvenile mind I'd made several miscalculations and those bad calls almost destroyed all the work that Clem and Doris had accomplished. What an idiot I'd been! I'd been selfish and I'd been negligent in helping Doris. I realized at that late date that if I'd been more involved in her research, I'd have been more focused and not allowed the Bob temptation to enter the picture. What a jerk I was! One misstep because of me, and Clem would have had to serve the full 10 years.

What was I thinking? I felt sorry for Bob but I felt sorrier for Clem.

There was no comparison:

Clem had been my hunting partner for the past 18 years . . .

Bob was a friend I'd made by chance and known for just over a year . . .

Clem had introduced me to life . . .

Bob had introduced me to the three Ds: Darla, Glorie Day, and Daiquiris . . .

So even though there was no real serious comparison, I *will* admit that my sensual memory bank, because of Bob, was packed with delightful deposits . . .

I called his number and his usual happy-go-lucky "*Hello!*" had been replaced with a solemn "*This is Bob . . .*" with no smile or laughter included.

I tried to sound cheerful as I said, "*Hey, Bob. It's Kirk. How you doing, man?*"

I heard his voice brighten and that was good to hear. He said, "*Mario Andretti! What a relief to hear your voice! I thought everyone would erase my number from their black books, and here you are, calling to see how I'm doing! Thanks, man!*"

My calling him had turned out to be harder than I thought it'd be. Bob had always been a friend, not a fiend! The whole Saturday night fiasco would cause me some sleepless nights since Clem and Doris had always taught me to never discount a true friend. The speech I was about to speak was against my religion and my whole philosophy of how I lived. I said, "Listen, Bob, I called to wish you good luck fighting the legal system, but you already know my feelings in that ring. My other feelings are important, too. I like and admire you. You and I have always shared the same interests and I never thought I'd say goodbye . . . but I have to."

I heard him take a deep breath and he said, "*I'm not happy to hear you say this . . . But I was going to call and suggest the same thing. Your family's in a tough spot right now. You don't need to be worrying about me. You need to worry about your father!*"

I couldn't believe it. And then he said something that I still think about, "*I love you, Kirk. Listen, you were like a son to me when Clem wasn't available. I enjoyed our time together and I'm just sorry I wasn't a better role model for you . . .*"

I instantly said, "*I love you back, Bobby. And you were important to me at a time when I needed good advice and help.* (I took a breath.) *Hey, do me a favor and think of me whenever you make a green Daiquiri, okay? They always cooled me off!*"

Bob laughed a sad laugh, and then he said, "*Stay cool, Mario!*" and he quietly hung up.

Unbelievable . . .

My heart tightened up and it took me about five minutes before I could finally relax and breathe. What a week-end! Steve, Bill, Barry, Concepción, Coach Craig and Coach Vickers, Clint Eastwood, Bobby Hatfield, Doris, Chris and Tim, and finally Bob Gilbert . . .

CHAPTER ELEVEN

WE HAVE TO ACCEPT WHAT HAPPENS, 1967

In Clem's absence I had learned many things about how the world worked. I'd learned we never know all the whys or wherefores and that sometimes we need to simply wait and see . . .

Just like that, it was Wednesday, March 22, 1967, and it was time for us to go to Austin. I was driving all the girls in my Malibu Super Sport and we were traveling at a high rate of speed going west on Highway 10 and leaving Houston behind us.

For the first half hour while I drove I was blessed to hear what my two sisters had been up to.

I tried to tune them both out as I remembered Doris's warning when she'd introduced us to the Texas Criminal Court of Appeals last Christmas, "*Now don't get too excited. A hearing is no guarantee that an early release will be granted.*" What had she meant? To *not* keep the faith? Was our driving to Austin a pointless exercise? Just when my ears were about to explode from "*the modern college experience*" as presented by both sisters, I was pleased when Doris took over the discussion, "*I want to thank you* (to Micki and Anne) *for sharing your wonderful stories, and I'm pleased that you both are doing so well and fitting in socially at your campuses. Now, like I told you at Christmas, we have one thing to accomplish today.* (to all of us) *You must remember that our mission is to take care of Clem. We must say and do whatever is necessary to make these judges release him.*"

I looked in my rearview and saw Micki and Anne nod. Doris continued, "*But first I need to share with you some of the things that I've learned about this court.*"

I exited the 4-lane Highway 10 and joined the two-lane Highway 71. I saw a highway sign that read AUSTIN 125.

Doris continued, "*To begin with, we are privileged to have this opportunity, so don't fall asleep! Don't ask to use the bathroom! Don't eat or drink or do anything that will distract me while I'm submitting our case to them. You mustn't speak. You won't be allowed to ask questions or to comment on whatever you hear. The judges have the documents that I thought they should see and I hope they've studied all the reasons they should grant Clem's release."

Micki asked a good question, *"Then why are WE here?"*

I glanced over at Doris and I noticed how nervous she appeared. She said, *"To show support for Clem. I have a lot to say and I'm confident the judges will be interested in the reasons I'll share with them for why your father needs to come back home."*

My turn, *"Will Frank Briscoe be there?"*

Doris answered, *"No, I don't think so, and anyway, since he ran for Congress he's no longer the District Attorney. Why would the judges want to listen to him?"*

My turn to answer, *"Because he was the District Attorney who prosecuted Clem! I would suggest we expect him to be there so we don't show our surprise when he is."*

Her response made me apprehensive, *"Well, there's no reason for these judges not to do the right thing."*

I was about to argue that (to these judges) hearing what the prosecuting attorney had to say would *be* the right thing to do if they wanted to understand why Clem was indicted to begin with, and why Clem was found guilty.

Before I could be heard though, Sister Anne asked, *"Can we find a gas station? I'm thirsty and I need a rest room."*

I looked at her in my rearview and said, *"Don't worry. We'll find one in a couple of miles."*

I could see that Doris didn't like being interrupted. Her presentation was more important than rest rooms or Frank Briscoe or anything else.

She continued, *"I've worked very hard gathering evidence for why Clem should be granted this parole and I've printed 3 extra copies of our plea in case any Judge forgot to bring the copy I'd previously sent them."*

I said, *"That's nice but I'm gonna suggest you keep those outta sight. Your extra copies might offend them, suggesting to them that they can't be trusted with your paperwork."*

She paid no attention to what I'd just said. Instead she held up copies of newspaper clippings from all the Houston papers' Sports Sections whenever my name was mentioned, and she said, *"I wanted to show them how hard you've worked to celebrate the McClelland name and how positive you were that good press could and would ultimately override all the bad."*

Then she flipped to another group of papers. She'd asked Velma to contact my Junior and Senior High Coaches so they could write these judges and tell them about Clem's involvement with my playing team sports. She explained, *"I wanted to share with you how hard Velma Brennan worked to gather these letters. One day we sat in her office at Lee and, after reading what your Coaches had to say, we both cried. Let me read some excerpts to you . . ."*

Coach Don Wilson, *"Early on, as I watched Judge McClelland's anguish, I watched his son. I told Clem, when we all knew he was going away, that I'd watch over Kirk. It's time again for Clem to do that."*

Coach Bartosh, "*What a fine athlete and what a wonderful heart, but this fine young man needs his Dad. No one can raise Kirk the way Clem can. Please send him home!*"

Coach Craig, "*I've never known a player who coached me while I was coaching him. In Kirk's case he was taught by the best, his father Clem, the best coach of us all.*"

Velma Brennan, "*I tried to help Doris McClelland guide Kirk and I even tried to fill Clem's shoes by advising Kirk on everything from what aftershave to wear to what college he should attend. This is a critical time for a fine boy to become a fine man. Please let Clem come back to help Kirk be able to do just that . . .*"

I looked and saw that all the letters were written on school letterheads addressed to the CCA.

Doris went through her remaining files and she summarized what else she planned to cover, "*I'll tell them about all the work Clem did as a Shriner for the Crippled Children's Hospital, and how much work he did as a Deacon for the First Presbyterian Church . . .*"

I interrupted her, "*It's all very positive, Doris and you've done a great job in gathering all these props, but it sounds like you plan to give a speech.* (I scratched my head) *Is it a good idea for you to preach to these guys?*"

She wagged her finger at me and said, "*It's a good idea for you to have faith in your mother! I've been working for this day for almost two years and we mustn't do or say anything wrong!*"

I was picking up on her anxiety and I felt she was struggling to keep herself under control, "*I must convince them to let your father come home! You all need to know . . . our family's survival depends on it!*"

Again I glanced at Doris and I saw her hands shaking as she returned every news clip or letter of support to its proper folder. The file was impressive and I was proud of all she'd done, but I still wondered and I had to ask, "*Are you sure that none of your children will be asked any questions?*"

She nodded.

I pressed, "*But how can you know that? If I was one of these judges, I'd ask whoever was in the room why they thought Clem should be released early.*"

I saw Doris sit up straighter as she tried to compose herself.

She answered me, "*I'll tell you what. You sit there and look handsome, and I'll do the rest!*"

Then we exited Highway 71 to join Highway 35. We drove past Lake Travis and I saw it was filled with sailboats and water-skiers. After two turns we drove down the main drag toward the State Capital with its impressive dome, and we parked at "*the court of last resort*" for all criminal cases, the Texas Criminal Court of Appeals, based inside the Supreme Court building.

The McClellands exited the Malibu and, with a sigh and a prayer, we walked hand-in-hand into that daunting place. It was a stately structure with huge staircases.

It was as silent as a church and then I heard some people whispering, not talking, down one of its corridors.

I saw an information kiosk and next to it was a marble stand with each of the courtrooms' scheduled hearings posted for all to see.

Under Courtroom 5, it read "**McCLELLAND—10:00 a.m.**"

I found and opened a white brochure that listed each court's location in the building. We walked up a staircase to the second floor where I opened a tall wooden door and we entered a bright, white room with one long bench and nine seats where the three judges waited for us. There were several onlookers, a court reporter, and Frank Briscoe who sat in the left front row.

Micki and Doris stumbled a bit. I'd tried to warn them that Briscoe would be there so their shock wouldn't be noticeable, but that strategy had failed. When he saw Doris, Briscoe smiled his devilish (insincere) smile, and nodded a condescending nod to me and my sisters.

Micki hissed, "*What's he doing here?*"

Doris raised her hand to hide her disappointment and, fortunately, I was by her side so I could direct her and my sisters to the right front row where a clerk pointed we should be seated.

As we sat I took stock of the three judges who awaited our presentation: The judge on the left was a white male in his 50s, I guessed, with a bald head and a subdued smile on his face. The judge on the right was a black man in his 60s with a head of gray hair speckled with a few hints of darker hair. There was no emotion on his face at all. Finally, the middle Judge was a woman who looked similar to Doris in age and deportment. She had no visible emotion either, but her eyes spoke volumes about all that she'd seen and heard and understood. I instantly recognized she'd be the decider for all things Clem, and I wasn't sure if that would benefit us.

I saw her nameplate and squinted my eyes to be sure I read it correctly: *MAGGIE MAY CARTER.*

There were two bailiffs, one on each end of the bench. Each Judge also had an assistant who sat behind them, I presumed for note-taking and topping off the judges' legitimate thirsts.

These people went right to work and the Bald Judge pointed to the front rail and said, "*Please come forward and stand right there if you would.*"

We moved to the front rail. I stood on the right and Micki stood on the left with Anne and Doris between us. I was nervous and that was healthy. I wanted to have my senses on edge if, for whatever reason, I'd be needed to support what Doris would present. My Debate teacher was there in spirit showing me the way, if it came time for me to perform, and I silently thanked him.

The Bald Judge asked Doris, "*I presume you are Mrs. McClelland?*"

I could sense she was all nerves as she said, "*Yes, Your Honors.*"

The Bald Judge smiled and said, "*As is the norm in a plea such as this, we three judges here have read all the documents including the brief and the trial transcript that you made available to us.*"

The Bald Judge gently waved his hand at Doris and said, "*Please begin.*"

Doris smiled and ran her hand through her hair, trying to compose herself. What I saw on her face, I hoped, was kickoff jitters. Then the whistle blew and she went to work introducing each of us, "*This is our oldest daughter, Micki.*"

Micki surprised me when she said, "*Good morning, judges!*" with a bright smile. All three smiled back at her. Good job.

Doris continued, "*She is attending Temple University in Philadelphia, uh,* (she hesitated and then looked at the Black Judge) *where the comedian Bill Cosby graduated a few years back.*"

Doris nodded at Anne and said, "*This is our second daughter, Anne, who is attending Rice University in Houston which is also my alma mater.*"

Anne bowed and smiled at the judges. Nice gesture, with a good eye-to-eye performance.

Then Doris turned to me and put her hand on my left shoulder as she said, "*And this is Kirk who will graduate this year as Valedictorian of his class at Robert E. Lee High School in Houston.*" Yeah, thanks to Velma's Bowl Game . . .

The three perfect dears all sat down behind Doris.

She was on her own. I hoped she could pull it off.

She began with, "*Let me start by . . . um . . . thanking Your Honors for allowing us this opportunity to speak today. As you probably saw when you examined our papers, the last . . . um . . . 2 years have taken a toll on our family and . . . uh, we're close to the end of what little savings Clem and I had.*"

I looked at the three judges. The Bald Judge seemed to be paying full attention, the Black Judge appeared to have little or no interest in what Doris had to say, and the Female Judge, Maggie May Carter, was looking down at her pad and appeared to be taking notes.

Doris stumbled a bit, "*We . . . uh . . . are here to ask for Clem's early release from his 10 year sentence . . . so he can return home . . . and again provide for his family, to help us ensure our children's future.*"

Doris took a breath and I continued to watch Judge Carter as she persisted to make notes on her notepad. Except they weren't note notes. Judge Carter was just like Clem. I found out later that she was sketching a rendering of her sailboat. I'd also learn later that this activity was normal for her as she listened to many different people (even though she'd **try** to stay involved with their important issues). She'd just finished drawing her boat's name on its bow, **Blind Justice**, when Doris began to stammer even worse.

Doris spluttered, "*We . . . um . . . need . . . We need to ask you . . . um . . . to consider . . .*"

Judge Maggie May Carter, with her experience of listening to thousands of pleas, determined that Doris was "*lost at sea.*" She looked up from her pad and interrupted Doris saying, "*Mrs. McClelland, we've read your transcripts. We are fully aware of your financial situation AND we are fully aware of the incredible contributions you and your husband have made to your community. The fact that you were the Chairwoman of The March of Dimes for four years running shows me a great deal about what a kind and giving person you are. But this is about your husband, not you. This is about whether or not he should come home.*"

Then Judge Carter pointed at Frank Briscoe and said, "*Before you and your family arrived, the former District Attorney of Houston stood right where you're standing and he told this court **NOT** to grant your husband an early release. He made several valid legal and moral points for keeping Clem McClelland locked behind bars . . .* (Doris began to cough, probably due to that image crossing her mind) *. . . So what WE all need* (she looked left and right at the other judges) *is one reason why your husband deserves to be let out early.*"

I, like Doris, was in shock. Why weren't we told that Briscoe would testify before we arrived? Why weren't we allowed to hear his "*valid legal and moral points*" so we'd have the chance to at least challenge them? This man had ruined the last seven years of our lives and there he was, right on schedule, pursuing the chance to ruin the next eight.

Doris hadn't expected to have her speech interrupted, because she didn't make motions to judges on a daily basis. She was out of her depth. The CCA arena was for seasoned professionals not for housewives with big hearts and little experience. Between that and Briscoe's presence, Doris had lost her train of thought. It had jumped the tracks. She was done.

After hearing Judge Carter's last request, Doris stammered as she tried to answer, "*He deserves it because he's a fine man, a good Christian man . . . I want him to come home . . .*"

Judge Carter nodded. "*Uh-huh.* (She looked behind Doris) *Let's hear from your children. Which of you would like to share with this court why you think your dad deserves to come home?*"

I bent to my right as I sat there, trying to see Doris's face. I couldn't see it. I looked to my left at my two sisters who considered each other and then both of them considered me.

Suddenly I could tell that both of them had chosen me to be the substitute (or back-up) player for the team. I saw Judge Carter smile and lean around Doris in order to see me. She curled her finger and motioned for me to rise, "*Tell us . . .* (She looked down at the file for my name.) *. . . uh . . . KIRK. Why should we grant your father an early release? Didn't they teach you in Civics class that a jail sentence should be served and not shortened?*"

I stood up and answered her, "*Yes, ma'am, they did.* (I went into my Debate mode) *But if Your Honor would allow me . . .* (I nodded to the other judges) *. . . Excuse me. I meant Your Honors . . .*"

I looked hard at all three of them, "*Clem McClelland deserves to come home because he has always accomplished great things. He can't do great things from behind bars.* (I smiled at all three judges with my best back-up smile) *The world deserves to have him out here, not in there.*"

Judge Carter thought about that and then looked down at the folder Doris had given each of the judges. She said, "*I see here that you won The American Legion Award. It just so happens* (she turned and pointed at the Black Judge) *that Judge Henry Mayfield also won this award at his Junior High, so I guess that gives you a positive link-up with our bench today . . .*"

I smiled and nodded at Judge Mayfield as Judge Carter continued, "*I have several letters in front of me that were sent from a Velma Brennan, a Coach Gil Bartosh, and a funny one from a Coach Babe Craig and there are lots of newspaper clippings that show you've been hard at it.*"

I tried to stay focused and replied, "*Yes, ma'am.*"

She smiled at me and caught me off guard when she said, "*So tell me the truth. Are you a good person?*"

I answered, "*I try to be.*"

Judge Carter smiled at me and said, "*I said the truth.*"

I said, "*I'd hate to say something that would keep Clem from coming home, but you know, you're right.* (I took a deep breath) *I have a long way to go before I'll be what you'd call a good person. That's why I need my Clem back, Judge Carter.*"

I heard Anne catch her breath, as usual. I continued, "*We need your help, Judge.* (I looked at all three judges) *We need the help of all you judges. Clem told me many times: Help is what every good Judge should always try to give.*"

Judge Maggie May Carter was skeptical

I stood there while Judge Maggie May Carter waded through the clippings and letters and then she closed the file. She looked left, then right at the other judges and spoke softly to them. They nodded. Judge Carter looked at me and said, "*Mr. McClelland, to my mind you seem too good to be true. I need to verify some information from these files and then we'll contact you with our decision. That will be all for now. You and your family may return to your home in Houston.*"

Judge Carter hit the gavel and just like that the hearing was over.

The judges began picking up their files and with the help of their assistants, they filed out of the courtroom through the rear doors that led into their Chambers.

While my sisters helped Doris, I had one more confrontation. I moved to my left and was able to catch Frank Briscoe as he walked toward the exit to Courtroom 5. I noticed he was wearing his same plain grey suit.

I said, "*Hello, Mr. Briscoe. Can I have a moment?*"

He turned toward me and I saw he had a thick leather briefcase that he quickly closed as I approached him. He greeted me saying, "*The judge's son and heir. Hey, too bad about your mother. She didn't help your father's bid for freedom. If anything she alienated all of them.*"

I defended her, "*I'm sure the judges know she's not familiar with court procedure. YOU don't cut people any slack, but I bet they do.*"

Briscoe grinned at me, "*Let's see . . . What do you want to ask me? Was your father innocent? Did the big bad wolf blow your house down? That's what this "interview" is all about, isn't it?*"

It was my turn and I smiled at him, "*You know, you've always envied Clem because he's a better man than you'll ever be. My question is, since he's no threat to anyone any more, what's the point of keeping him locked up?*"

I saw that Frank was enjoying our skirmish. He was in full prosecutorial mode as he said, "*I knew I needed a high class case to show Houston I'd keep the streets safe, and your dad was perfect. In my office my assistants had his picture framed and hung it on my wall with the words "The Glistening Target" as its caption. I love that picture and it still motivates me.*"

He smiled as he reflected on what for him was a fond memory. He continued, "*I remember thinking a great deal about your father in the early 50s. He got his law degree at Texas just like I did, he had a wife and kids, he had a corner office at the county courthouse, and it was obvious whenever I spoke to him that in his mind he was always above criticism.*"

I confronted him, "*So you cheated?*"

He laughed at my naiveté, "*Cheated? I didn't have to cheat! I just won!*"

I countered by handing him a piece of paper, "*I hoped I might see you so I could give you this. It's a copy of the new Code of Criminal Procedure that became effective last January.*"

He smirked, "*I've seen it. So what?*"

I took the paper back and read it, "*Under this new Code passed by the Texas legislature, no Justice of the Peace can convene a Court of Inquiry. Only District Judges! AND all witnesses are entitled to the same protections as in felony prosecutions! Clem loved it when this passed.*"

I stared at him, "*It made you and your entire office look impotent! History will show that because of my father no one will have to suffer this Court of Inquiry nonsense ever again.*"

Frank clucked his tongue, "*He was living The American Dream and that made him an easy target for me. He was important for my self-esteem. And if you still wonder why I need him to stay in the jug, be aware I plan to run for mayor one of these days. The smarter voters will remember I'm the one who put that "horrible Judge" away so they could sleep safely at night.*"

By then I'd had enough of Mr. Briscoe and I respectfully thanked him for his time. Not because his views were helpful but because I was raised to be polite, even to former D A's.

He reached out to shake my hand, and I shook his as he said, "*Good luck*" and walked away.

I watched him stop to talk to the Bald Judge who was waiting for him at the door to our courtroom. They spoke briefly and shared a laugh about something, probably Doris.

As I watched him shake the Bald Judge's hand I saw Briscoe exit the tall doors to that hall of justice. I shook my head at how this man had harmed my family and how he'd convinced himself that he could do anything he wanted as long as it helped him stand tall and attract votes.

I moved out the same doors and caught up with Doris and my sisters as they walked toward the Malibu. It was time for us to leave that place . . .

May 27, 1967 was a Saturday and it started off wet. Then, as the day progressed, the sun peeked out from behind the storm clouds. It was early evening and we were at the Sam Houston Coliseum, the same arena where Clem's Circus had had its successful run nine years before.

Doris and I were backstage with the other students who would sit on the raised Graduation Platform facing the 5,000 or so students, parents and teachers assembled on the other side of the golden curtains. She'd been very helpful, assisting me to get dressed into my graduating cap and gown by first combing my hair with her hand and then placing the cap at a sexy angle on top of my head.

I was impatient with this ritual, though, so I whispered, "*Are you done, yet? Jesus . . .*"

Doris angrily whispered back, "*Get ahold of yourself, young man! Remember where you are! The Sam Houston Coliseum is one of Clem's favorite places!*"

Yeah, she was right. I remembered his wonderful Circus as "*Clem's Last Stand*" before all the Briscoe trouble started.

I apologized and then kissed Doris a thank you kiss and she left me to go sit in a box reserved for the Valedictorian's family. Micki and Anne were already there waiting for her.

An hour later I was bored and looked around at the other *Platform students* and I didn't see anyone there that I'd invite over for dinner. I did see Grace Stewart, but when I flashed her my special "*Gee, I know I'm cute*" smile, she rolled her eyes and turned her back on me.

We'd already suffered the individual name calling, diploma-receiving exercise and I was ready to shed my hot golden graduation outfit and find a refreshment stand for some liquid relief.

I noticed that our Graduation Platform was located close to the Center Ring of Clem's Three Ring Circus. Me and the other five straight-A students sat in the center of the Platform with a row of Teachers and Principals and the Lee Coaches sitting behind us.

I looked out into the crowd of students and I was able to locate the important ones to me.

I was able to find Steve, Tim, Tom, MaryAnn, Larry Klump, and Chris. I waved to all of them except Larry.

The Robert E. Lee General's Band had just finished playing our fight song when Velma Brennan, with a big smile, walked up to the podium and began the next part of the program.

Velma said, "*And now we come to the highlight of our Graduation ceremony this evening, the awarding of our annual Outstanding Graduate Award.*"

As she spoke I had grown bored with all the ceremonial nonsense and like I always did, I misbehaved. I watched Chris make an "*I Love You*" sign with his hand to me and laugh. I saw MaryAnn blow an air-kiss to me and I blew one back. I saw Larry make a middle finger gesture that I answered with a chin flick gesture which I knew meant "*get lost asshole.*"

Velma was still talking, "*This is the highest award that any student at Robert E. Lee can achieve and it represents not only excellence in academics but also leadership and service in school clubs, athletics, and other school organizations.*"

I remember that I tried real hard not to, but I yawned. Several of my friends like Steve and Chris saw me and pointed at me, silently laughing.

I looked over and saw the special box seats that Doris and Micki and Anne occupied in the McClelland box. I saw the one empty chair in the family box and felt a tightening in my chest. I thought of Frank Briscoe and how he had deprived me of my Clem for far too long. I thought of my partner Clem and told myself that I'd give anything for him to be there with his family as we all experienced the joy of celebrating me.

That thought made me smile and I tuned-back-in to Velma as she said, "*Now for those of you who are falling asleep as I describe this award, let me tell you . . .*

(she whispered) *this is not an easy one to win!*"

Velma was in performance mode and had a huge grin on her face as she continued, "*You've got to be so good, so motivated, so special, so spectacular in everything you do that no teacher will feel the urge to vote against you. Because if any one teacher DOES vote against you, you're out!*"

She laughed and said, "*I don't know about you but I don't think I could survive that kind of heat!*"

I remember I laughed, as did the entire audience of over 5,000. I remember I looked over to see if Doris was laughing at Velma and that's when I saw a figure standing in the wings about 20 yards behind the McClelland box. I looked again and focused . . . It was Maggie May Carter!

All I could think of was, "*What's she doing here?*" I tried to get Doris's attention to get her to turn around to see Judge Carter, but that's when Velma turned and looked right at the group of Valedictorian-wannabes, saying, "*So who DID survive and win this award? Who, against all odds, made it through the gauntlet with no votes against, and all votes "Aye"?*"

Velma turned back to look at the audience of parents and students and, smiling, she said, "*Ladies and Gentlemen, it is with great pleasure and admiration that I present to you this year's winner of the Outstanding Graduate Award. Mr. Clement Kirk McClelland!*"

I didn't see that one coming and my surprised jaw dropped below my knees. Everyone around me, except Grace Stewart, was patting me on my back, congratulating me. The entire audience of 5,000 people were up on their feet clapping and whistling. I stood up and I waved a big wave to my friends. Then I walked up to Velma so she could hand me the Award.

As she was about to hand it to me, I lifted her up off the ground and gave her a huge hug.

I owed that woman a great deal of gratitude.

Then as I held her up with both my hands, I kissed her and the crowd laughed. She laughed too, and pushed me away so she could wag her finger at me as she handed me my Award.

Then Coach Bartosh and Coach Babe Craig came up behind me and both slapped me on my back. Coach Craig made Coach Bartosh laugh when he said, "*That's a real nice trophy, Mac! Hey, don't you ever forget, I voted for you!*"

With this new trophy in my hand I held it up to show to Doris so she could see it and I could see her reaction. That's when I saw him. At first he was just a tall 6'4" figure walking toward the McClelland family box. I was thanking people all around me for their positive reactions and then I swiveled my head to see who the tall figure was. My eyes locked with his and I saw that it was Clem. I froze. Doris told me later that when she saw my reaction to him it made her turn.

In the excitement she didn't know who or what I was looking at, but when she saw Clem she almost fainted. Micki and Anne looked behind the box and both started screaming. Then all three rushed to his side and began to hug and kiss him. From the look on his face I could tell he knew he'd finally made it home. Off to the side and behind our box stood Judge Maggie May Carter. She watched me, then she looked toward Clem. She saw Clem salute me and she saw me laugh and return the salute. That's when Judge Carter laughed.

Clem continued to hug Doris while he looked and waved proudly at me. I looked back, and my tears began to flow. I remember I said, "*That's my Clem!*" and then I lost it. Velma told me later that when she saw me crying, she thought the tears in my eyes were because I had won. She was right. My Clem was home . . .

Clem arrived in time for my Graduation
(Doris took the picture)

Valedictorian Award

Outstanding Graduate Award May 1967

AFTERWORD

"Clem McClelland was unopposed when he ran for Probate Judge in his last two terms. What made him unbeatable also made him a glistening target to Frank Briscoe.

In 1966 Frank Briscoe ran for Congress against George Herbert Walker Bush in the Seventh Houston Congressional District, and he lost to Mr. Bush.

Frank Briscoe also ran for the Mayor of Houston twice, and he lost both times.

The Houston Press was Frank Briscoe's tool for attacking Clem McClelland's name and reputation. This paper went out of business in 1965, the same year Clem McClelland reported to begin serving his sentence at the Texas Penitentiary in Huntsville.

The Texas Legislature in 1965 debated the antiquated 1876 law, which allowed Frank Briscoe's Court of Inquiry to convene in Houston in June of 1962. The 1876 law was banned January 1, 1966, to ensure that all witnesses are entitled to the same protections as those in felony prosecutions, and to allow only *District Judges* to request Courts of Inquiry. No other District Attorney in Texas will be allowed to use this unconstitutional decree again.

Clem's parole was signed by Governor John Connolly in May of 1967. Clem was also granted a full pardon by Governor Preston Smith in 1972, ten years after Clem's conviction in 1962. These two Texas Governors, by their parole and their full pardon, expressed their personal views concerning Frank Briscoe's Court of Inquiry."

**DISTRICT ATTORNEY
FRANK BRISCOE**

ABOUT THE AUTHOR

A graduate of the University of Southern California Film School, Kirk, over the past forty years, has written, produced, and directed over five hundred Commercials and Documentary films from his home base in Sarasota, Florida, for clients around the world.

His first published book was titled **ON MAKING A MOVIE-BREWSTER MCCLOUD**, which is about his experiences with director Robert Altman in his hometown of Houston, Texas. It was a paperback published by Signet Film Series in 1970.

His present novel, **BRING CLEM HOME: THE FALL OF A TEXAS JUDGE**, is also a Houston story that covers the first eighteen years of his life.

CPSIA information can be obtained
at www.ICGtesting.com
Printed in the USA
BVHW090221271121
622650BV00012B/411